Culture and Content in French

FRAMEWORKS FOR
INNOVATIVE CURRICULA

Edited by

Aurélie Chevant-Aksoy and
Kathryne Adair Corbin

LEVER
PRESS

Copyright © 2022 by Aurélie Chevant-Aksoy and Kathryne Adair Corbin

Lever Press (leverpress.org) is a publisher of pathbreaking scholarship. Supported by a consortium of liberal arts institutions focused on, and renowned for, excellence in both research and teaching, our press is grounded on three essential commitments: to be a digitally native press, to be a peer-reviewed, open access press that charges no fees to either authors or their institutions, and to be a press aligned with the ethos and mission of liberal arts colleges.

This work is licensed under the Creative Commons Attribution-NonCommercial 4.0 International License. To view a copy of this license, visit http://creativecommons.org/licenses/by-nc/4.0/ or send a letter to Creative Commons, PO Box 1866, Mountain View, CA 94042, USA.

DOI: https://doi.org/10.3998/mpub.12467264
Print ISBN: 978-1-64315-025-3
Open access ISBN: 978-1-64315-026-0

Published in the United States of America by Lever Press, in partnership with Amherst College Press and Michigan Publishing

Contents

Member Institution Acknowledgments	v
Acknowledgments	vii
Introduction Aurélie Chevant-Aksoy and Kathryne Adair Corbin	1

Part I: Immersion and Improvisation — 23

Chapter 1: Teaching Culture through Food: A Kinesthetic Approach to the College Language Classroom   25
   Aria Dal Molin

Chapter 2: Improv Games Adapted to the Bridge Classroom   51
   Jeremie Korta

Part II: Literature and Film — 83

Chapter 3: Some Benefits to Going Narrow Instead of Broad. Rethinking Cultural Instruction in the French Language Classroom: Andrée Maillet as a Case Study   85
   Rebecca Josephy

Chapter 4: *La Chanson engagée*: Waging War on War! Using Songs to Teach French Language and Culture   113
   Christophe Corbin

Chapter 5: Teaching Francophone and French Cultures through Project-Based Learning   145
   Eliza Jane Smith

Part III: Visual Arts and Mass Media   177

Chapter 6: The French Classroom as a Newsroom: A Multiliteracies Framework   179
   Kathryne Adair Corbin

Chapter 7: Of Presidents and Internet Memes: Fostering Student-Centered Learning, Cultural Competency, and Critical Thinking through the Use of Images   205
   Heidi Holst-Knudsen

Chapter 8: Culture with Pictures: *Blogs BD* for Multiple Literacies in the French Language Classroom   261
   Aurélie Chevant-Aksoy

Part IV: Digital Technologies   283

Chapter 9: Engaging Students Inside and Outside of the Classroom with YouTube   285
   Audra Merfeld-Langston

Chapter 10: Charting the Course: Online Maps as a Tool in the French Culture Classroom   315
   Carrie O'Connor

Chapter 11: Developing Intercultural Communicative Competence via Video-Based Synchronous Communication among L2 French Learners   333
   Virginie Cassidy and Hongying Xu

Appendices   361
About the Contributors   363

Member Institution Acknowledgments

Lever Press is a joint venture. This work was made possible by the generous support of Lever Press member libraries from the following institutions:

Adrian College
Agnes Scott College
Allegheny College
Amherst College
Bard College
Berea College
Bowdoin College
Carleton College
Claremont Graduate University
Claremont McKenna College
Clark Atlanta University
Coe College
College of Saint Benedict / Saint John's University
The College of Wooster
Denison University
DePauw University
Earlham College
Furman University
Grinnell College
Hamilton College
Harvey Mudd College
Haverford College
Hollins University
Keck Graduate Institute
Kenyon College
Knox College
Lafayette College Library
Lake Forest College
Macalester College
Middlebury College

Morehouse College
Oberlin College
Pitzer College
Pomona College
Rollins College
Santa Clara University
Scripps College
Sewanee: The University of the South
Skidmore College
Smith College
Spelman College
St. Lawrence University
St. Olaf College
Susquehanna University
Swarthmore College
Trinity University
Union College
University of Puget Sound
Ursinus College
Vassar College
Washington and Lee University
Whitman College
Willamette University
Williams College

Acknowledgments

We thank our mentors at University of California, Santa Barbara—Catherine M. J. Nesci, Jean Marie Schultz, and Sarah Roberts—who have inspired us as scholars, teachers, and mentors.

We are grateful to Beth Bouloukos and our editors at Lever Press for their support and guidance. We thank our peer reviewers whose comments and suggestions helped us improve our manuscript.

Finally, we are thankful for all the contributors who have worked diligently and patiently on this volume. We have been inspired by their resourcefulness, creativity, and dedication to bring something new to the classroom. We would like to acknowledge Carrie O'Connor whose life was tragically cut short in September 2020. Her legacy will continue to inspire her colleagues and students alike as a model of engagement, curricular innovation, and collaboration.

Aurélie Chevant-Aksoy
First, I would like to extend my thanks to my dear friend and colleague Kathryne Adair Corbin.

This volume would not have existed without her positive energy and unfailing work ethic. Working with Katy is truly a privilege and a joy. I am also grateful for my colleagues and students, who are constant sources of inspiration. In particular, I acknowledge Stacey Katz Bourns and Nicole Mills, who set the bar for teaching excellence so high. Finally, I thank my families, the Chevants and the Aksoys, for their love and support. I'm especially grateful for my husband, Can, for being my editing ears and eyes throughout this whole process.

Kathryne Adair Corbin
I am especially grateful for my colleague and dear friend Aurélie Chevant-Aksoy, whose initial conference paper led to many post-panel discussions and ultimately this project. Without her perspicacity and determination, this work would not be possible. I am thankful for the creative and fruitful exchanges with student research assistants whose ideas and reflections push me to experiment, refine, and replace. I acknowledge Alison Cook-Sather and the Andrew W. Mellon Teaching and Learning Institute at Bryn Mawr College for lending support so I could work through renditions of new courses, as well as my student partners in the Students as Learners and Teachers program for their questions, observations, and feedback. Many thanks to Jacob Coleman for helping us track down rights for images. Finally, I am extremely grateful for the everlasting support of my family.

INTRODUCTION

Aurélie Chevant-Aksoy and Kathryne Adair Corbin

As new globalized realities are being shaped every day, language instructors must constantly reassess how to teach discrete aspects of languages curricula in interactive and innovative ways. While the field of modern languages is aware of the impact of globalization on language instruction, as Erin Kearney points out, "language learning in ML [Modern Languages] education is often discussed as and assumed to be a linear process, the staged acquisition of linguistic (mostly grammatical and lexical) forms, with learners moving from one well-defined phase to another and, eventually, from the concrete, immediate and referential to the abstract and symbolic."[1] Despite the influence of the World-Readiness Standards for Learning Languages and the push for the "5 Cs" (Communication, Cultures, Connections, Comparisons, Communities), the linear process outlined by Kearney is clearly visible in approaches to teaching culture in which "culture is largely side-lined in favor of a focus on linguistic form or is seen simply as the broad backdrop against which language use occurs."[2]

What is the real value in learning culture in a language course? Studying cultures helps us to gain a deeper understanding of others in this world we share—as well as to gain a deeper understanding of ourselves. Through the study and practice of culture, we reflect upon, and indeed continue to construct, identities, traditions, ideas, and beliefs that compose the foundation of our selves and form the basis of our interactions with social others. When the study of culture and languages can intermix, we learn to communicate with empathy while asserting our own identities. The resulting goal for the language classroom, then, is for students to achieve both linguistic competence and critical culture awareness. For, as Katherine Arens suggests, many students will not find much use for the target language upon completion of a language requirement, but they will in fact find themselves, years later, recalling cultural differences and various aspects of cultural identity.[3]

Furthermore, this is also often the main reason why students study a language from the outset: they delight in exploring cultural artifacts such as movies and music; they are eager to travel and discover other cultures; they want to meet new people and exchange ideas about cultures different from their own. Indeed, the language, for some second language (L2) learners, is often simply a vector toward the ultimate goal: cultural competence.

REFLECTIONS ON THE RECENT HISTORY OF TEACHING CULTURE

Considering culture as a backdrop for teaching grammar and vocabulary is not a newly found problem. As the twentieth century ushered in rapid innovations in language teaching, the United States experienced a surge of language learning during the Second World War and Cold War periods, when proponents of the direct and audio-lingual methods advocated for the development of four disparate skills: listening comprehension, reading comprehension, writing, and speaking. In this pedagogical skill-based system, culture often appeared as the "fifth skill"—the ability to perceive, understand, and accept cultural differences—lagging behind reading, writing, listening, and speaking. Additionally, until the 1960s, the teaching of culture focused on "big C culture," as students learned a language "to be able to one day read the foreign literature in the original, become a cultured, educated person, and be able to hold sophisticated conversations with educated native speakers."[4] In the 1980s, the next important step in teaching culture in modern languages education came about, with a significant move away from a "grammar-translational teaching style, concentrating on some carefully chosen big C culture content" to a communicative approach and "the admission of more little c culture into the curriculum."[5] However, even though instructors were now more encouraged to teach information about the native speaker's daily life and practices as much as canonical literary works, culture was still considered more of an addendum to the main curriculum.

It was not until the 1990s that researchers such as applied linguist Claire Kramsch[6] and anthropologist Michael Agar[7] defended the idea that language and culture were reciprocally related. In parallel, in 1996, the National Standards promoted by the American Council on the Teaching of Foreign Languages (ACTFL) proposed five new main goals that motivated teachers to reconsider how to integrate culture in the process of foreign language (FL) learning: Communication, Cultures, Connections, Comparisons, and Communities (commonly known as the 5 Cs). Under these guidelines, the Cultures goal includes "the philosophical perspectives, the behavioural practices, and the products—both tangible and intangible—of a society."[8] Still, the focus on the 5 Cs triggered some misconceptions and ill-adapted practices in modern language teaching. Genelle Morain argues that, through this reinterpretation of Cultures (as perspectives, behavioral practices, and products), even though teachers have no problem "grasping the concept of products" and teaching behaviors in social situations, there is often confusion in distinguishing a product from a practice.[9] Morain adds that it is difficult to identify cultural perspectives because "values are never put into words, unstated assumptions are not recognized, and 'shared cultural attitudes' are not analyzed" by native speakers.[10] With this in mind, how can teachers speak with confidence about other cultures' perspectives and views of the world, especially with textbooks that rarely contain any information on values, attitudes, and beliefs in L2 culture(s)? The end result is that teachers often "concoct a perspective based on a personal experience" and/or "'discover' a perspective derived from a widely-held stereotype."[11] Cultural knowledge appears then as bits of trivia, stereotypes, and homogenized facts.

In 2007, the report of the Modern Language Association (MLA) called for "replacing the two-tiered language-literature structure with a broader and more coherent curriculum in which language, culture, and literature are taught as a continuous whole."[12] The report also supported alliances with other departments and the development of interdisciplinary courses to "reinvigorate language departments as valuable academic units central to the humanities and to the missions of institutions of higher learning."[13] Although this structural and curricular change has been central to much research in teaching foreign languages, the reality is that programs' structures and textbooks' formats continue to perpetuate the distinction between language, culture, and literature. Therefore, it is necessary for teachers to have access to resources that help blend the curriculum. Kramsch emphasizes the importance of revisiting within the curriculum and course content the meaning of language, culture, and communication[14] and adds that "FL learning today is caught between the need to acquire 'usable skills' in predictable cultural contexts and the fundamental unpredictability of global contexts."[15] She also raises the following question: "How can FL teachers take into account the changing contexts of language use for which they are preparing their students, without losing the historical and cultural awareness that comes from studying one national language, literature and culture?"[16] Within the teaching of languages, instructors must navigate teaching culture through perennial cultural and historical staples while constantly introducing new cultural markers that are reshaping cultures every day.

RECENT INITIATIVES IN THE GLOBAL CONTEXT

While preparing this volume and exploring useful pedagogical approaches toward the aforementioned goals, we turned to scholars whose work built upon the notions of "translingual and transcultural competence."[17] Therefore, this section focuses on two main overarching contemporary positionings that the authors of this volume relied on to explore innovative ways to teach culture: multiliteracies (including digital literacies) and intercultural and symbolic competences.

Multiliteracies and Digital Literacies

Some scholars proposed a multilingual approach to the teaching of languages, emphasizing translingual and transcultural competence through which students are trained to reflect upon the world and their place in it through the perspective of cultural others. This approach includes "heteroglossia (or the ability to use multiple voices, registers, and styles), multiliteracy (or the ability to use various genres and create new ones), and multimodality (or the ability to make meaning not just through language but also through visuals, music, gestures, film, and video)."[18] While the New London Group was the first to introduce the term "multiliteracy" in "A Pedagogy of Multiliteracies: Designing Social Futures," Rick Kern's work has been central to the development of a curriculum centered on multiliteracies.[19] Within this framework, Kern defines literacy as:

> the use of socially-, historically-, and culturally-situated practices of creating and interpreting meaning through texts. It

entails at least a tacit awareness of the relationships between textual conventions and their contexts of use and, ideally, the ability to reflect critically on those relationships. . . . It draws on a wide range of cognitive abilities, on knowledge of written and spoken language, on knowledge of genres, and on cultural knowledge.[20]

A multiliteracies framework serves the purpose of reconciling the teaching of "communication" with the teaching of "textual analysis."[21] To help instructors understand what this pedagogy implies in the classroom, Heather Willis Allen and Kate Paesani revisit the four "pedagogical acts" (situated practice, overt instruction, critical framing, and transformed practice), first introduced by the New London Group.[22] These four components are particularly useful to plan classroom activities, are neither hierarchical nor sequential, and can overlap. In situated practice activities, students are immersed in contextualized learning, and they use familiar knowledge to make sense of new knowledge. In over-instruction activities, a teacher introduces formal concepts with texts, and students focus on the form of the text to make meaning. Students interpret the social and cultural contexts that created the meanings of the text in critical framing activities. Finally, in transformed practice activities, students engage in creating new texts (based on the existing ones) or reshaping the existing texts.[23]

Additionally, Allen and Paesani note, within this framework, language use is always contextualized and involves both linguistic and socio-cultural knowledge, and conventions "are viewed as culturally situated, shaping how people read and write, and evolving over time."[24] They argue that, conventions include linguistic resources yet extend beyond these to include schematic resources related to a broad spectrum of written and spoken genres (e.g., advertisement, novel, editorial, conversation, etc.), their organizational patterns, and their particular ways of using language."[25] Accordingly, by providing access to multiple voices and offering new ways to make meaning through language and various forms of media and texts, the multiliteracies approach can help faculty (and programs) bridge the traditional divide between language and culture.

When rethinking modern language education through the lens of a multiliteracies framework, Chantelle Warner and Beatrice Dupuy add that instructors should also study and use information and communication media that globally mediate processes of language development and scholarly engagement. Instructors should consider embedding in their curriculum "not only the types of visual media . . . e.g., film, images, and posters, but . . . any new literacy practices enabled through digital communications media."[26] In 2008, Steven Thorne and Jonathon Reinhardt introduced their "bridging activities" initiative focused "on developing learner awareness of vernacular digital language conventions and analyzing these conventions to bridge in-class activity with the wider world of mediated language use."[27] Thorne and Reinhardt applied the New London Group's cycle of situated practice, overt instruction, critical framing, and transformed practice as a model for their initiative and set up a three-phase cycle of activities centered on observation and collection, guided exploration and analysis, and creation and participation:

> Observation activities ask students to develop awareness of their own internet use habits and to collect texts of interest. Guided exploration and analysis activities lead students to notice and critically examine the linguistic and social features of the observed and collected texts. In creation and participation activities, students join internet communities and participate in text creation, which leads to new observations and analyses.[28]

The authors suggest looking into instant messaging, blogs and wikis, remixing (mixing different types of media such as books, movies, comics, video games), and online gaming to help implement the bridging activities initiative. Overall, by integrating a multiliteracies framework (including digital literacies), instructors can work toward dismantling the distinction between language and literature with their curricula and programs and ensure that language teaching always involves linguistic and socio-cultural knowledge.

Intercultural and Symbolic Competences

In addition to looking into multiliteracies and digital literacy approaches to rethink the ways we teach culture in the language classroom, we also turned to Kearney's work on intercultural learning. Kearney built her idea of "approaching culture via multiple narratives"[29] upon Michael Byram's model of Intercultural Communicative Competence (ICC) and Kramsch's model of Symbolic Competence. As Kearney explains, Byram's 1997 monograph, *Teaching and Assessing Intercultural Communicative Competence*, establishes that learning a language is "about more than grammar and vocabulary, or even the ability to perform in communicative situations."[30] Kearney adds that "in [Byram's] view, culture learning in ML education does have to do with communicative exchange, but it also, and more centrally, concerns the ability to relate to others."[31] Byram proposes an Intercultural Communicative Competence model that involves knowledge (*savoirs*), attitude (*savoir être*), and skills (*savoir comprendre + apprendre/faire*) that lead to critical cultural awareness (*savoir s'engager*). Therefore, the ICC model focuses on the learner's ability to identify how social groups and identities function (*savoirs*), to interpret and relate information and experiences from different cultures (*savoir comprendre*), to keep an open mind and challenge one's beliefs (*savoir être*), to acquire new knowledge about different cultures through interaction (*savoir apprendre*), and to critically evaluate one's culture and other cultures (*savoir s'engager*).[32] As Kearney summarizes, "overall, developing knowledge, skills, certain dispositions and awareness can promote, in Byram's mind, a kind of engaged citizenship . . . , an ability to be transformed and to be transformative in one's social and intercultural communities."[33] Instructors contributing to this volume were thus encouraged to develop activities in which students would compare cultures, examine social processes, and exchange stereotypes, cultural misunderstandings, and cultural similarities and differences. In Byram's model, intercultural learners are both ethnographers and informants as they allow "their own knowledge and experience to serve as the vantage point from which they can gain a new perspective; this is akin to Kramsch's third place . . . , which is based in neither a native nor an 'other' culture entirely."[34]

In 1993, as Kramsch investigated processes of intercultural dialogue in classroom settings, she introduced the notion of "third place" and explained that learners need to take both an insider's and an outsider's view on their own culture and the other cultures:

> Through dialogue and the search for each other's understanding, each person tries to see the world through the other's eyes without losing sight of him or herself. The goal is not a balance of opposites, or a moderate pluralism of opinions but a paradoxical, irreducible confrontation that may change one in the process.[35]

However, in later work Kramsch revisits her notion of "third place": "[T]he notion of third culture must be seen less as a place than as a symbolic process of meaning-making that sees beyond the dualities of national languages (L1–L2) and national cultures (C1–C2)."[36] Thus, by 2008, Kramsch advocated for symbolic competence as a way to expand upon communicative competence. In this new approach, "symbolic competence does not do away with the ability to express, interpret, and negotiate meanings in dialogue with others, but enriches it and embeds it into the ability to produce and exchange symbolic goods in the complex global context in which we live today."³⁷ At that time, she focused on the importance of literary imagination at all levels and in all its manifestations (linguistic, textual, visual, acoustic, poetic). To that, Kramsch later added the importance of translation and the recommendation that teachers design more "exercises in translation, transcription, transposition—exercises that would systematically practice the transfer of meaning across linguistic codes, discourse frames, media, and modalities."³⁸ Such exercises directly position learners to operate between their first language (L1) and L2 as they reference languages according to grammatical relationships as well as culturally embedded meanings.

In 2010, Kearney advocated for transcultural understanding through a multiple cultural narratives approach. In this case, subjects are explored from a variety of narratives in which different mediatic forms, styles, and voices—both complementary and dissonant—present a veritable cultural mosaic. This array of polyphonic complexities presents students with a rich cultural fabric that provides the basis for their critical inquiry. In 2016, Kearney described this approach through teaching models underpinning the following:

> development of semiotic awareness and symbolic competence, such as (1) identifying culturally symbolic forms and reference points (words, phrases, images); (2) hypothesizing about possible meanings of these forms; (3) animating cultural narratives, one type of symbolic form, through voicing and embodiment; (4) repositioning the students or teacher in classroom discourse to project them into the plotlines of cultural narratives and (5) developing a broader approach to the interpretation of meaning and a metalanguage for this analytic process.³⁹

In the examples provided in her book, Kearney describes how students work on linguistic expressions and making meaning of new points of view as well as complete a narrative writing assignment within a global simulation project.[40] Overall, providing students with exercises using multiple voices to critically inquire and create is key because it connects them to individual and broader social scales of meaning and allows them to move within and across cultures.

CHAPTERS

As we have seen, defining "culture" and deciding how to teach it has been (and continues to be) a contentious topic among foreign language education researchers. As we mentioned previously, and echoing Kramsch, we acknowledge that instructors teach the standard language and that it can be a challenge to avoid stereotypical forms when teaching culture. We also recognize the critical need to sustain the multitude of narratives and experiences that feed language instruction and to work constantly with the diverse formats to access them. For these reasons, in this volume we present educators at all levels of language instruction with examples of activities to integrate culture, literature, and language as part of a cohesive and continuous curriculum. This volume does not study modernist and postmodernist approaches to teaching culture in the language; nor does it analyze developments in teaching culture within the field of applied linguistics. Rather, our goal is to offer pedagogical ideas to encourage teachers to venture outside of their comfort zones and revisit canonical texts and engage with culture(s) in nontraditional and innovative ways using diverse media and narratives. We embrace the motto inspired by Kramsch that "*bricolage* is the name of the game"[41] because we believe that a globalized context of teaching calls for a diversity of cultural resources and hybridized pedagogical tools. Therefore, we encouraged authors to explore pedagogical approaches around their own interpretations of culture(s) within the realm of multiliteracies, multimodality, and intercultural competence.

Contributors to this volume are secondary- and college-level instructors of French, Italian, and Chinese with backgrounds in applied linguistics, literary and cultural studies, teaching language for specific purposes, and study abroad. Like most college professors, the authors have taught courses at all levels of the curriculum, often bridging disciplines as well as the rigid divide that still exists in most standard university language departments between "literature" or content courses and "language" courses. Their combined expertise and specific presentations in the following chapters emphasize the possibilities for flexibility and creativity that can reinvigorate offerings, leading to a broader and more coherent curriculum. Moreover, each contributor reflects upon critical theoretical objectives pertaining to various modalities and pedagogies and their practical uses in language classes. While this volume is not a case study in applied linguistics, we do hope readers will benefit from these theoretical perspectives and their practicalities in the classroom to expand their own inquiries and further their research.

In the first part of this volume, "Immersion and Improvisation," the authors look at teaching culture with kinesthetics, music, and theatrical extemporization. In the first chapter, "Teaching Culture through Food: A Kinesthetic Approach to the College Language Classroom," Aria Dal Molin proposes an empiricist-inspired, experiential learning approach to teaching French culture in the intermediate-level language classroom. Dal Molin suggests teaching culture through *dîner et un film* (dinner and a movie), a collaborative scaffolded project in which students engage in meaning-making around cultural forms, texts, and representations inspired by the PACE model: Presentation, Attention, Co-Construction, Extension.[42] Dal Molin explains how she adapted the PACE model's four-step process of "guided participatory" learning[43] to the teaching of culture in her projects and demonstrates the use of lived-through experiences as cultural "texts" to promote active production of meaning and understanding through shared social interactions, ultimately promoting reflective international citizens with a keen interest in a heteroglossic world.

In "Improv Games Adapted to the Bridge Classroom," Jeremie Korta describes his experimental approach to teaching culture in bridge courses using drama techniques, improvisational games, and class projects. He demonstrates how the practice of drama and improvisational games in the language classroom helps to integrate these disparate fields and provide a possible method in which to "develop language competencies holistically" within a multiliteracies pedagogical framework.[44] Thus, this chapter will, first, make the case for drama techniques and improvisational theatre games in second-language acquisition (SLA) and, second, present a series of improvisational games, adapted to teach language and culture interactively.

In the second part of this volume, authors turn their attention to literature and film, expanding the canon to include both lesser-known authors and literary forms and some of the most successful works of French literature and cinema as objects of inquiry. In her chapter, Rebecca Josephy responds to two central questions: How do instructors integrate culture while not glossing over its intricacies and without reducing culture to a series of authors that seem to be chosen specifically for their social identities? And what exciting and innovative ways exist to incorporate a deep and sustained understanding of culture, and especially francophone culture, into the French language classroom? In "Some Benefits to Going Narrow Instead of Broad. Rethinking Cultural Instruction in the French Language Classroom: Andrée Maillet as a Case Study," Josephy proposes to design a language course around a single noncanonical author, thus creating a project-based cultural exploration centered on a single francophone author and their writings. Josephy outlines her experience integrating cultural content in a French grammar review course through the use of a series of short stories by the little-known francophone Québécois author Andrée Maillet.

Delving into the use of songs in the French language classroom, Christophe Corbin, in "*La Chanson engagée*: Waging War on War! Using Songs to Teach French Language and Culture," investigates how songs can provide stimulating entry points to topics under study in a given course as well as an opportunity to examine cultural specificities. Considering the broader theme of war, Corbin takes the anonymous song "La Chanson de Craonne," Georges Brassens's "La Guerre de 14-18," and Boris Vian's and Renaud's renditions of "Le Déserteur" as examples of songs that reflect societal norms at the time of their performance. As a new breed of hero—or anti-hero, depending on one's perspective—emerged from the growing pacifist trend of the 1960s, French songs, a powerful and easily transmittable medium of popular culture, celebrated the figure of men who refused to fight or who regarded a given war as unjust. In his chapter, Corbin offers a case study of each of the aforementioned songs as well as possible ways to teach French language form (register, vocabulary, and grammar) and the context (political controversies and social questions) that generated it.

Eliza Jane Smith's chapter, "Teaching Francophone and French Cultures through Project-Based Learning," centers on project-based learning and culturally centered projects with authentic materials, mainly film and literature, in beginner language courses as a means of effectively exposing students to various aspects of francophone and French culture while still adhering to rigid curriculum standards with regard to grammar and the four skills. By describing how students complete four projects that revolve around cultural discussions of the content and questions of genre, the author shows that, in addition to strengthening students' overall communicative competence, the use of project-based learning (PBL) in the language classroom ultimately helps bridge the content gap between language classes and advanced literature and culture courses.

The third part of this volume tackles visual arts and mass media through multiliteracies frameworks. Kathryne Adair Corbin's approach to teaching culture encourages criticality and transcultural learning through reflecting on social practices and identities.[45] In "The French Classroom as a Newsroom: A Multiliteracies Framework," the author explores how students can "reflect upon the world and themselves through the lens of another language and culture"[46] by becoming journalists who read, analyze, and report the news and write opinion pieces that explore the communities where they live. Corbin illustrates how developing one's language skills is also deeply cultural, for much meaning is embedded in structures and word choices—a key tool for journalists who must construct culturally embedded news material to share via text and video every day. Her course "Tous journalistes" serves as a model to redesign an advanced grammar, conversation, and composition course to include diverse forms for critical making that engage and challenge students as learners of language and culture through discussion, process-based writing, grammar lessons, and critical inquiry.

Heidi Holst-Knudsen's chapter, "Of Presidents and Internet Memes: Fostering Student-Centered Learning, Cultural Competency, and Critical Thinking through the Use of Images," is grounded in a literacy-based foreign language curriculum[47] and in cognitive research dedicated to multimedia learning.[48] Holst-Knudsen demonstrates how to use memes in the French language classroom using a pedagogical sequence centered on an original photograph of French president Emmanuel Macron that spread rapidly on the internet through various forms. The chapter also illustrates why and how memes are fertile points of departure for stimulating communication, presenting culture, analyzing discursive strategies, and encouraging cultural comparison and critical analysis while also focusing on language production and grammatical competence.

In "Culture with Pictures: *Blogs BD* for Multiple Literacies in the French Language Classroom," Aurélie Chevant-Aksoy introduces French *blogs BD*, comics in the form of blog entries, as a pedagogical tool providing easy access to authentic linguistic and cultural material. Following a multiliteracies framework,[49] the author demonstrates how to utilize *blogs BD* in beginner to advanced levels to immerse students in authentic French language use; to make cross-cultural assessments; to alert students to the social, cultural, and historical contexts of communication; and to promote community building in French language outside the classroom.

The fourth and final part of this volume explores teaching culture through digital technologies and digital tools. First, Audra Merfeld-Langston illustrates practical strategies for integrating a variety of authentic target-language YouTube videos into French-language courses, including for different age groups and different language ability levels. Her chapter, "Engaging Students Inside and Outside of the Classroom with YouTube," highlights how incorporating YouTube videos allows instructors to address all of ACTFL's 5 Cs with their students while fostering the development of many areas outlined by the Partnership for 21st Century Skills, such as social and cross-cultural skills, creativity and innovation, and flexibility and adaptability. The author includes sample activities to use in class, which can be stand-alone exercises or smaller components that build on a larger theme throughout a unit.

Investigating the growing field of place-based education and its more recent offshoot, virtual place-based education, Carrie O'Connor focuses her chapter, "Charting the Course: Online Maps as a Tool in the French Culture Classroom," on the application of Google My Maps in an advanced French for business course. The author not only explains the course's final project, for which students researched and analyzed sites according to a particular theme, but also provides further innovative uses of the digital mapping tool in a variety of language-learning environments, noting the possible disadvantages and pitfalls in using online platforms. In this multiliteracies learning environment, students engage with the language and content that will support them later in their professions (business, in this case). As O'Connor explains, "Interaction with online shared maps... supports each of the four literacies commonly referred to under the umbrella of multiple literacies: visual, textual, digital, and technological."

Finally, in "Developing Intercultural Communicative Competence via Video-Based Synchronous Communication among L2 French Learners," Virginie Cassidy and Hongying Xu report on the development of ICC among intermediate-level L2 learners of French through a semester-long, weekly, video-based synchronous computer-mediated communication (CMC) with native speakers of French. Using the model established by Byram in *Teaching and Assessing Intercultural Communicative Competence*, in which the author makes the case for the concept of an "intercultural speaker" rather than a "near-native speaker," Cassidy and Xu explain how their study not only evaluates how ICC can be achieved without studying abroad but also displays how culture can be part of any course.

Finally, we reiterate our support of the MLA Ad Hoc Committee on Foreign Languages and hope the contributions to this volume will serve to support individual instructors as well as departments that seek to transform curricula in order to better reflect the changes that are already occurring in the profession—and to maintain their place as vital players in the pursuit of a cross-disciplinary education. As such, language departments will be better positioned to offer "valuable academic units central to the humanities and to the missions of higher learning."[50]

NOTES

1. Erin Kearney, *Intercultural Learning in Modern Language Education: Expanding Meaning-Making Potentials* (Bristol, UK: Multilingual Matters, 2016), 11.
2. Kearney, 11.
3. Katherine Arens, "The Field of Culture: The Standards as a Model for Teaching Culture," The Modern Language Journal, 94, no. 2 (2010): 322.

4. See Claire Kramsch, "Language and Culture in Second Language Learning," in *The Routledge Handbook of Language and Culture*, ed. Farzad Sharifian (London: Routledge, 2015), 403–404.
5. Gabriella Kovács, "Culture in Language Teaching: A Course Design for Teacher Trainees," *Acta Universitatis Sapientiae, Philologica* 9, no. 3 (2017): 76.
6. At the time, Kramsch introduced the concept of creating a third place between the native and target cultures, that at "the intersection of multiple native and target cultures, the major task of language learners is to define for themselves what this 'third place' that they have engaged in seeking will look like, whether they are conscious of it or not." In other words, the classroom—in regards to both setting and material—provide students with an opportunity to occupy a "third place" where they can operate between native and target languages and cultures in order to think critically about both. Claire Kramsch, *Context and Culture in Language Teaching* (Oxford: Oxford University Press, 1993), 233.
7. Michael Agar, *Language Shock: Understanding the Culture of Conversation* (New York: William Morrow, 1994).
8. National Standards in Foreign Language Education Project, *Standards for Foreign Language Learning: Preparing for the 21st Century (SFFLL)* (Lawrence, KS: Allen Press, 1996), 47.
9. Genelle Morain, "Appendix C: Goal 2: *Cultures*: A Perspective on the Cultural Perspectives," in *Bringing the Standards into the Classroom: A Teacher's Guide*, 2nd ed., ed. Marcia Harmon Rosenbusch (Ames: Iowa State University, 1997), 35–36.
10. Morain, 36.
11. Morain, 37.
12. Modern Language Association Ad Hoc Committee on Foreign Languages, "Foreign Languages and Higher Education: New Structures for a Changed World," *Profession* (2007): 234–245, https://www.mla.org/flreport.
13. Modern Language Association.
14. Kramsch, "Language and Culture," 413.
15. Kramsch, 409.
16. Kramsch, "Language and Culture," 410.
17. See the report of the 2007 MLA Ad Hoc Committee on Foreign Languages for definitions of "translingual" and "transcultural competence."
18. Kramsch, "Language and Culture," 412.
19. Chantelle Warner and Beatrice Dupuy, "Moving toward Multiliteracies in Foreign Language Teaching: Past and Present Perspectives . . . and Beyond," *Foreign Language Annals* 51, no. 1 (2018): 119.

20. Richard Kern, *Literacy and Language Teaching* (Oxford: Oxford University Press, 2000), 16.
21. Richard G. Kern, "Literacy as a New Organizing Principle for Foreign Language Education," in *Reading between the Lines: Perspectives on Foreign Language Literacy*, ed. Peter C. Patrikis (New Haven, CT: Yale University Press, 2003), 43.
22. Heather Willis Allen and Kate Paesani, "Exploring the Feasibility of a Pedagogy of Multiliteracies in Introductory Foreign Language Courses," *L2 Journal* 2, no. 1 (2010): 119–142. Mary Kalantzis and Bill Cope suggested a reframing of the four curricular components as pedagogical acts. They refer to these reconceptualized components of the multiliteracies pedagogy as experiencing, conceptualizing, analyzing, and applying: experiencing the known and the new, conceptualizing by naming and theorizing, analyzing functionally and critically, and applying appropriately and creatively (http://newlearningonline.com/learning-by-design/pedagogy). Mary Kalantzis and Bill Cope, *Learning by Design* (Altona, Victoria: Common Ground Publishing, 2005); and Bill Cope and Mary Kalantzis, "'Multiliteracies': New Literacies, New Learning" *Pedagogies* 4, no. 3 (2009): 164–195.
23. Allen and Paesani, "Exploring the Feasibility," 122.
24. Allen and Paesani, 124–125.
25. Allen and Paesani, 125.
26. Warner and Dupuy, "Moving toward Multiliteracies, 123.
27. Steven L. Thorne and Jonathon Reinhardt, "'Bridging Activities,' New Media Literacies, and Advanced Foreign Language Proficiency," *CALICO Journal* 25, no. 3 (2008): 561.
28. Thorne and Reinhardt, 566.
29. Stacey Katz Bourns, Cheryl Krueger, and Nicole Mills, *Perspectives on Teaching Language and Content* (New Haven, CT: Yale University Press, 2020), 214.
30. Kearney, *Intercultural Learning*, 33.
31. Kearney, 33.
32. Michael Byram, *Teaching and Assessing Intercultural Communicative Competence* (Clevedon, UK: Multilingual Matters, 1997), 38.
33. Kearney, *Intercultural Learning*, 35.
34. Kearney, 37.
35. Kramsch, *Context and Culture*, 231.
36. Claire Kramsch, "The Symbolic Dimensions of the Intercultural," *Language Teaching* 44, no. 3 (2011): 355.
37. Claire Kramsch, "From Communicative Competence to Symbolic Competence," *Modern Language Journal* 90, no. 2 (2006): 251.

38. Kramsch, "Language and Culture," 412.
39. Kearney, *Intercultural Learning*, 144.
40. Kearney, 144–145.
41. Claire Kramsch, "Third Culture and Language Education," in *Contemporary Applied Linguistics: Language Teaching and Learning*, ed. Vivien Cook and Li Wei (London: Continuum, 2009), 238.
42. Bonnie Adair-Hauck and Richard Donato, "The PACE Model: A Story-Based Approach to Meaning and Form for Standards-Based Language Learning," *French Review* 76, no. 2 (December 2002): 265–276.
43. Adair-Hauck and Donato.
44. Kate Paesani, Heather Willis Allen, and Beatrice Dupuy, *A Multiliteracies Framework for Collegiate Foreign Language Teaching* (Upper Saddle River, NJ: Pearson, 2016), 21.
45. Modern Language Association, "Foreign Languages," 4.
46. Modern Language Association, "Foreign Languages," 237.
47. Byram, *Teaching and Assessing*; Richard Kern, "Reconciling the Language–Literature Split through Literacy," *ADFL Bulletin* 33, no. 3 (Spring 2002): 20–24; and Paesani, Allen, Dupuy, *Multiliteracies Framework*.
48. Richard E. Mayer, *Multimedia Learning*, 2nd ed. (New York: Cambridge University Press, 2009).
49. New London Group, "A Pedagogy of Multiliteracies: Designing Social Futures," *Harvard Educational Review* 66, no. 1 (Spring 1996): 60–93; Kern, *Literacy and Language Teaching*; and Paesani, Allen, Dupuy, *Multiliteracies Framework*.
50. Modern Language Association, "Foreign Languages," 234–245.

REFERENCES

Adair-Hauck, Bonnie, and Richard Donato. "The PACE Model: A Story-Based Approach to Meaning and Form for Standards-Based Language Learning." *French Review* 76, no. 2 (December 2002): 265–276.

Agar, Michael. *Language Shock: Understanding the Culture of Conversation*. New York: William Morrow, 1994.

Allen, Heather Willis, and Kate Paesani. "Exploring the Feasibility of a Pedagogy of Multiliteracies in Introductory Foreign Language Courses." *L2 Journal* 2, no. 1 (2010): 119–142.

Arens, Katherine. "The Field of Culture: The Standards as a Model for Teaching Culture." *Modern Language Journal* 94, no. 2 (2010): 321–324.

Bourns, Stacey Katz, Cheryl Krueger, and Nicole Mills. *Perspectives on Teaching Language and Content*. New Haven, CT: Yale University Press, 2020.

Byram, Michael. *Teaching and Assessing Intercultural Communicative Competence*. Clevedon, UK: Multilingual Matters, 1997.

Cope, Bill, and Mary Kalantzis. "'Multiliteracies': New Literacies, New Learning." *Pedagogies* 4, (2009): 164–195.

Kalantzis, Mary, and Bill Cope. *A Pedagogy of Multiliteracies: Learning by Design*. New York: Palgrave Macmillan, 2015.

Kearney, Erin. *Intercultural Learning in Modern Language Education: Expanding Meaning-Making Potentials*. Bristol, UK: Multilingual Matters, 2016.

Kern, Richard. *Literacy and Language Teaching*. Oxford: Oxford University Press, 2000.

———. "Literacy as a New Organizing Principle for Foreign Language Education." In *Reading between the Lines: Perspectives on Foreign Language Literacy*, edited by Peter C. Patrikis, 40–59. New Haven, CT: Yale University Press, 2003.

———. "Reconciling the Language—Literature Split through Literacy." *ADFL Bulletin* 33, no. 3 (Spring 2002): 20–24.

Kovács, Gabriella. "Culture in Language Teaching: A Course Design for Teacher Trainees." *Acta Universitatis Sapientiae, Philologica* 9, no. 3 (2017): 73–86.

Kramsch, Claire. *Context and Culture in Language Teaching*. Oxford: Oxford University Press, 1993.

———. "Culture in Foreign Language Teaching." *Iranian Journal of Language Teaching Research* 1, no. 1 (2013): 57–78.

———. "From Communicative Competence to Symbolic Competence." *Modern Language Journal* 90, no. 2 (2006): 249–252.

———. "Language and Culture in Second Language Learning." In *The Routledge Handbook of Language and Culture*, edited by Farzad Sharifian, 403–416. London: Routledge, 2015.

———. "The Symbolic Dimensions of the Intercultural." *Language Teaching* 44, no. 3 (2011): 354–367.

———. "Teaching Foreign Languages in an Era of Globalization: Introduction." *Modern Language Journal* 98, no. 1 (Spring 2014): 296–311.

———. "Theorizing Translingual/Transcultural Competence." In *AAUSC 2010: Critical and Intercultural Theory and Language Pedagogy*, edited by Glenn S. Levine and Alison Phipps, 15–31. Boston: Heinle, 2012.

———. "Third Culture and Language Education." In *Contemporary Applied Linguistics: Language Teaching and Learning*, edited by Vivien Cook and Li Wei, 233–254. London: Continuum, 2009.

Lange, Dale L. "Planning for and Using the New National Culture Standards." In *Foreign Language Standards: Linking Research, Theories, and Practices*, edited by June K. Phillips and Robert M. Terry, 57–135. Lincolnwood, IL: National Textbook Company and American Council on the Teaching of Foreign Languages, 1999.

Mayer, Richard E. *Multimedia Learning*. 2nd ed. New York: Cambridge University Press, 2009.

Modern Language Association Ad Hoc Committee on Foreign Languages. "Foreign Languages and Higher Education: New Structures for a Changed World." *Profession* (2007): 234–245. https://www.mla.org/flreport.

Morain, Genelle. "Appendix C: Goal 2: *Cultures*: A Perspective on Cultural Perspectives." In *Bringing the Standards into the Classroom: A Teacher's Guide*, 2nd ed., edited by Marcia Harmon Rosenbusch, 35–37. Ames: Iowa State University, 1997.

National Standards in Foreign Language Education Project. *Standards for Foreign Language Learning: Preparing for the 21st Century (SFFLL)*. Lawrence, KS: Allen Press, 1996.

New London Group. "A Pedagogy of Multiliteracies: Designing Social Futures." *Harvard Educational Review* 66, no. 1 (Spring 1996): 60–93.

Thorne, Steven L., & Jonathon Reinhardt. "'Bridging Activities,' New Media Literacies, and Advanced Foreign Language Proficiency." *CALICO Journal* 25, no. 3 (2008): 558–572.

Paniagua, Alejandro. "Innovation in Everyday Teaching: No More Waiting for Superman." *Brookings* (blog), February 8, 2018. https://www.brookings.edu/blog/education-plus-development/2018/02/08/innovation-in-everyday-teaching-no-more-waiting-for-superman/.

Thorne, Steven L., & Jonathon Reinhardt. "'Bridging Activities,' New Media Literacies, and Advanced Foreign Language Proficiency." *CALICO Journal* 25, no. 3 (2008): 558–572.

Warner, Chantelle, and Beatrice Dupuy. "Moving toward Multiliteracies in Foreign Language Teaching: Past and Present Perspectives ... and Beyond." *Foreign Language Annals* 51, no. 1 (2018): 116–128.

PART I

IMMERSION AND IMPROVISATION

CHAPTER ONE

TEACHING CULTURE THROUGH FOOD
A Kinesthetic Approach to the College Language Classroom

Aria Dal Molin, University of South Carolina

INTRODUCTION: TEACHING CULTURE THROUGH FOOD

On the first night of my study abroad trip to Vannes, France, when I was sixteen, I found myself sitting across the dinner table from my French maman and papa, with my French "sister," Marie, on my left and her six-year-old sister, Cécile, on my right. My two years of high school French had not adequately prepared me for the linguistic aspects of the experience, but my linguistic shortfalls did not preclude the cultural exchanges that would take place over the course of the meal. Indeed, what I learned that night far surpassed essential grammar and vocabulary and had a lasting impact on my understanding of French-speaking cultures as well as on my own conception of self.

Study abroad experiences are one of the most efficient methods of teaching a second language (L2) culture. Unfortunately, due to restrictions on time and money that limit access to such experiences, foreign language (FL) instructors must come up with effective alternate methods for teaching culture in the FL classroom. This chapter proposes a method of teaching culture in the FL classroom centered on food, cuisines, and somatic experiences that moves students beyond textbook learning and seeks to emulate the same dynamic interpretative possibilities and personal self-reflection that study abroad opportunities often provide.

The purpose of teaching culture is to stimulate inquiry—both into the L2 culture and into one's awareness of the self—and must have the socially transformative goals of what B. Kumaravadivelu and Michael Byram have called "global cultural consciousness" and "intercultural citizenship."[1] That is to say, it is no longer desirable to simply focus on target-culture competence; instead, pedagogy needs to promote language learners who are able to critically interpret the heteroglossic reality of the world around them on individual and global levels. A more nuanced approach to teaching culture is necessary in order to move away from learning as acquisition and concentrate instead on cultural complexity, hybridity, and the interaction of different perspectives. A large body of contemporary research uses semiotic principles to understand the intercultural dimensions of language education.[2] A dialogic-semiotic approach to teaching culture envisions culture as a process rather than a product and seeks to examine "culture meaning not as locked into a certain image or text but as emergent through human engagement with learning materials."[3] Kramsch's work on the intercultural dimensions of language education points out that "semiotic fluidity presents a challenge to the traditional normativity of FL education"[4] and therefore necessitates nontraditional activities in the classroom that give students the opportunity to engage in cultural inquiry and meaning-making on their own. When language learners come to use and experience a new system of signs, they, in turn, begin to change and transform since "language constructs the historical sedimentation of meanings that we call our 'selves.'"[5]

Indeed, in a vein similar to this conception of the mutable nature of texts and cultures, Scottish philosopher and empiricist David Hume (1711–1776) proposed the idea that knowledge itself is neither constant nor fixed, and even the most basic convictions about the natural world must be arrived at through repeated experiences rather than through inductive reasoning.[6] Empiricism, or the philosophy that learning comes through sensorial experience, lends itself nicely to pedagogical approaches to culture since Hume envisioned knowledge as "beliefs" rather than as static, immutable facts. Furthermore, John Stewart Mill (1806–1873) acclimatized Hume's empiricism to nineteenth-century English language philosophy by arguing that one obtains knowledge through reasoning of and inferences gained from direct sensorial experiences.[7] Kramsch's theory of the "Multilingual Subject" is similarly based on the visceral, physical, subjective experience of the language learner. Admittedly, previous approaches to language learning have already involved capitalizing on the physical experience of the language learner (i.e., Total Physical Response, Community Language Learning, the Direct Method, etc.). Kramsch's theory, however, sets itself apart from these past approaches due to its emphasis on perception and individual experience in learning and using a new language. In an interview on her theory of the Multilingual Subject, she reminds language teachers of the following:

> [T]he bodies they have in front of them in the classroom are, in fact, acquiring the language with all their senses; not just their brains but their eyes, their ears, their touching, their smell, their taste, and that they [teachers] should appeal to the senses in a much greater way than they usually do.[8]

The educational approach of experiential learning, which was founded in the 1970s but has gained more influence in the past decade, especially in American colleges and universities,[9] similarly takes advantage of the somatic experience of language learning but is insufficient in the confined space of the language classroom. To this end, Byram asserts that it is not the job of the language teacher to attempt to recreate or replace the sensations of firsthand experience within the classrooms; rather, the task is to "facilitate learners' interaction with some small part of another society and its cultures, with the purpose of relativizing learners' understanding of their own cultural values, beliefs and behaviors and encouraging them to investigate for themselves the otherness around them."[10] In-class activities need, therefore, to be grounded in inquiry, interaction, and interpretation, through which learners make meaning of polysemous and flexible cultural forms. Accordingly, I propose an empiricist-inspired approach to teaching French culture in the L2 classroom that emphasizes personal, subjective, somatic experiences and builds toward the goal of fostering intercultural skills and a reflexive understanding of culture, self, and other. Students work together in a process of meaning-making around cultural forms, texts, and representations and have the opportunity to reflect on their perspectives with their peers, which requires learners to critically analyze their own beliefs and engage with alternate viewpoints. An approach to culture learning in the L2 classroom inspired by PACE (Presentation, Attention, Co-Construction, Extension) is helpful since the method was designed to build interpretive skills through student-centered inductive instruction. The PACE method brings the students to the fore in the process of examining cultural meaning as emergent through human engagement with the learning material.

A PACE-INSPIRED MODEL FOR TEACHING FRENCH CULTURE

In the early 2000s, Bonnie Adair-Hauck and Richard Donato designed a pedagogical model named PACE, which they describe as "contrasting with both explicit and implicit teaching."[11] In fact, Adair-Hauck and Donato's model navigates a middle ground of instruction that forestalls placing the instructor in the all-knowing, authoritative seat of the "Atlas Complex" yet also avoids creating an instructional free-for-all in which students are unsure if their attempts at communication are meaningful. Based on cultural-historical psychologist Lev Vygotsky's cognitive theories of communication and the development of higher psychological processes, the PACE model insists on creating a "dynamic, reciprocal, and interactive" approach to FL instruction to take into account "how learning takes place between people in the world outside of the classroom."[12] In Adair-Hauck and Donato's article describing the storytelling-based method to teaching grammar, the last section, "Cultural Interpretation," acknowledges an inadvertent benefit to this model of instruction. They noticed that language students in the past had to "put in their time" in language-only classes before finally being able to be exposed to cultural aspects of the language learning process. They observed that by using the PACE model, learners begin to explore the interrelations of language and culture early on thanks to the authentic texts employed in the model's first phase.[13] Therefore, the PACE model in its conception was always already intended for the teaching of culture, even if its founders focused mainly on the model's uses for grammatical instruction.

The PACE model is a four-step process that encourages student inquiry through the formation of predictions, hypotheses, and "the creation of interpersonal language learning experiences for the students."[14] The acronym PACE stands for the four phases of instruction: Presentation, Attention, Co-Construction, and Extension. Broadly speaking, the first half of PACE instruction employs "guided" *presentation* of authentic materials to the students using only the target language, wherein the instructor takes an "instructional detour" in order to call to *attention* the specific linguistic exploration that the story-based teaching will provide. The final two stages—Co-Construction and Extension—call on the students to hypothesize about the forms they are learning in the lesson and, finally, to *extend* these hypotheses and put them to use in creative and interpersonal ways.

I propose using the study of French cuisines and food culture, loosely following the PACE model's method of *co-construction*, as a means to engage kinesthetic college learners in intermediate-level language classes. The initial periods of formal learning take place inside the classroom, but this approach also requires small group learning in meetings between students outside of class time. This method stresses the learning of culture through tangible group experiences that link initial periods of theory with real-world practice. Through instructor-guided *dîner et un film* (dinner and a movie) projects scaffolded according to PACE's four phases, students learn to make sense of cultural forms, texts, and representations. The informal social environment of the project fosters the transformative goals of reflexivity and intercultural skill-building by helping students to critically explore the self and other in a heteroglossic global world. The goal in applying a PACE-inspired approach to teaching French culture is to place the students at the center of cultural inquiry in order to collaboratively construct cultural meaning through comparative analysis, self-reflection, and dialogue with their peers. In this way, the *dîner et un film* project relies more heavily on a Vygotskian psycholinguistic approach to instruction than even the original PACE instruction, since it was Vygotsky himself who acknowledged the powerful tool that is conversation between human beings outside of the classroom in active social externalism.[15]

THE FORGOTTEN LEARNING STYLE

There are several kinds of learning styles, but visual, auditory, and kinesthetic (VAK) styles are commonly used to classify participants in the learning process. Identifying students' preferred learning styles and teaching to diverse learning styles in the classroom have been shown in recent studies to enable more effective education.[16] For years our profession has been wrestling with how to teach to all learning styles in the classroom. In particular, there is very little consensus on the best ways to teach culture to the L2 learner.[17] Much progress has been made for visual and auditory learners through the integration of visual aids, audio-visual demonstrations, and literature-based learning in the language and culture classrooms. Textbooks, too, have improved over the decades by offering a multitude of paratextual features in the forms of videos, music, and online workbook activities and supplements, which often include listening opportunities, short video clips, art, blogs, vlogs, and voice recordings. Kinesthetic learners, however, have not benefited from the same expansion of options in and beyond the FL classroom due to limited classroom activities offering physical learning opportunities to the students.

Arguably, kinesthetic learners are the most neglected of the learning styles in the typical college language classroom. Theater practicum courses in FL departments aiming to teach language through theater and performance are one of the few examples of language courses geared toward kinesthetic learners.[18] Study abroad opportunities, too, reach this style of learner, as they offer interpersonal and direct engagement with the student. This chapter offers a practical guide to *dîner et un film* projects that can be implemented in intermediate-level French language courses as an innovative technique to teach culture in the classroom as well as to furnish learning opportunities that appeal to this neglected learning style. This classroom example shows that teaching intermediate French students culture through food offers a tangible, multifaceted opportunity that appeals especially to kinesthetic learners by creating interpersonal, hands-on learning environments comprising interaction and movement.

WHY USE FOOD TO TEACH FRENCH CULTURE?

This project employs food as historical and sociological testimony in active dialogue with the past and present forms of French-speaking cultures. Learning a foreign culture is a process whereby knowledge is created through the transformation of experiences.[19] The seemingly trivial and familiar acts of eating and cooking, I argue, offer experiences ripe with cultural insight into behaviors, values, attitudes, and perspectives.

Cuisine is not simply food; it is a social product, an aesthetic artifact, and a cultural tradition that reflects the geography, agricultural practices, values, and customs of a society. Fabio Parasecoli's analysis of food and popular culture aligns with Kramsch's semiotic framework of language learning as it considers comprehending a culture in terms of analyzing and making sense of a multitude of symbols engaging with one another:

> One of the basic tenets of semiotics is that everything in a culture can be considered as carrying meaning and that as humans we are constantly engaging in semiosis, the process of making sense of the reality that surrounds us. Signs need to be considered within their context, as parts of a system, in which each component's role is somehow defined by the other elements in it.[20]

Teaching students through cooking and cuisines, Parasecoli argues, forces them to think outside of the consumable product itself and consider "networks of simultaneous relation with not only other objects, behaviors, and representations, but also with norms, values, discourses, embodied experiences, social relations, organizations, economic and political structures."[21] The products must be considered within a system of food production (how food is created), nutritional values (which foods are chosen for consumption), behaviors of consumption (how food is consumed and in what environment), food preparation (who prepares the food and how), the history behind recipes (who taught them to prepare food in this way), the social implications of certain foods (who eats what types of food and when), and the connections with the environment. As Priscilla Clark puts it, cuisine is "a *process* which involves several distinct products, specific functions and separate actors."[22] Therefore, reflections on important cultural points, such as perspectives on history, environment, social class, gender roles, age, religion, and moral values, are sneakily entrenched within a food unit in an FL class. Food and cuisine are carriers of cultural information whose meaning can only emerge through a complex process of interaction, reflection, critical analysis, and meaning-making. Therefore, lessons and discussions on cuisine ultimately lead to considerations of regions, history, geography, agriculture, and sociology.

However, French-speaking countries' cuisines, like French-speaking cultures more generally, are not a static, unmoving cultural artifact but are in continual evolution while also remaining in dialogue with the past. For insights into the history of a culture's cuisine, Clark argues, one must look to its literature. She maintains that French cuisine is inextricably interwoven into French literature, "from Rabelaisian feasts, the banquet of *Le Bourgeois gentilhomme*, the *petits soupers* of the eighteenth-century novels, Sadean orgies to the laden tables of Balzac, Flaubert, Maupassant, Zola, Proust's madeleines with tea at his grandmother's house, Colette and many more."[23] Whereas interviews with local French chefs and consultation of French cookbooks will help supply students with cultural input regarding contemporary cuisines and food consumption, excerpts from French literature will help engage with social history and traditions linked with the past. Joseph Berchoux's *Gastronomie*, Jean Anthelme Brillat-Savarin's *Physiologie du goût*, *L'art de la cuisine française au XIXe siècle*, Honoré de Balzac's "Nouvelle théorie du déjeuner," and Alexandre Dumas's *Grand Dictionnaire de cuisine* all contributed in various ways to the diffusion of the cultural ideal of French cuisine in the nineteenth century. The method proposed in this chapter therefore encourages instructors to use food in the French language classroom as historical as well as sociological testimony.

Finally, since every culture has its own culinary traditions, food is a particularly adept theme for fulfilling goals of reflexivity and intercultural analysis in the FL classroom. In this way, lessons on French culture must first be based on self-discovery and self-inquiry into the cultures of food associated with the individual students. They start by examining their own relationship to food and culinary traditions and then move on to other perspectives.

THE *DÎNER ET UN FILM* PROJECT FOR INTERMEDIATE-LEVEL FRENCH STUDENTS

The PACE-inspired *dîner et un film* project was designed with the following learning objectives in mind:

1. Foster lively interaction between students in the FL classroom that centers students in the process of meaning-making of cultural forms, texts, and representations.
2. Develop students' intercultural skills by having them critically analyze their own beliefs with alternate viewpoints.
3. Have students reflect on their own impressions of culture through intracultural discussions among peers in a "whole language"[24] context.

Over the course of a few weeks, intermediate-level French language students were put into small groups, selected a French-speaking region for their group, completed several in-class pre-presentation preparatory research activities, participated in a classroom interview with a French chef, selected a regional menu for their group meal, and prepared the meal as a group in an informal learning environment outside of class time. To conclude, students in each group prepared a presentation on their region to reveal their intercultural findings.[25] In what follows, I will describe how I implemented this PACE-inspired approach to teaching culture through the *dîner et un film* project in an intermediate-level French culture course in order to make the instruction of culture an active discovery learning process that encouraged learners to make sense of the target culture through kinesthetic engagement with the learning materials.

As mentioned above, the PACE model is a four-step process that guides the student through four phases of instruction (Presentation, Attention, Co-Construction, and Extension) in order to facilitate a student-centered hypothesis-building and interpretation-shaping process. As a preparatory phase to this project, students first reflected on their own eating habits and American food cultures. The instructor prepared a school-sponsored "dinner dialogue" at her house, and the students were each assigned to contribute a dish or a drink that they believed represented their cultural heritage or that was a staple in their households growing up. The class gathered and conducted a conversation around the students' own personal food traditions entirely in the L2 language. The instructor provided students with prompts and sample questions to consider before coming to the discussion (see appendix 1.1 on Fulcrum). The dinner dialogue proved fruitful for stimulating intercultural dialogues around regional variances in cuisines and traditions in America as well as demanding students to reflect critically on their own personal perspectives. The class focused the majority of the conversation on the subtle cultural differences between various regions of the United States, and students grappled with the difficulty of how to accurately define "American cuisine" and America's relationship to food. Students expressed frustration with the stereotype that "American food" is associated with fast food and extended these considerations to stereotypes of French cuisine. The class happened to include two non-American students, one from China and one from Italy; thus, these students were able to contribute personal information regarding their own local food traditions, especially on how these traditions are manipulated and translated in Chinese and Italian restaurants in the United States. As a pre-cultural discussion activity, this preliminary step allowed the students time to get acquainted with the general subject at hand and to start reflecting upon their local cultures before moving on to the target culture. It also planted the seeds for reconsideration of homogeneous cultural stereotypes.

As a homework assignment, after the dinner dialogue, students wrote a reflection piece in the L2 on what they learned over the course of the dinner and made predictions regarding what they might learn about French-speaking cultures over the course of the assignment. They also came up with at least five questions regarding French cuisines and French food culture that they would pose to a French chef at the next class meeting (for examples, see appendix 1.2 on Fulcrum). These preliminary writing assignments help students accumulate the vocabulary with which to discuss topics of food, cuisine, and culture. They also allow students to start making cross-cultural comparisons and having insights on their own rather than receiving the information from a book or from the instructor.

The second phase of the assignment encompassed the Presentation phase of the PACE model, in which the instructor provides authentic cultural forms, texts, and representations of which the students must make sense. The instructor invited a French chef who resided locally into the classroom to answer questions that the students had prepared regarding French cuisine and cultural traditions. Each student was required to ask the chef at least one question during the class period. The discussion evolved gradually from personal questions regarding the chef's upbringing in Lyons, France, to differences between working as a chef in France and in the United States. He discussed the contents and construction of a standard French menu compared with menus for French restaurants in America, as well as ordering habits of customers in each country. Students appeared invested in the interview, and a lively discussion around the chef's experience with different French cuisines and the difference between *la haute cuisine* and local, regional specialties arose.

To complement the interview, students were assigned excerpts from authentic cultural material foreshadowing some structures and conceptions of the history of French cuisines.[26] The excerpts from these texts were specifically selected by the instructor to highlight structures of the philosophy of French cuisine in the nineteenth century. For instance, many of the excerpts focused on the elaborate rules and regulations regarding the preparation of certain dishes and how and in what circumstances they should be consumed. The excerpts drew attention to the creation of the word "restaurant," compared with other dining establishments available, such as cabarets, inns, and *tables d'hôte*. They also highlighted the social implications of certain foods and meals to reveal that socialization is an integral part of the French meal. For instance, Brillat-Savarin wrote in 1826, "Tell me what you eat, and I'll tell you what you are,"[27] a phrase that serves to underscore the connection between behaviors of consumption and conceptions of self. Balzac's tongue-in-cheek "Nouvelle théorie du déjeuner" remarks on the intellectual vogue of the frugal "modern" breakfast as a "culinary symbol" of "intellectual 'methodism.'"[28] Balzac's observation on the trend-setting younger generation's reduction of the number of meals consumed in a day also helps establish the theme of changing culinary habits/vogues and the ever-shifting conceptions of cultural traditions more generally.

At the next class meeting, students came to class prepared to discuss what they had learned from both their interview with the French chef and from the excerpts from the French literature. It was insufficient to simply be present in the interview and read the excerpts before class since, as Byram and Kramsch point out, language classes must teach "critical language awareness, interpretive skills, and historical consciousness."[29] To that end, the instructor asked students to summarize what they had learned from the interview and compare it to the vision of cuisine portrayed in the historical accounts so that they could situate the chef's personal experiences within a historical framework. A discussion of these literary excerpts together with the interview with the French chef helped to problematize the static notion of food cultures for the students. Thus, in the Presentation phase, comparisons of differences between historical texts and personal accounts allowed the instructor to guide students to develop an awareness of the dangers of declarative stereotyping and offered students opportunities to engage critically with the cultural representations. This phase of the project promoted personal critical analysis and intercultural skills by reducing learners' essentializations of food cultures.

After the Presentation stage of the assignment, students were broken into small groups, assigned a region for their group to study, and supplied the following research scenario:

> Le département d'hospitalité, tourisme, et arts culinaires de votre université va envoyer deux étudiants à un stage dans un restaurant de votre région. L'université vous a engagé à faire découvrir aux deux futurs stagiaires la culture culinaire et la culture générale de votre région afin de les préparer pour leur premier voyage en France. N'oubliez pas que la culture (surtout culinaire) change d'une région à l'autre en France.
>
> [The department of hospitality, tourism, and culinary arts of your university is planning to send two students to an internship in a restaurant in your region. Your university has hired you to introduce the two future interns to the culinary and general cultures of the region to prepare them for their first trip to France. Keep in mind that culture (especially culinary) changes from region to region in France.]

The Attention phase of the PACE model is positioned after the Presentation of authentic material with the goal of getting learners to "perceive and attend to the language forms under exploration."[30] In the case of this adaptation of the PACE model for teaching culture, cultural forms are substituted for "language forms." Students were then tasked with researching the geography, landscape, weather, major agricultural products, population, and economy of their assigned region through online research and the use of the library and library databases in order to make connections between behaviors of consumption and the environment. The students were forewarned that part of their extensive final presentation project would entail an in-depth description of these aspects of their region of study.

To accompany the nineteenth-century literature on French cuisine, more contemporary depictions of French eating habits according to regions was provided in the form of recipe books.[31] First, the instructor asked students to analyze the structure of a French meal from their region according to the information provided in the introductions of the recipe books. Cross-cultural discussion among the groups compared the length, structure, and organization of a French meal with meals prepared in their own homes within their own cultures. Then, the instructor had the students gather a list of common ingredients, spices, or cooking techniques emphasized in the recipes within their assigned book. Students discussed within their groups how this information corroborated the online research they had done for their region, which led to deeper questions regarding how the environment, weather, and geography affect not just what but how a population chooses to eat. Each group then chose at least one *entrée*, a *plat principal*, and a dessert from their region to prepare on the night of the project. Movies set in each region were also distributed to the groups at this point in the project.[32]

As previously mentioned, the Co-Construction phase of this project takes place in an informal environment outside of the classroom. Students must arrange to meet outside of class to prepare their meal together, eat dinner, and watch their film. The process must also be documented with video and photos taken by the participants, and the entire night should be conducted in the L2. These materials will then be employed during the Extension portion of the assignment, in which the students report on their experiences and introduce their regions to the rest of their classmates. During the Co-Construction phase, students gather in a simulated experiential learning environment that exists between the students' own cultures and that of the "other." In a way, the simulated space of the *dîner et un film* project creates a physical manifestation of Kramsch's notion of an "intercultural third place"[33] in which culture meaning becomes emergent through human engagement with learning materials. This third space has been theorized as an intermediary place wherein students reflect upon their own culture and the other cultures.

The instructor scaffolded students' hypothesis-making in the Co-Construction phase by supplying discussion prompts to use during the meal (see appendix 1.3 on Fulcrum) and film response sheets to fill out and discuss after the viewing (see appendix 1.4 on Fulcrum). In *The Multilingual Subject*, Kramsch points out that second-language acquisition (SLA) research traditionally pays more attention to the language learner's process of acquisition than to the individuals who are learning the language by separating the minds, bodies, and social behaviors of the learners into different domains of inquiry.[34] A semiotic approach to teaching culture means that the instructor does not have a fixed interpretation or meaning in mind so that projects place the individual language learner's experience at the center of the process, and meanings emerge through physical engagement with the material. As the students discuss the provided prompts in the L2 over the course of the meal and examine the cultural material represented in the film, the learners are not only inquiring about, interacting with, and interpreting the cultural forms in order to make sense of their meanings, but they are also cultivating their emerging learner identities in the L2. In the simulated in-between space of the dinner and a movie, the students are given room to relativize the otherness of the "other" culture by partaking in the language, cooking the meal, enjoying the food, and analyzing the cinematographic representations. The use of the L2 in the discussions throughout the evening allows students to experience both an insider's and an outsider's perspective. Angela Scarino describes this reflexive process of meaning-making as "moving between the diverse linguistic and cultural systems in the mix with learners drawing upon their entire repertoire in order to make meaning" since the language learner is both the user and learner of the language.[35] This phase focuses on students becoming active participants in culture learning so that they can move beyond "self v. other" forms of thinking and comprehending.

To finish the projects, the Extension stage "affords the learners opportunities to use their new skills creatively and interpersonally."[36] After discussing and collaboratively hypothesizing cultural findings regarding their region with their group, the students then extend their conclusions in a formal presentation and a written reflection. The requirements for the presentation were as follows:

> 1. Présentez des aspects culturels et géographiques de la région. 2. Présentez des aspects de la cuisine de la région (et en quoi les caractéristiques géographiques ont un impact sur les aliments cultivés dans la région). 3. Présentez le menu que votre groupe a préparé et réfléchissez aux aspects/ingrédients des plats qui sont spécifiquement liés à la région. Quels aspects/ingrédients en font des recettes régionales ? 4. Résumé du film. 5. Analysez les aspects régionaux du film (décors, dialectes, nourriture, vêtements, etc.). Portez une attention particulière à la relation des personnages avec la nourriture et les repas.
>
> [1. Present the cultural and geographical aspects of the region. 2. Present the aspects of the region's cuisine (and how the geographical characteristics have an effect on the food grown in the region). 3. Present the menu that your group cooked and

reflect upon which aspects/ingredients of the dishes are specifically linked to the region. What makes them regional recipes? 4. Summary of the film. 5. Analyze the regional aspects in the film (scenery, dialect, food, clothing, etc.). Pay special attention to the characters' relationships with food and meals.]

The formal presentation offered students a chance to report on the project's initial "problem" of teaching the hospitality students about the region in which they will be living and working. The students described the menu they chose to prepare and accompanied their explanations with pictures and videos taken from their meal, clips from the film, and explanations of specific ingredients that they found were important to the regional cuisine and how those ingredients reflected geographic, economic, social, and historical factors. Then, the groups described the film that they watched and its depictions of the region as well as the relationship that the characters had with food and meals within the film. The students interpreted the parameters of these oral presentations in different ways. Many students used visual representations through slide shows and PowerPoints, whereas other groups chose to theatrically enact the information they learned through performing their own original skit about the region.

The last portion of the assignment allowed students to articulate their experiences from the projects and the meanings they made of the cultural forms through written reports in the L2. The theory guiding these writing assignments was founded on Erin Kearney's assertion that "cultural forms are polysemous and cultural meanings are flexible and not only owned or produced by native speakers."[37] Therefore, rather than having students submit a formal, fixed report summarizing their findings regarding the culture and cuisine of their particular region as well as an analysis of the importance of food, cooking, and food products connected to the region presented within the film, the instructor asked students to focus on what they had learned about themselves as well as about the target culture over the course of the project (see appendix 1.5 on Fulcrum). They were prompted to confront some of the cultural beliefs they had come into the project with, about both their own culture and that of the other, in an effort to analyze how the project changed, transformed, or reinforced their perspectives on both themselves and French-speaking cultures. These written assignments gave students the opportunity to assess their own relationship with food in comparison with what had emerged about French cuisines.

CONCLUDING REMARKS

I began this chapter by referring to the importance of empiricism and learning through experience and the senses for teaching culture in an FL classroom because it is my opinion that culture, like Hume's consideration of knowledge, must be envisioned in terms of dynamic "beliefs" made sense of through repeated experiences rather than static, cultural "facts." Indeed, the constantly shifting nature of culture certainly contributes to the ambiguity regarding how one should go about teaching culture in a classroom and has undoubtedly influenced the conception and creation of this volume. It may well be that the study of a foreign language is synonymous with the study of another culture since, as Kramsch has famously asserted, "every single utterance is a speech act and every speech act is culturally meaningful."[38] However, in adapting the PACE model originally envisioned as a way to teach grammar as meaning and as meaningful to the instruction of culture as a process of meaning-making, this article has argued that culture, like grammar, is best made sense of through student-centered learning activities that encourage the students to come up with hypotheses themselves using their own personal experiences with the cultural forms. As Mill posited, learning takes place through inferences gained from experiences. Culture that is lived and language that is spoken are best taught through experiences. Although it was impossible to spy on the group discussions and determine the accuracy of the L2 used during the out-of-class portion of the project, the videos created by the students during the meal preparation at least gave evidence of students interacting in the L2. As Kramsch theorizes, the use of the L2 helps create a desire within the student for the identification with the other even if it is an imagined or hypothesized other.[39] This form of desire, founded on Julia Kristeva's famous theory,[40] pushes students to generate an identity for themselves and uncover new perspectives and new ways of thinking.[41]

Students appreciated the supportive environment of the out-of-class phase of the assignment. Many students expressed their appreciation for the dynamic aspects of the assignment, in which they were physically involved in the investigation of culture. Other students valued the authentic content of the Presentation phase of the assignment, in which they were able to interview the local French chef and engage directly with a native speaker. A common response in the opinion section of the final essay was the appreciation for the opportunity to "discover" aspects of French culture on their own rather than simply being "professed to" in the classroom environment. Indeed, many students affirmed that the project forced them to reconsider deeper questions such as the "concept of culture" in general through comparisons that they made between their own relationship with food and what they learned about French cuisines.

Adaptation of the PACE model for culture-oriented teaching in FL classrooms appears useful for bringing students to the center of the subjective, meaning-making process and for promoting intercultural skills by focusing on reflexivity and critical cultural analysis. This approach differs from previous research on intercultural exchanges in that it does not exalt interaction with native speakers of a language as the be-all and end-all of developing intercultural skills. Rather, by using the L2 in discussions with their peers during the dinner and after watching the film, participants in the project were able to "escape from the confines of their own grammar and culture"[42] and interpret and negotiate meaning through their own subjective and individual experiences of using a foreign language. The simulated space of the dinner and a movie assignment allows students adequate distance away from both self and the other in order to be able to confront some of the taken-for-granted cultural beliefs about both.

NOTES

1. B. Kumaravadivelu, *Cultural Globalization and Language Education* (New Haven, CT: Yale University Press, 2008), 164; and Michael Byram, "Intercultural Citizenship from an International Perspective," *Journal of the NUS Teaching Academy* 1, no. 1 (2011): 10–20.
2. See, especially, Claire Kramsch, *The Multilingual Subject* (Oxford: Oxford University Press, 2009); and Erin Kearney, *Intercultural Learning in Modern Language Education: Expanding Meaning-Making Potentials* (Bristol, UK: Multilingual Matters, 2016).
3. Csilla Weninger and Tamas Kiss, "Culture in English as a Foreign Language (EFL) Textbooks: A Semiotic Approach," *TESOL Quarterly* 47, no. 4 (December 2013): 700.
4. Claire Kramsch, "Teaching Foreign Languages in an Era of Globalization: Introduction," *Modern Language Journal* 98, no. 1 (Spring 2014): 300.
5. Kramsch, *Multilingual Subject*, 17.
6. David Hume, "An Enquiry Concerning Human Understanding," in *Enquiries Concerning the Human Understanding and Concerning the Principles of Morals*, 2nd ed., ed. Lewis Amherst Selby-Bigge (Oxford: Clarendon Press, 1902), 18.
7. John Stuart Mill, *The Collected Works of John Stuart Mill*, ed. John M. Robson (Toronto: University of Toronto Press, 1974), 7:7.
8. Claire Kramsch and Sascha Gerhards, "Im Gespräch: An Interview with Claire Kramsch on the 'Multilingual Subject,'" *Die Unterrichtspraxis / Teaching German* 45, no. 1 (Spring 2012): 75.
9. The University of South Carolina, for example, will now require at least 300 hours of experiential learning in order to graduate with leadership distinction (GLD). See "Experiential and Engaged Learning," University of South Carolina, accessed July 18, 2019, https://sc.edu/about/initiatives/usc_connect/choose_experiences/experiential_and_engaged_learning/index.php.

10. Michael Byram, Adam Nichols, and David Stevens, *Developing Intercultural Competence in Practice* (Clevedon, UK: Multilingual Matters, 2001), 3.
11. Bonnie Adair-Hauck and Richard Donato, "The PACE Model: A Story-Based Approach to Meaning and Form for Standards-Based Language Learning," *French Review* 76, no. 2 (December 2002): 268. For more information regarding the PACE model of story-based grammar instruction, see Bonnie Adair-Hauck, Richard Donato, and Phil Cumo-Johannsen, "Using a Story-Based Approach to Teach Grammar," in *Teacher's Handbook: Contextualized Language Instruction*, ed. Judith L. Shrum and Eileen W. Glisan (Boston: Heinle, 2005), 189–213; Bonnie Adair-Hauck and Richard Donato, "Foreign Language Explanations within the Zone of Proximal Development," *Canadian Modern Language Review* 50, no. 3 (1994): 532–557; and Bonnie Adair-Hauck and Richard Donato, "The PACE Model—Actualizing the Standards through Storytelling: 'Le Bras, la Jambe et le Ventre,'" *French Review* 76, no. 2 (December 2002): 278–296.
12. Adair-Hauck and Donato, "PACE Model: A Story-Based Approach," 268.
13. Adair-Hauck and Donato, 292.
14. Adair-Hauck and Donato, 292.
15. Lev Vygotsky, *Mind in Society: The Development of Higher Psychological Processes* (Cambridge, MA: Harvard University Press, 1978), 11; and Lev Vygotsky, "Tool and Sign in the Development of the Child," in *The Collected Works of L. S. Vygotsky*, ed. Robert W. Rieber (New York: Springer, 1999), 6:18.
16. Dodi Mulyadi, Dwi Rukmini, and Issy Yuliasri, "The Analysis of Students' Listening Proficiency Viewed from Their Different Learning Styles after Getting the Strategy Instructions," *Theory and Practice in Language Studies* 7, no. 12 (December 2017): 1200–1209.
17. Dale L. Lange, "Planning for and Using the New National Culture Standards," in *Foreign Language Standards: Linking Research, Theories, and Practices*, ed. June K. Phillips and Robert M. Terry (Lincolnwood, IL: National Textbook Company and American Council on the Teaching of Foreign Languages, 1999), 58.
18. See, for example, Nicoletta Marini-Maio and Colleen Ryan-Scheutz, *Set the Stage! Teaching Italian through Theater* (New Haven, CT: Yale University Press, 2010), for a practical guide to theater practicum language courses.
19. Peter Jarvis, John Holford, and Colin Griffin, *The Theory and Practice of Learning* (London: Kogan Page, 1998), 15; David Kolb, *Experiential Learning: Experience as the Source of Learning and Development* (Englewood Cliffs: Prentice-Hall, 1984), 24.

20. Fabio Parasecoli, "Food and Popular Culture," in *Food in Time and Place: The American Historical Association Companion to Food History*, ed. Paul Freedman, Joyce E. Chaplin, and Ken Albala (Berkeley: University of California Press, 2014), 327.
21. Parasecoli, 327.
22. Priscilla P. Clark, "Thoughts for Food, I: French Cuisine and French Culture," *French Review* 49, no. 1 (October 1975): 32.
23. Clark, 34.
24. The concept of "whole language" is employed by Bonnie Adair-Hauck in her article "Practical Whole Language Strategies for Secondary and University-Level FL Students," *Foreign Language Annals* 29, no. 2 (1996): 253–270.
25. In the first attempt at this project, due to the small size of the class, only regions of continental France were assigned to each group. However, this assignment could easily be adapted include discussions of francophone countries and their cuisines as well. In the future, I intend to expand the discussion of French cuisines to francophone cuisines in order to enlarge the discussion of French cultures.
26. The reading assignment included excerpts from Berchoux's *Gastronomie*, Brillat-Savarin's *Physiologie du goût*, *L'art de la cuisine française au XIXe siècle*, Balzac's "Nouvelle théorie du déjeuner," and Dumas's *Grand Dictionnaire de cuisine*.
27. Jean Anthelme Brillat-Savarin, *The Physiology of Taste* (1826), quoted and translated in Priscilla Parkhurst Ferguson, *Word of Mouth: What We Talk about When We Talk about Food* (Berkeley: University of California Press, 2014), 51.
28. Martina Lauster, *Sketches of the Nineteenth Century: European Journalism and Its Physiologies, 1830–50* (Basingstoke, UK: Palgrave Macmillan, 2007), 99.
29. Katra Byram and Claire Kramsch, "Why Is It So Difficult to Teach Language as Culture?," *German Quarterly* 81, no. 1 (Winter 2008): 21.
30. Adair-Hauck and Donato, "PACE Model—Actualizing," 284.
31. Julie Andrieu's *Le tour de France gourmand*, Gabriel Gate's *A Cook's Tour of France: Regional French Recipes*, Stéphanie Béraud-Sudreau's *La cuisine du Sud-Ouest*, Katia Podevin's *Carnet de recettes du Val de Loire*, Pierre Huguenin's *La vieille cuisine bourguignonne*, and Pierre Leroux's *Connaître et cuisiner les algues bretonnes* were distributed to groups according to their region, and students collectively assembled menus from these recipe books for their culinary projects.
32. Depending on the region, it may be difficult to find films set in places other than Paris. Some good titles of films set in various regions of France include

Bienvenue chez les Ch'tis (Normandie), *Les recettes du bonheur* (Occitanie), *Chocolat* (Bourgogne Franche-Comté), *Après Vous* (Paris), *Sous le sable* (Nouvelle Aquitaine), *Ma loute* (Hauts-de-France), *Manon des Sources* (Provence), *De rouille et d'os* (Occitanie), and *Alceste à bicyclette* (Nouvelle Aquitaine).

33. Claire Kramsch, *Context and Culture in Language Teaching* (Oxford: Oxford University Press, 1993), 236.
34. Kramsch, *Multilingual Subject*, 2.
35. Angela Scarino, "Learning as Reciprocal, Interpretive Meaning-Making: A View from Collaborative Research into the Professional Learning of Teachers of Languages," *Modern Language Journal* 98, no. 1 (2014): 388.
36. Adair-Hauck and Donato, "PACE Model—Actualizing," 286.
37. Kearney, *Intercultural Learning*, 37.
38. Kramsch and Gerhards, "Im Gespräch," 81.
39. Kramsch, *Multilingual Subject*, 17.
40. Julia Kristeva, *Desire in Language: A Semiotic Approach to Literature and Art* (New York: Columbia University Press, 1980).
41. Kramsch, *Multilingual Subject*, 17.
42. Kramsch, 18.

REFERENCES

Adair-Hauck, Bonnie. "Practical Whole Language Strategies for Secondary and University-Level FL Students." *Foreign Language Annals* 29, no. 2 (1996): 253–270.

Adair-Hauck, Bonnie, and Richard Donato. "Foreign Language Explanations within the Zone of Proximal Development." *Canadian Modern Language Review* 50, no. 3 (1994): 532–557.

———. "The PACE Model: A Story-Based Approach to Meaning and Form for Standards-Based Language Learning." *French Review* 76, no. 2 (December 2002): 265–276.

———. "The PACE Model—Actualizing the Standards through Storytelling: 'Le Bras, la Jambe et le Ventre.'" *French Review* 76, no. 2 (December 2002): 278–296.

Adair-Hauck, Bonnie, Richard Donato, and Phil Cumo-Johannsen. "Using a Story-Based Approach to Teach Grammar." In *Teacher's Handbook: Contextualized Language Instruction*, edited by Judith L. Shrum and Eileen W. Glisan, 189–213. Boston: Heinle, 2005.

Byram, Michael. "Intercultural Citizenship from an International Perspective." *Journal of the NUS Teaching Academy* 1, no. 1 (2011): 10–20.

Byram, Katra, and Claire Kramsch. "Why Is It So Difficult to Teach Language as Culture?" *German Quarterly* 81, no. 1 (Winter 2008): 20–34.

Byram, Michael, Adam Nichols, and David Stevens. *Developing Intercultural Competence in Practice.* Clevedon, UK: Multilingual Matters, 2001.

Clark, Priscilla P. "Thoughts for Food, I: French Cuisine and French Culture." *French Review* 49, no. 1 (October 1975): 32–41.

Ferguson, Priscilla Parkhurst. *Word of Mouth: What We Talk about When We Talk about Food.* Berkeley: University of California Press, 2014.

Hume, David. "An Enquiry Concerning Human Understanding." In *Enquiries Concerning the Human Understanding and Concerning the Principles of Morals*, 2nd ed., edited by Lewis Amherst Selby-Bigge, 5–168. Oxford: Clarendon, 1902.

Jarvis, Peter, John Holford, and Colin Griffin. *The Theory and Practice of Learning.* London: Kogan Page, 1998.

Kearney, Erin. *Intercultural Learning in Modern Language Education: Expanding Meaning-Making Potentials.* Bristol, UK: Multilingual Matters, 2016.

Kolb, David. *Experiential Learning: Experience as the Source of Learning and Development.* Englewood Cliffs: Prentice-Hall, 1984.

Kramsch, Claire. *Context and Culture in Language Teaching.* Oxford: Oxford University Press, 1993.

———. *The Multilingual Subject.* Oxford: Oxford University Press, 2009.

———. "Teaching Foreign Languages in an Era of Globalization: Introduction." *Modern Language Journal* 98, no. 1 (Spring 2014): 296–311.

Kramsch, Claire, and Sascha Gerhards. "Im Gespräch: An Interview with Claire Kramsch on the 'Multilingual Subject.'" *Die Unterrichtspraxis / Teaching German* 45, no. 1 (Spring 2012): 74–82.

Kristeva, Julia. *Desire in Language: A Semiotic Approach to Literature and Art.* New York: Columbia University Press, 1980.

Kumaravadivelu, B. *Cultural Globalization and Language Education.* New Haven, CT: Yale University Press, 2008.

Lange, Dale L. "Planning for and Using the New National Culture Standards." In *Foreign Language Standards: Linking Research, Theories, and Practices*, edited by June K. Phillips and Robert M. Terry, 57–136. Lincolnwood, IL: National Textbook Company and American Council on the Teaching of Foreign Languages, 1999.

Lauster, Martina. Sketches of the Nineteenth Century: European Journalism and Its Physiologies, 1830–50. Basingstoke, UK: Palgrave Macmillan, 2007.

Marini-Maio, Nicoletta, and Colleen Ryan-Scheutz. *Set the Stage! Teaching Italian through Theater.* New Haven, CT: Yale University Press, 2010.

Mill, John Stuart. *The Collected Works of John Stuart Mill.* Volume VII. Edited by John M. Robson. Toronto: University of Toronto Press, 1974.

Mulyadi, Dodi, Dwi Rukmini, and Issy Yuliasri. "The Analysis of Students' Listening Proficiency Viewed from Their Different Learning Styles after Getting the Strategy Instructions." *Theory and Practice in Language Studies* 7, no. 12 (December 2017): 1200–1209.

Parasecoli, Fabio. "Food and Popular Culture." In *Food in Time and Place: The American Historical Association Companion to Food History*, edited by Paul Freedman, Joyce E. Chaplin, and Ken Albala, 323–339. Berkeley: University of California Press, 2014.

Scarino, Angela. "Learning as Reciprocal, Interpretive Meaning-Making: A View from Collaborative Research into the Professional Learning of Teachers of Languages." *Modern Language Journal* 98, no. 1 (2014): 386–401.

University of South Carolina. "Experiential and Engaged Learning." Accessed July 18, 2019. https://sc.edu/about/initiatives/usc_connect/choose_experiences/experiential_and_engaged_learning/index.php

Vygotsky, Lev. *Mind in Society: The Development of Higher Psychological Processes.* Cambridge, MA: Harvard University Press, 1978.

———. "Tool and Sign in the Development of the Child." In *The Collected Works of L. S. Vygotsky*, edited by Robert W. Rieber, 6:3–26. New York: Springer, 1999.

Weninger, Csilla, and Tamas Kiss. "Culture in English as a Foreign Language (EFL) Textbooks: A Semiotic Approach." *TESOL Quarterly* 47, no. 4 (December 2013): 694–716.

CHAPTER TWO

IMPROV GAMES ADAPTED TO THE BRIDGE CLASSROOM

Jeremie Korta, Commonwealth School

This chapter presents a set of working techniques to bring improvisational games into the French language program and in particular bridge courses (200–300 level). In my ten years of teaching French language and literature courses at the collegiate level, I have observed and sought to remedy the continuing two-tiered configuration of "lower-level" language acquisition courses and "upper-level" courses focused on the analysis of literature and film still mostly effected through reading and writing in the target language.[1] My approach to bridging the well-documented pedagogical and cultural divide in foreign language departments has been to introduce drama techniques, improvisational games, and class projects that mobilize students in body and mind and as social actors to stake their own positions vis-à-vis culture and chosen cultural materials. My approach to teaching culture heeds Claire Kramsch's chief criticism that second-language acquisition (SLA) research "has traditionally given more attention to the process of acquisition than to the flesh-and-blood individuals who are doing the learning" dividing learners' "minds, bodies, and social behaviours into separate domains of inquiry."[2] The practice of drama and improvisational games in the language classroom helps to integrate these disparate fields and provide a possible method in which to "develop language competencies holistically" within a multiliteracies pedagogical framework.[3] The purpose of what follows is to share specific drama techniques that I have tested within the context of bridge-level French courses that aim to teach language and culture interactively. The techniques—inspired from improvisational games first developed by drama coaches and social activists[4]—invite students to engage more fully and "re-creatively" with cultural materials and hence to create new meanings for themselves through an enhancement of translingual and transcultural "competencies."[5] The first part of the chapter will make the case for drama techniques and improvisational theater games in SLA, drawing from past research and recent developments in SLA scholarship. The second part presents in detail a series of improvisational, or improv, games adapted to the teaching of culture for instructors who wish to experiment, or "cook" with them in their own classrooms.[6]

The improv games described below were tested and developed over several semesters teaching French language and culture through mostly dramatic texts and theatrical productions that students viewed and discussed in and outside of class. The games were likewise integrated into a drama club that I facilitated as an extracurricular activity for students of all levels, offering them the opportunity to further develop and integrate their cultural competencies in both process-oriented and product-oriented ways via workshops and a final production, respectively. The primary purpose of improv games within the context of SLA pedagogy is to invite students to challenge the tacit assumption (exacerbated by inter-departmental language/literature divides) positioning literature and the native speaker as the only authoritative sources of knowledge, "a perception that dominates their learning," as Margaret Keneman (2017) argues. Drawing from my own experience as first a student and then an instructor, I was and am still keenly aware of the severe limitations that seminar-style courses impose on disparate learning styles. These games responded to an imperative to "raise the confidence-level and motivation of shy and/or weaker learners" by "complement[ing] their verbal skills through non-verbal aspects"[7] such as enhanced physical engagement and sensitivity to somatic metaphors, elements we will explore in detail below. Dramatic texts, from the anonymous medieval *La Farce de Maître Pathelin* to Yasmina Reza's *"Art,"* were selected for classes (and drama club) for their ability to lend themselves to the "embodiment of language and spatio-temporal structures [that] are instrumental in the creation of learning opportunities."[8] Literature from French farce and the Franco-Italian *commedia dell'arte* tradition, with its timeless stock characters and heightened physicality,[9] was explored beginning with Pathelin, Corneille (*L'Illusion comique*), and Molière (*Dom Juan, Monsieur de Pourceaugnac, Le Bourgeois gentilhomme*) while students, by virtue of character explorations and improvisational techniques, uncovered resonances in Ionesco and the contemporary theatre of Yasmina Reza and performed them in final class productions via the kinds of guided activities we present in this chapter. Following a multiliteracies approach,[10] the guided activation of improv games aims to foster a classroom environment in which students may learn not only how textual form contributes to meaning but also how that meaning may be harnessed by future authors, and by themselves, in a two-way creation and transformation of socio-linguistic knowledge.

WHY IMPROV GAMES?

The improvisational games outlined in this chapter are meant to spark a playful, at times "transgressive,"[11] engagement with language and cultural artifacts. They harness the importance of a physical, or somatic, awareness in the foreign language (FL) classroom and attempt to respond to the need for students to engage the language and culture in ways that play to their strengths and "multiple intelligences."[12] The games are both process oriented and product oriented, allowing students to dwell on and re-signify language at its smallest units (vowels, consonants, and phonemes), yet inviting them to assimilate their acts of re-accenting and re-signifying within the context of a full-fledged mise-en-scène of an excerpt or a re-writing of dramatic texts, as a semester-end project.

The earliest games explored in detail below integrate breath, heightened attention to the somatic production of language, and the social construction of an ensemble engaged in a common pursuit: the re-creative exploration of linguistic features and cultural materials in the FL. These early games invite the teacher and students together to turn away from a more cognitively based approach to SLA and reassimilate the body into the learning process, taking to heart that "when seen as a phenomenon of mind alone, learning is stripped of half of its medium and educational potential."[13] The idea that we learn and think somatically is not new and has been demonstrated by cognitive scientists such as George Lakoff and Mark Johnson[14] and Antonio Damasio,[15] whose work has offered renewed justification and an empirical basis for the practice of drama in the FL classroom.[16] The properties of concepts, Lakoff and Johnson argue, "are created as a result of the way the brain and body are structured and the way they function in interpersonal relations and in the physical world."[17] In *The Multilingual Subject*, Kramsch demonstrates how French language students conceptualize their personal experience of acquiring a new language through somatic metaphors: "Learning a foreign language makes these students more conscious of their bodies ... and of the language's body."[18] The improvisational games presented in this chapter both take for granted and reinforce the notion that learning in general, and SLA in particular, should lend a renewed focus on the "bodily-kinaesthetic intelligence" that students already have but perhaps too rarely or too superficially get the chance to activate in the FL classroom.

It can be argued, as numerous SLA researchers have done, that "promot[ing] a full sensory, physical, and emotional appreciation of the language" through even the most fundamental improvisational drama games like the ones presented in this chapter is in itself a form of "cultural education" that goes beyond and provides more lasting results than a "purely cognitive method."[19] These drama or improv games aim to invite the "interplay between body and language in general that leads to doubts, questions, and insights for learners interacting with themselves and others and their linguistic and cultural identity."[20] Already at the level of sound—its production and reception—improv games give students the opportunity to *play* and *experiment* with vowel sounds and phonemes unique to French, feeling and transmitting them through their own breath and body while positioned within a collaborative ensemble. These kinds of games help students create a space in which the "idealization of the native speaker"[21] is not predominant and the smallest language elements are seen to carry context-depending meaning and hence may be further re-signified by students through physical gesture and collaboration. In games proposed here, the (fictional) notion of a correctly pronounced vowel or phoneme is implicitly laid to rest as students layer on, experiment with, and eventually comment upon collaboratively produced breathing patterns, intonations, and gestures within the context of literary and cultural analysis. This kind of "spontaneous social symbolic play,"[22] having been introduced and encouraged at the elemental level of vowels and phonemes, may then be built upon as the activities proceed through more and more complex engagement with and reflection on textual materials. Crucially, the earliest improv games introduced in this chapter also help the student begin activating and reflecting upon *non-verbal* aspects of language, whether in the FL or their own. As students take up and explore the space of the classroom (forgoing their desks), they experiment with sociospatial relations and proxemics, aspects of the games that later play a role as students create their own interpretations and mise-en-scènes of the plays studied in class.

As previously mentioned, these improv games were activated both in a bridge (late second-year, early third-year) course and in the context of a year-long drama club that had the time to be more process oriented in the fall, before becoming decidedly product oriented in the spring (with a public performance as its final aim). The bridge course also had as its term project either a mise-en-scène, the performance of an original monologue in which students took on and transformed one of the voices they had been studying, or a dramaturgical project in which students were invited to imagine in the most multisensory way possible the production of a major scene in a play read for class.[23] These collaborative final projects assimilated activities that had been explored throughout the semester: improv games, discourse analysis, and the semiotic analysis and imagined production of light and set design. *Le Mariage de Figaro* and *On ne badine pas avec l'amour*, thanks to their circulation of bodies and objects charged with affect and symbolism, lent themselves especially well to student explorations of the semiotics of lighting and set design. Some, such as Ionesco's *La Cantatrice chauve*, were perfect for activities such as playing with the most elemental building blocks of language. Ionesco's famous absurdist play, for instance, disintegrates into a (typically very energetic[24]) hodgepodge of decontextualized proverbs, lexemes, and phonemes before wondering which way to exit ("C'est pas par là! / C'est pas ici!"). However bizarre and alienating the final scene feels to students at first, it may be harnessed to provide an entry point to "symbolic competence" in the FL at perhaps the most elemental level, giving students license to break apart, play with, and put back together the linguistic elements of the dramatic texts they are reading. In a similar vein, drawing from *L'Illusion comique*, my bridge course (and drama club) students found license to play with sound and intonation from the elements of alexandrine verse, a potentially intimidating dramatic form for students at the intermediate (200–300) level who made up the ensemble. The games described in this chapter eventually invited students to take great pleasure, for instance, in Matamore's linguistic polyvalency, embodying in performance what they observed (and observing what they performed) rather than analyzing features of the verse by simply counting syllables. Similar to Ionesco's anarchic final scene, Matamore, too, breaks down Corneille's alexandrine into atomic bits ("Faîtes, lattes, chevrons, montants, courbes, filières") or fractures it in ways that are most effectively understood by the student through mise-en-scène and physical character exploration ("Les voilà, sauvons-nous!").

In what follows, I present several improvisational "warm-up games." While building on this first set of games to introduce more and more complex improvisational drama activities, I also take time with my class (and here) to reflect on how these games—from those playing with vowel and phoneme to those playing with character and movement and beyond—may be harnessed to open up unexpected avenues of reflection on literary form and meaning while building the students' symbolic competency through playful "transgression" of language and gesture in the classroom environment.

THE IMPROV EXERCISES

Dagger and Ball Exercises

Dagger and ball exercises are fundamental improvisational theatre techniques that help forge a sense of play and ensemble from the very start. Both linguistically, in its focus on the physical production of vowels and phonemes, and socially, in its effort to create a sense of cohesion, playfulness, and common purpose, these exercises may serve as a starting point for integrating theatre techniques into the FL classroom.[25]

a) *Throwing and catching*. Without yet incorporating sound or speech, the first improv game "merely" accustoms students to the challenges of remaining attentive to their environment. This is often the students' favorite moment as they gleefully shove their desks to the side and back of the room, then gather to define a circular empty space in the center with the teacher-facilitator positioned as a member of the team. As Janet Shier notes in her own practice,[26] this phase-transition in the classroom suddenly allows the students to focus their attention on one another (without any being the constant center of attention) and away from the teacher. It also suggests a reconfiguration of the classroom as an "empty space"[27] in which students may harness a collaborative, collective agency in their performative engagement with language and cultural materials.

To begin: draw an imaginary dagger from an imaginary scabbard. Feel its weight, its handle, and the cold edge of its blade. Practice throwing and catching together. To do so, establish eye contact with a partner in the circle, then throw the dagger at them blade first! Naturally, we are all samurais with lightning-fast reflexes, so your partner catches the dagger by the blade by clapping her palms in front of her face. Continue practicing throwing and catching. The dagger should be thrown and caught almost simultaneously, as it whizzes across the room in an instant. Encourage students to feel the weight of the dagger and to appreciate the speed at which it travels through the air between them. Coach them to avoid unnecessary tension in the neck or shoulders. Eventually, the exercise should reach a flow state in which students are throwing and catching with hardly a beat in between. When it finally comes back to the instructor, she ends the game by putting the imaginary dagger back into the imaginary scabbard.[28]

b) *Throwing vowels and phonemes*. This game builds upon the former, seeking to go further in providing students with an opportunity to observe linguistic elements of the FL, activate meaning at an early stage, and harness both sound and meaning in a symbolically empowering way (holding and throwing the dagger; performing meaning as an ensemble). The instructor invites the students to propose a vowel or to draw one from the text being studied. Uniquely French vowel sounds are important (/y/, /ə/, /e/, /ɛ/, /ɑ/, etc.), but ones that already carry meaning in the language are especially recommended to start (such as a tragic or curious "/o/!"; a surprised, frightened, or complicit "/ɑ/!"; a perplexed "/ə/?"; or a giddy "/i/!"). As before, students throw and catch the dagger, but this time that same dagger is carrying their sound away from them. As students imitate the rapid-fire trajectory of the imaginary dagger somatically, the vowel sounds should ideally utilize short bursts of breath controlled by the diaphragm. You may encourage students to place the thumb they are not throwing with over their navel to make sure they feel their diaphragms engage as they launch their vowel sounds across the space to their partners. When students feel comfortable with throwing about one vowel sound at a time, the instructor can invite them to choose the vowel sound they want to try, thus getting a collective mix of sounds and expressions piercing across the space, increasing or decreasing the tempo as desired, with students always maintaining eye contact with one another.

When you have reached a stopping point with vowels, try phonemes: /mə/, /sə/, /kə/, /mɑ/, /sɑ/, /lɑ/, and so forth. The phonemes need not carry meaning in and of themselves. The aim at first is simply to externalize the sounds, sending and receiving them energetically across the space. However, the game can and should eventually be harnessed to explore character through elementary sounds and phonemes that recur and carry special meaning in the text. If we are studying *L'Illusion comique*, I may suggest, for example, the exclamatory and anaphoric "que!" and "quel/le/s

!" that begin Isabelle's soliloquy lamenting her plight and denouncing her father's unjust actions[29] or her shift from addressing an absent Clindor ("ton," "ta," "tes," "toi") to lamenting her present situation ("mon," "ma," "mes," "moi") before finally threatening to haunt her father from beyond the grave with another string of possessive adjectives (and ineffectual action verbs, to which we will return). Clindor's active thought process may be explored in a similar way by analyzing and activating the anaphoric sounds that structure his prison speech,[30] as may Isabelle's successful linguistic maneuverings in her tirade of act V that begins with "Eh bien, cours au trépas." While reflecting upon the semiotic diversity of vowel and phoneme in these and other excerpts, students can begin to inhabit the characters at various moments in the plays read, performatively stepping through the "linguistic moves" in their arguments with one another and with themselves.

c) *Throwing and catching lexical and phonological words.* Generalizing from the preceding exercises, invite each student to suggest a word in the text they have been reading for class, especially one the pronunciation of which they find difficult or confusing or one that they have identified as sensorily charged: Dorante's description of Alcandre's cave is a wonderful excerpt to plumb for words full of sensory charge and affect ("grotte," "obscure," "affreux," "épais")[31] and can color the entire game, so may the infinitives a desperate Isabelle hurls at her absent father that characterize the colorful ways she plans to haunt him from beyond the grave ("épouvanter," "s'attacher," "jeter," "te reprocher," "t'appeler," "t'accabler," etc.).[32] The instructor can provide a warm-up by having each student in the circle energetically send the word across the room, fixing the horizon, a classmate, or an object. The instructor immediately repeats the word (with whatever adjustment needed implied in her pronunciation) and invites the entire class to do the same together. Each student gets a turn trying out their word before the instructor resumes the dagger exercise, inviting the students to send one or more words across the room. (It is important that the student send the dagger on the stressed, i.e., final, syllable of their word.)

The instructor may then build from lexical to phonological word, where by "lexical" I mean any word as it is presented in a dictionary, and by "phonological" I mean "a string of sounds that behaves as a unit for certain kinds of phonological processes, especially stress or accent."[33] Demonstrating some examples from the chosen text, invite students to find a complete syntactical unit in the text they are studying. Taking the blustering Matamore as an example, I might suggest, from Matamore's first tirade,[34] "Mon armée," "Il est vrai," "vous rêvez," "assez fort," and students will come back with further examples: "que ce bras," "le seul bruit," "de mon nom," "les batailles," and so forth. Before launching back into the dagger exercise, I ask my students what the significant word is in their unit of text. Which one does Matamore want Clindor to hear the most? (And which one does the actor want the audience to hear the most?) Even if they don't all come back with the final word, most will come back with the last lexical word in their syntactical unit: "armée," "vrai," "rêvez," "fort," "bruit," "batailles," "courage," and so on for the first fourteen verses of the monologue. Having established that the meaningful word to get across is the final one, we crucially gain a picture of the persona Matamore is trying to construct for himself and of the *effect* Matamore is trying to have on Clindor at this moment. I then have students boil down the final words to a handful of implied imperatives, inviting them to imagine what he wants to *make* Clindor *do*. I may have to coax them to be imaginative, but we eventually have a host of examples, such as "tremble!" "pleure!" "taisez-vous!" "cachez-vous!" and "écoute-moi!" (Rather than focus on emotion—e.g., "sois impressionné !"—the imperatives should be active.)

Armed, as it were, with these implied imperatives, we may return to the dagger exercises, this time without the dagger! I have students "throw" their units of text to one another (without moving their arms anymore), taking care to put the accent on the final word (and indeed the final syllable): "ah, poltron," "mes soldats," "et tu m'oses parler" (or "et tu m'oses"), and so forth. This time, however, those units of text are charged with the intention to affect the other physically through the student's preferred imperative. For example, the student directs "ah, poltr**on**" at her classmate and thinks "tremble!" As a result, the dagger game becomes a "speech-act" game in which students, invited to inhabit and perform meaning through a character's linguistic choices and their own "bodily-kinaesthetic intelligence," activate "the performative power of speech-acts."[35]

d) *Ball exercises*. A good physical counterpart to the dagger exercises are what we can simply call "ball exercises." While tossing an imaginary dagger punctuates a given phoneme by activating the diaphragm suddenly, ball exercises are meant to help students sustain breath while practicing vocalization and articulation of longer phrases. They also help students explore the natural arc of the language, especially in alexandrine form, in which a momentary suspense at the caesura may coincide with the apex of the imaginary ball's trajectory. When working with a text that is not alexandrine or in verse, the instructor may invite the students to deconstruct the text into meaningful chunks—those "phonological words" that can meaningfully be followed by a short breath—having offered some examples to clarify the idea.

To initiate the game, the instructor gets students to toss around an imaginary ball of given weight, size, and texture (is it a tennis ball? a tired helium balloon? a dense billiard ball? a heavy bowling ball? is it hot? cold? metallic? fuzzy?). As before, the class may begin with a vowel, then build to phonemes, lexemes, and phonological words. It is advisable, however, to begin the exercise by tossing the ball around to "get a feel" for it before informing the chosen text with our new gesture. Coach students to feel the weight of the ball in their hands, arms, and shoulders, maintaining their knees slightly bent and their feet at shoulder-width's distance in an "active" stance (heavier balls should not be thrown by collapsing the shoulders, which will impede the breath, but by bending the knees and keeping the chest open). As they practice throwing the imaginary ball, coach students to really *feel* when the ball has left their hands, when it is at its highest point, and when it finally lands in their classmate's hands. They should remain actively engaged throughout the throw until the ball has been received, at which point they may "let go." Eye contact should be maintained throughout between the thrower and the catcher.

Preparing a few key excerpts of a lengthy passage ahead of time, such as Isabelle's denunciation of her father's injustice in *L'Illusion comique* (act IV, scene i), I invite students to work through them, one hemistich at a time, exploring at what syllable to release their "ball," at what syllable it lands, and whether there is an apex or "climax" to the arc (especially if they try to toss the entire alexandrine). What does the trajectory of the toss look like? Does it float or sink immediately? What is the character trying to "get rid of"? To whom are they tossing the "ball," whatever it is? When Isabelle addresses an absent Clindor, does it "feel" different than when she addresses herself? When she addresses her father, how has the texture, the weight, the temperature, even the color of the "ball" evolved? These ball exercises invite students to continue engaging the language kinesthetically, imagining with every sense how characters work through an argument. They are also a great segue into movement and character exercises that get them engaging one another as an ensemble in a physically collaborative re-creation of meaning.

Movement Exercises

The speech exercises presented above could just as well have been called breath exercises to denote the accent they place on use of breath support to produce, color, and play with language and encourage meaningful, personalized speech. The movement exercises I present now could by analogy be called body exercises given the accent they place on engaging the whole body in space with a view to creating new meaning-making opportunities within the context of literary and cultural analysis. Of course, the previous speech exercises already engaged the body in important ways, and the exercises described here will continue to integrate proper breath support. As students work through the dagger and ball passing games, for instance, they not only use their arms and core strength but also learn how to produce language through controlled activation of one critical muscle: the diaphragm. In the movement exercises below, we will be working from an activation of the whole body in movement through space as a kind of blank canvas (in the tradition of Jacques Lecoq) to produce new meanings as a group and with an eye toward a kinesthetic exploration, discovery, and re-creation of culture and cultural materials.

The following movement exercises are intended to enhance students' transcultural competence through personalized understanding and expression of characters developed in the text that they are reading. Beginning with a simple exploration of walking through space—a neutral gait that we may consider our blank canvas—students begin writing upon this movement certain variations that I coach them to discover. Similarly to the experimentation and analysis that accompany the introductory dagger and ball tossing exercises, students are again encouraged to make connections between the new physical lexicon they invent and the text they read to stimulate the emergence and clarification of original ideas.

a) *Neutral walk.* This is our blank canvas for the remainder of our subsequent "walking" exercises upon which students are invited to build meaning and eventually express their understanding of the text. Within the same Brooksian "empty space" as for our dagger and ball exercises, students walk "normally" about, exploring just what that means for them. Their gaze is on the imaginary horizon, breathing regular, their attention turned toward letting go of tension (shoulders, neck, and facial muscles) and actively feeling the floor with the soles of their feet. Encourage students to begin exploring the space in a non-trivial way, that is, without moving as a mass in a circle (which groups will have a tendency to do), instead being mindful of new spaces as they open and moving into them. Eyes remain on the horizon rather than on one another. This silent but attentive activity is intended to allow the student to explore and discover their own blank canvas upon which they can build and interpret further kinesthetic discovery. Without it, movement exercises and analysis run the risk of feeling pre-encoded from the outside rather than emerging from the kind of "spontaneous symbolic play"[36] that these games are meant to stimulate.

b) *Tactile walks*. Having invited students to identify their own spatio-temporal "template" in the neutral walk, the instructor can then evoke an environment previously explored within the context of a "dagger" or "ball" exercise or a classic brainstorming activity. Transitioning from a neutral walk, students then explore physically how their body reacts to the evocation of, for example, Alcandre's cave in the opening lines of *L'Illusion comique*, from the point of view, most interestingly, of Pridamant who encounters the hall of mirrors for the first time. How does the space feel, in every sense of the word (not just affectively but sensorily)? Is it thick? dark? sticky? crystalline? How does their body move through such a space? Most effective are those scenes in a text that are sensorily and affectively charged by one or more characters, moments in which the plot stops to dwell on the emotional state of a given character or the power dynamic between characters (cf. Clindor and Matamore in act II, scene ii), heightening anticipation and demanding resolution. Indeed, a tactile walk exercise is useful in eventually bringing students to consider the differences between plot-driven scenes and those that dwell on the affective tensions pulling at one or more characters. Other examples in *L'Illusion comique* could be Clindor's prison scene mentioned previously or Matamore's faint-hearted attempt to stalk Isabelle. Some passages, such as the latter one ("Les voilà, sauvons-nous !"[37]), are particularly amenable to a tactile walk as the instructor or a student reads the passage "in character" and following an initial exploration (from Matamore's point of view) of the space around Isabelle's desired yet threatening home (crawling as it is with "ces diables de valets") evoked by a host of sensory key words ("coulons-nous," "le corps me frissonne," "le vent faisait ce bruit," "des ombres de la nuit").

After performing a tactile walk, students are invited to reflect upon and draw from their kinesthetic discoveries: How did the space feel? What color was it? What did they see (or prefer not to see)? How did their movements feel? easy? difficult? burdened? light? (Questions such as "What movements did you make?" are to be rigorously avoided since movement must, throughout all of these exercises, be harnessed and cultivated as a vehicle for renewed discovery, not implied to be the sole purpose of the exercise.) Finally, if the passage was read in its entirety during the tactile walk, the students may reread the text again (or listen to it reread), informed this time by their new kinesthetic and affective investment. Invite students to recall their tactile walk as they listen or read. What in the passage provoked changes in the space? How and when did it shrink or expand? When did its texture change? Reflecting on the bipolar Matamore in the scene just mentioned, for example, students may be brought to observe the fragmented verses and unpredictable shifts in attention and emotion. In Clindor's prison scene, they may reflect on what senses prevailed when for them in his soliloquy, what in the text inspired such sensory shifts, and what those shifts might imply about the character's evolving emotional state and objectives.

c) *Biased walks*. The following exercise is particularly well suited to a play like *L'Illusion comique* with its strong characters inspired by the "masks" of *commedia dell'arte*. However, if the instructor insists that the movements students are encouraged to explore need not hew to the dictates of realism, there is no reason that through it students cannot explore character in any play or text. Beginning from our neutral walk, start exploring walks biased by a given part of the body. I have the students lead their movements, as if pulled by an invisible string, by (for example) the knees, the pelvis, the chest, the head. Next, I try walks *resisted* by parts of the body (as if a string were pulling them back). Encouraging them alternatively to dial up and down their biased walk from "neutral," I ask them how the world around them is changing as they explore their biased walk. How is their relationship with others changing? Do they want to be close to others? Do they prefer to avoid them? How does their walk change in the vicinity of others? It is much more effective to ask these questions intended to stretch the student's kinesthetic imagination, to validate their choices, and to explore collaboratively rather than reductively asking why they are moving the way they are.

Armed with a palette of "biased walks," I have students explore one or more characters in the play or text by inviting them to assign one or two of the biased movements they have been exploring to the chosen character. Two biased movements can be assigned to a single character one at a time or, more fun still, simultaneously! After having read, for example, act II, scene ii of *L'Illusion comique*, in which we meet Matamore and Clindor for the first time, students are invited to explore their movements, assigning and exaggerating biased walks as they see fit, interacting with other Clindors and Matamores in the space. What do they discover in the process of their spontaneous play, through their own movements and in their interactions with one another? What words resonate as they explore physically and spatially? These exploratory questions may be asked during the exercise and elaborated upon after. As in the tactile walk, this exercise may also be performed as a kinesthetic framework from which to renew the students' textual analysis of a dialogue or monologue. As the instructor reads a monologue, for instance, students explore a chosen character through biased walks (the walk can also slow to a virtual halt), reflecting subsequently on what was driving or holding the character back, how their physical discoveries stemmed from linguistic features of the text—salient words that "drove" them, assonance, rhyme, apostrophe—and further deepened their personal understanding of the character they inhabited. It is often instructive, in both the tactile and biased walk activities, for half of the students to watch the other half (and then switch), having the audience elaborate on what they saw. Students can then alternate and juxtapose their exploration and elaboration of cultural meaning from both emic (insiders') and etic (outsiders' "objective") perspectives.[38]

IMPROVISATION EXERCISES AND "CANOVACCI"

The final exercises I present here are adapted from the kind of "talking-head" improvisational games that one can come across in improv workshops (for the "interview" game) and from the tradition of *commedia dell'arte* and its activation of improvised scenes from pre-existing scenarios or *canovacci* (*canevas* in French). They are probably best suited for an advanced group of students: I have used them successfully in a second-semester 300-level bridge course and in theatre workshops conducted in French. I include them here after the exercises above that focus in on speech and movement because I consider the latter as building blocks of the former, and this in multiple ways. Speech and movement games encourage students to problem-solve using breath and physicality, thus stimulating them to engage the language and develop ideas in ways that would not be possible in a traditional classroom setting.[39] They encourage teamwork in problem-solving, removing the pressure that easily seeps into the classroom from an often competitive, self-centered academic environment.[40] For these reasons, they may serve to encourage the individual student in her spontaneous activation of language and in developing original ideas. They also help create an environment of cooperation in which everyone is involved in the game. Without these "warm-ups," students could understandably be overwhelmed or confused by the games described here, and those involved as the "audience" could misunderstand their implicit role as active members of the process.

a) *Character interviews.* I first came across a version of this game, widely known in the theatre world as "hot-seating," in an actors' workshop at the Théâtre Lucernaire in Paris and subsequently activated an adapted version of the game in my bridge classes and student francophone companies, always with delightful results. The adapted exercise, or game, invites two to four students in front of the classroom, seated or standing and in the persona of a chosen character, to be interviewed by the instructor-host and class-audience. The interview should not take the tone of an interrogation, of course; rather, it ought to take the relaxed form of a late night talk show or of the kinds of interviews one comes across in reality TV shows (or "mock" reality TV shows, such as *The Office*). The results are particularly fun for students when the characters they assume would not be particularly appealing in "real life." Thus, when I interviewed students doing Matamore or Dom Juan (Molière), they often took the physical demeanor of their character without being asked to and revelled in their provocative responses. Other students enjoyed answering questions within their chosen persona that invited them to tell the class what they "really thought" about the characters in their world. In fact, the energy that the game liberates is so potent, I always play it with students as the final exercise of class! To prepare for the interview, students are assigned a character ahead of time. I ask a group of students to be ready to propose a staged reading of a scene that we have already read and discussed in class, asking that they read the scene out loud together several times outside of class to practice pronunciation and to work out the proxemics of the scene, or how the relationships between the characters are represented in (evolving) spaces between them. As another preparatory exercise, I also ask students to write a paragraph in the voice of a character they choose, making sure that those students preparing a staged reading for that week write from the point of view of the character they are meant to take on. The topic of the paragraph will vary and may be chosen with the interview in mind: the history of a character's relationship with another/others, the one thing that a character wants most out of another character and how they intend to acquire it, and so forth. The prompt may trigger certain grammar structures (*what a character expects to do*: future simple; *what a character feels about a situation or another fellow character*: subjunctive; *what a character wishes were the case and/or their regrets and recriminations*: imperfect, pluperfect, and conditional, etc.); it may also encourage students to incorporate certain stylistic elements utilized by a given character and brainstormed previously. With these preparatory exercises, students come to class with a wealth of ideas that come out in the interview game, prompted by the right questions. To begin the interview, I invite the ensemble to first take their place in front of their "audience." I thank them for coming (to "play" the "game" with them, of course: an essential detail!). Then I begin asking questions beginning with the most banal and following their lead when a topic seems to interest them most. As there are two to four students involved in the interview, I can pause with one and ask a follow-up question from another, especially if they were recently implicated in an answer, and so forth. Students who act as "audience" are expected to ask a question of one of the characters. When the interview comes to a natural end, I thank them for their time and let them regain their seats.

The interview game can be activated within the context of a larger sequence of activities that together foster the kind of "ethnographic attitude" stimulated by FL classroom drama games.[41] It encourages students to step into their characters more fully and playfully when engaged in a staged reading. It enhances students' understanding of the obstacles facing each character and their linguistic strategies to overcome them. Having written lexically, stylistically, or syntactically directed monologues from the characters' points of view allows students during and following the interview game to invest the linguistic strategies they analyzed in the text with active meaning. In a later staged reading, students will be better equipped to playfully "manipulate symbolic representation" as they collaboratively activate the text along with the socio-linguistic strategies it implicitly contains.[42]

b) *Improvised scenarios.* The final game that I want to describe here is more of a template: not a single game, but a collection *ad libitum*, and inspired by the traditional theatrical practice of *commedia dell'arte*. I describe it here as a place from which I hope instructors may be inspired to construct their own improvisational games suited for the level and cultural materials they are using. *Commedia dell'arte* was historically performed by actors in fairs and courts who followed a scenario laid out in what was called a *canovaccio* in Italian. Based on the scenario, they would perform the same basic premise every time but with varying details that could change moment to moment since lines and stage directions were rarely written out in full. Performers and teachers of *commedia dell'arte* such as Antonio Fava and Barry Grantham have published examples of *canovacci*,[43] and I have drawn from them to prepare similar scenarios on which students could base a semi-improvised performance in the target language.

Following the character development exercises explored in tactile and biased walks, as well as the interview game, students are better equipped to explore and heighten the conflict or conflicts represented within a given scene. Take, for example, the first-time Maître Pathelin walks into his "frenemy" Guillaume's fabric shop in *La Farce de Maître Pathelin*, which was part of a bridge course curriculum. Writing the *canovaccio* first requires an analysis of power dynamics and dramatic reversals in the scene, something that students may already have begun to explore in their character exploration through tactile and biased walks, for example. Pathelin is vain and hungry (something like an Harlequin character in *commedia*), while Guillaume is vain and avaricious (something like Pantalone). The power struggle in the scene is, at its most elemental, a socio-economic one: Guillaume is a wealthy bourgeois with plenty of wares, and Pathelin is penniless and has only his guile. Unable to pay for what he wants (fabric for clothes and thus job prospects), Pathelin flatters until, in the scene's dramatic reversal of the situation, he gets his hands on the priciest fabric without having paid a dime. The *canovaccio* inspired by this scene then involves only a few elements: the characters Pathelin and Guillaume, the contested object, and the dramatic reversal. Students are then invited to imagine different commercial objects and different paths to and resolutions from the dramatic reversal within the scene. The contested object can be anachronistic, such as a BMW (the play was first performed in the late fifteenth century), or even absurd, such as a cassette tape. The point is for students to explore how and how long to heighten the tension in the scene until it reaches its breaking point. They are given plenty of time in class to collaboratively brainstorm for their improvisation: deciding what Pathelin wants and why, the socio-linguistic strategies he can use to approach the object he is after and those Guillaume uses to parry his advances, how to build and sustain tension in the scene, and what finally causes the latter to capitulate to the former. While the *canovaccio* itself should be constructed previously as well as some preliminary character exploration and analysis of socio-linguistic features of the text (for instance, how Pathelin speaks with his wife versus how he speaks with Guillaume, the etiquette to which both Pathelin and Guillaume hypocritically adhere), the brainstorming and performance itself should not be split into two periods. A single timeframe will be seen to stimulate a more spontaneous and transgressive symbolic play (while having the added virtue of being more in line with the historical tradition of *commedia dell'arte* and the practice of contemporary pedagogues such as Antonio Fava). The improvised performance itself can be analyzed either during or after its completion, freezing the scene momentarily to interview a character and clarify their intention or offer a suggestion, or repeating the scene with an alternate reversal or outcome. In a different (monolingual) context, this kind of audience intervention was theorized and practiced by Augusto Boal as a method to empower spectators by involving them in re-imagining representative scenes of social struggle and lopsided power dynamics—what Boal called "forum theatre."[44] This activity is inspired by Boal in its intent to position students as "spect-actors"[45] or "participant observers,"[46] offering them a framework in which to both inhabit and observe cultural elements and thereby enhance intercultural competence.

CONCLUSION

Adapting and engaging these and other improvisational theatre games in my bridge courses and drama workshops have offered a number of advantages in the classroom environment and beyond. They may be used punctually to get students moving and actively engaging with the language out from behind their seats and with one another; they may offer a kind of experiential module complementary to traditional textual analysis in classroom activities; they may finally inform the work done throughout an entire term toward a semester-end performance that collaboratively involves the entire class. Many of these "games" were activated in the context of the French and Italian drama club I directed for five years at the collegiate level, which was usually geared toward a production in which students in the FL could take pride in and ownership of their performance. The games were also implemented with a view toward final projects in a bridge (300-level) course in which students had a choice to either (1) activate their physical lexicon developed over the course of the semester within the context of a staged excerpt, (2) integrate the socio-linguistic markers and strategies studied over the course of the semester within their own monologues and transformed voices, or (3) envision and justify the meaning-making choices of a full-fledged production by taking on the role of director and dramaturg for a critical scene in a play.

While my primary aim in this chapter was to present improvisational drama games adapted to bridge courses in French, any number of other improvisational games could potentially be adapted from teachers such as Viola Spolin, Keith Johnstone, Barry Edelstein, Patsy Rodenburg, and Augusto Boal and implemented in a progressive manner as illustrated above (working from speech games, to movement games, to improvised scenarios), and I encourage interested readers to take inspiration from those sources as well as the numerous scholars and pedagogues who have made similar use of drama techniques. While the games may change, the goal of improv games in this context remains the same: to stimulate a more spontaneous approach to the target language and the interpretation of its cultural materials through the enhancement of body-kinesthetic "intelligence" and ensemble building and to encourage students to take an active part in the meaning-making potential of SL learning, fostering opportunities for them to enhance symbolic competency and a tolerance for ambiguity and semiotic complexity. Indeed, as a performing artist and workshop director at the Théâtre Lucernaire (Paris) once explained to me of his improvisational, *canovaccio*-like approach to performing Molière for contemporary audiences, "le texte ce n'est qu'un prétexte." In the same way, these improv games may offer a potent way to give spontaneous, indeed transgressive, language production a leg up over too great a respect for the text and textual analysis while also affording opportunities for more profound understanding of cultural materials and greater ownership by the student over her learning process.

NOTES

1. For the groundbreaking article on this dilemma, see Heidi Byrnes, "The Cultural Turn in Foreign Language Departments: Challenge and Opportunity," *Profession* (2002): 114–129. The standard configuration of collegiate FL programs and suggestions to rethink it are taken up in the MLA report "Foreign Languages and Higher Education: New Structures for a Changed World," *Profession* (2007): 234–245.
2. Claire Kramsch, *The Multilingual Subject* (Oxford: Oxford University Press, 2009), 2.
3. Kate Paesani, Heather Willis Allen, and Beatrice Dupuy, *A Multiliteracies Framework for Collegiate Foreign Language Learning* (Upper Saddle River, NJ: Pearson, 2016), 21.
4. See conclusion and references.
5. For a detailed performance-based approach to language-learning, see Les Essif, *The French Play: Exploring Theatre 'Re-creatively' with Foreign Language Students* (Calgary: University of Calgary Press, 2006); for "translingual" and "transcultural competence," see, in particular, Claire Kramsch, "Theorizing Translingual/Transcultural Competence," in *Critical and Intercultural Theory and Language Pedagogy*, ed. Glenn S. Levine and Alison Phipps (Boston: Heinle, 2012); for drama as a tool for enhancement of translingual and transcultural competence, see Margaret Lynn Keneman, "Le Pouvoir du Théâtre: Foreign Languages, Higher Education, and Capturing the Notion of Symbolic Competence," *L2 Journal* 9, no. 2 (Summer 2017): 84–106.
6. Janet Shier proposes drama techniques with which to "cook" in the FL classroom, that is, adapting and applying them without a "recipe" as the occasion demands. See Janet Hegman Shier, "The Arts and the Foreign-/Second-Language Curriculum: An Interdisciplinary Approach to Actively Engage Students in Their Own Learning," in *Body and Language: Intercultural Learning through Drama*, ed. Gerd Bräuer (Westport, CT: Greenwood Publishing, 2002), 200–201.
7. Stefanie Giebert, "Drama and Theatre in Teaching Foreign Languages for Professional Purposes," *Recherche et pratiques pédagogiques en langues de spécialité* 33, no. 1 (Spring 2014): 138–150, https://doi.org/10.4000/apliut.4215. For silent activities as methodological alternatives within the practice of drama in the FL classroom, Giebert points to Cameron R. Culham, "Coping with Obstacles in Drama-Based ESL Teaching: A Non-Verbal Approach," in Bräuer, *Body and Language*, 95–112. For the use of non-verbal activities as a drama technique for the acquisition of intercultural competence in the FL classroom, we also point to Manfred Lukas Schewe, "Teaching Foreign Language

Literature: Tapping the Students' Bodily-Kinesthetic Intelligence," in Bräuer, *Body and Language*, 73–94.
8. Leo van Lier, "The Semiotics and Ecology of Language Learning: Perception, Voice, Identity and Democracy," *Utbildning & Demokrati* 13, no. 3 (Fall 2004): 79, previously cited by Keneman, "Le Pouvoir du Théâtre," 89.
9. For a study of the "masks" or stock characters of *commedia dell'Arte* and an overview of commedia as a living, contemporary practice, see Antonio Fava, *The Comic Mask in the Commedia dell'Arte: Actor Training, Improvisation, and the Poetics of Survival*, trans. Thomas Simpson, ed. Jenny Gherpelli (Evanston, IL: Northwestern University Press, 2007).
10. Paesani, Allen, and Dupuy, *Multiliteracies Framework*, 21.
11. Keneman, "Le Pouvoir du Théâtre," 94.
12. Howard Gardner, *Frames of Mind: The Theory of Multiple Intelligences* (New York: Basic Books, 1983). See Schewe, "Teaching Foreign Language Literature," 73–74, who points to Gardner in support of drama in the FL classroom; in the same volume, see also Gerd Bräuer, introduction to Bräuer, *Body and Language*, x–xiii. For further support of drama toward SLA and intercultural competence based on the activation and enhancement of "bodily-kinaesthetic intelligence," see Marianne Jensen and Arno Hermer, "Learning by Playing: Learning Foreign Languages through the Senses," in *Language Learning in Intercultural Perspective: Approaches through Drama and Ethnography*, ed. Michael Byram and Michael Fleming (Cambridge: Cambridge University Press, 1998), 178–192.
13. Bräuer, introduction, x.
14. George Lakoff and Mark Johnson, *Philosophy in the Flesh: The Embodied Mind and Its Challenge to Western Thought* (New York: Basic Books, 1999).
15. Antonio R. Damasio, *Descartes' Error: Emotion, Reason, and the Human Brain* (New York: G. P. Putnam's Sons, 1994). See also Giebert, "Drama and Theater," who points to Damasio in support of drama activities in the FL classroom.
16. See, for example, Giebert, "Drama and Theatre," and Matthew DeCoursey (cited by Giebert), "Dramatic Art for Second Language Education: Appropriate Process Objectives for Hong Kong Schools," *Asia-Pacific Journal for Arts Education* 11, no. 11 (2012): 250–270.
17. Lakoff and Johnson, *Philosophy*, 37.
18. Kramsch, *Multilingual Subject*, 66.
19. Jensen and Hermer, "Learning by Playing," 178–179.
20. Bräuer, introduction, ix–x. See also Norah Morgan and Juliana Saxton, *Teaching Drama: A Mind of Many Wonders* (Portsmouth, NH: Heinemann, 1987),

cited by Bräuer in support of the position that body-language interplay is an effective tool for teaching intercultural competence through drama.
21. Keneman, "Le Pouvoir du Théâtre," 88. See also Keneman, "Finding a Voice in the Foreign Language Classroom: Reading, Writing, and Performing Slam Poetry to Develop Critical Literacies," in *Integrating the Arts: Creative Thinking about FL Curricula and Language Program Direction*, ed. Lisa Parkes and Colleen M. Ryan (Boston: Cengage Learning, 2015), 108–130.
22. Betty Jane Wagner, *Educational Drama and Language Arts: What Research Shows* (Portsmouth, NH: Heinemann, 1998), cited by Bräuer, introduction, xi. See also the groundbreaking work on "symbolic play" by the educator Jean Piaget, *Play, Dreams, and Imitation in Childhood* (New York: W. W. Norton, 1962).
23. See Keneman, "Le Pouvoir du Théâtre," 92–93, for a related warm-up exercise.
24. See *La Cantatrice chauve*, directed by Jean-Luc Lagarce (Arte Editions, 2007), for a particularly frenetic end to the play.
25. For similar preparatory exercises, see Shier, "Arts," 193–194.
26. Shier.
27. Peter Brooks, *The Empty Space: A Book about the Theatre: Deadly, Holy, Rough, Immediate* (New York: Scribner, 1995).
28. Such details may seem silly, but I have observed that students relish the instructor's involvement in the game. If she does not take "seriously" the rules of the game, students will naturally feel cheated or as if they are being condescended to or forced to do something arbitrary. The importance of respecting the rules of the game in such a context can be appreciated by a glance back to chapter 1 of Johan Huizinga's *Homo Ludens* (1938), for example, esp. 11–12; see also Jensen and Hermer, "Learning by Playing," 179.
29. The excerpt in question is act IV, scene i, and may be found in the Gallimard edition of Pierre Corneille, *L'Illusion comique*, ed. Jean Serroy (Paris: Folio Classique, 2000), 117–119.
30. Act IV, scene vii, in Corneille, 136–138.
31. Act I, scene i, in Corneille, 51–52.
32. Act IV, scene i, in Corneille, 117–119.
33. Mark Aronoff and Kirsten Fudeman, *What Is Morphology?* 2nd ed. (Chichester, UK: John Wiley & Sons, 2011), 40. Phonological words are usually longer than lexical words and consist in a complete syntactical group, a building block of meaning in the sentence. Though the nuances may be complex, I find that students understand this concept intuitively. For phonological words in French and their effect in the articulation of verse poetry, see, in

particular, Jean-Claude Milner and François Regnault, *Dire le vers* (Paris: Verdier/Poche, 2008), 29–38.
34. Act II, scene ii, in Corneille, *L'Illusion comique*, 66–67.
35. Keneman, "Le Pouvoir du Théâtre," 88.
36. In addition to the educators already cited who have developed and defended the idea of "spontaneous symbolic play," I point to the foundational drama teacher Viola Spolin, who based her practice on improvisational games: "Through spontaneity we are re-formed into ourselves. It creates an explosion that for the moment frees us from handed-down frames of reference.... Spontaneity is the moment of personal freedom when we are faced with a reality and see it, explore it and act accordingly.... It is the time of discovery, of experiencing, of creative expression." Viola Spolin, *Improvisation for the Theatre*, 3rd ed. (Evanston, IL: Northwestern University Press, 1999), 4.
37. Act III, scene vii, in Corneille, *L'Illusion comique*, 107.
38. See Sonia Cunico, "Teaching Language and Intercultural Competence through Drama: Some Suggestions for a Neglected Resource," *Language Learning Journal* 31, no. 1 (Summer 2005): 25.
39. See, for example, Bräuer, *Body and Language*; and Jensen and Hermer, "Learning by Playing."
40. For the importance of collaborative teamwork in drama activities, see Shier, "Arts"; and Essif, *French Play*.
41. See Cunico, "Teaching Language," 24, who also cites Byram and Fleming, *Language Learning*, 143.
42. Keneman, "Le Pouvoir du Théâtre," 94.
43. Fava, *Comic Mask*; and Barry Grantham, *Commedia Plays: Scenarios, Scripts, Lazzi*, (London: Nick Hern, 2006).
44. Augusto Boal, *Theatre of the Oppressed*, trans. Charles A. McBride and Maria-Odilia Leal McBride (New York: Theatre Communications Group, 1993); and Augusto Boal, *Games for Actors and Non-Actors*, 2nd ed., trans. Adrian Jackson (New York: Routledge, 2002), xxiv–xxv, 241–245.
45. Boal, *Games*, 19.
46. Byram and Fleming, *Language Learning*, 143, cited by Cunico, "Teaching Language," 23.

REFERENCES

Anonymous. *La Farce de Maître Pathelin*. Translated by Alain Migé. Paris: Éditions Larousse, 2013.

Aronoff, Mark, and Kirsten Fudeman. *What Is Morphology?* 2nd ed. Chichester, UK: John Wiley & Sons, 2011.

Boal, Augusto. *Games for Actors and Non-Actors.* 2nd ed. Translated by Adrian Jackson. New York: Routledge, 2002.

———. *Theatre of the Oppressed.* Translated by Charles A. McBride and Maria-Odilia Leal McBride. New York: Theatre Communications Group, 1993.

Bräuer, Gerd, ed. *Body and Language: Intercultural Learning through Drama.* Westport, CT: Greenwood Publishing, 2002.

Brooks, Peter. *The Empty Space: A Book about the Theatre: Deadly, Holy, Rough, Immediate.* New York: Scribner, 1995.

Byram, Michael, and Michael Fleming, eds. *Language Learning in Intercultural Perspective: Approaches through Drama and Ethnography.* Cambridge: Cambridge University Press, 1998.

Byrnes, Heidi. "The Cultural Turn in Foreign Language Departments: Challenge and Opportunity." *Profession* (2002): 114–129.

Corneille, Pierre. *L'Illusion comique.* Edited by Jean Serroy. Paris: Folio Classique, 2000.

Culham, Cameron R. "Coping with Obstacles in Drama-Based ESL Teaching: A Non-Verbal Approach." In *Body and Language,* edited by Gerd Bräuer, 95–112. Westport, CT: Greenwood Publishing, 2002.

Cunico, Sonia. "Teaching Language and Intercultural Competence through Drama: Some Suggestions for a Neglected Resource." *Language Learning Journal* 31, no. 1 (Summer 2005): 21–29.

Damasio, Antonio R. *Descartes' Error: Emotion, Reason, and the Human Brain.* New York: G. P. Putnam's Sons, 1994.

DeCoursey, Matthew. "Dramatic Art for Second Language Education: Appropriate Process Objectives for Hong Kong Schools." *Asia-Pacific Journal for Arts Education* 11, no. 11 (2012): 250–270.

Edelstein, Barry. *Thinking Shakespeare: A Working Guide for Actors, Directors, Students . . . and Anyone Else Interested in the Bard.* New York: Theatre Communications Group, 2018.

Essif, Les. *The French Play: Exploring Theatre 'Re-creatively' with Foreign Language Students.* Calgary: University of Calgary Press, 2006.

Fava, Antonio. *The Comic Mask in the Commedia dell'Arte: Actor Training, Improvisation, and the Poetics of Survival.* Translated by Thomas Simpson, edited by Jenny Gherpelli. Evanston, IL: Northwestern University Press, 2007.

Gardner, Howard. *Frames of Mind: The Theory of Multiple Intelligences.* New York: Basic Books, 1983.

Giebert, Stefanie. "Drama and Theatre in Teaching Foreign Languages for Professional Purposes." *Recherche et pratiques pédagogiques en langues de spécialité* 33, no. 1 (Spring 2014): 138–150. https://doi.org/10.4000/apliut.4215.

Grantham, Barry. *Commedia Plays: Scenarios, Scripts, Lazzi*. London: Nick Hern, 2006.

Huizinga, Johan. *Homo Ludens: A Study of the Play Element in Culture*. Mansfield Centre, CT: Martino Publishing, 2014. First published in Dutch in 1938.

Jensen, Marianne, and Arno Hermer. "Learning by Playing: Learning Foreign Languages through the Senses." In *Language Learning in Intercultural Perspective: Approaches through Drama and Ethnography*, edited by Michael Byram and Michael Fleming, 178–192. Cambridge: Cambridge University Press, 1998.

Johnstone, Keith. *Impro: Improvisation and the Theatre*. London: Routledge, 1987.

Keneman, Margaret Lynn. "Finding a Voice in the Foreign Language Classroom: Reading, Writing, and Performing Slam Poetry to Develop Critical Literacies." In *Integrating the Arts: Creative Thinking about FL Curricula and Language Program Direction*, edited by Lisa Parkes and Colleen M. Ryan, 108–130. Boston: Cengage Learning, 2015.

———. "Le Pouvoir du Théâtre: Foreign Languages, Higher Education, and Capturing the Notion of Symbolic Competence." *L2 Journal* 9, no. 2 (Summer 2017): 84–106.

Kramsch, Claire. "From Communicative Competence to Symbolic Competence." *Modern Language Journal* 90 (2006): 249–252.

———. *The Multilingual Subject*. Oxford: Oxford University Press, 2009.

———. "Theorizing Translingual/Transcultural Competence." In *Critical Intercultural Theory and Language Pedagogy*, edited by Glenn S. Levine and Alison Phipps, 15–31. Boston: Heinle, 2012.

Lakoff, George, and Mark Johnson. *Philosophy in the Flesh: The Embodied Mind and Its Challenge to Western Thought*. New York: Basic Books, 1999.

Milner, Jean-Claude, and François Regnault. *Dire le vers*. Paris: Verdier/Poche, 2008.

Modern Language Association Ad Hoc Committee on Foreign Languages. "Foreign Languages and Higher Education: New Structures for a Changed World." *Profession* (2007): 234–245. https://www.mla.org/flreport.

Molière. *Le Bourgeois gentilhomme*. Paris: Flammarion, 2016.

Morgan, Norah, and Juliana Saxton. *Teaching Drama: A Mind of Many Wonders*. Portsmouth, NH: Heinemann, 1987.

Paesani, Kate, Heather Willis Allen, and Beatrice Dupuy. *A Multiliteracies Framework for Collegiate Foreign Language Learning*. Upper Saddle River, NJ: Pearson, 2016.

Piaget, Jean. *Play, Dreams, and Imitation in Childhood*. New York: W. W. Norton, 1962.

Rodenburg, Patsy. *Speaking Shakespeare*. London: Palgrave Macmillan, 2004.

Schewe, Manfred Lukas. "Teaching Foreign Language Literature: Tapping the Students' Bodily-Kinesthetic Intelligence." In *Body and Language*, edited by Gerd Bräuer, 73–94. Westport, CT: Greenwood Publishing, 2002.

Shier, Janet Hegman. "The Arts and the Foreign-/Second-Language Curriculum: An Interdisciplinary Approach to Actively Engage Students in Their Own Learning." In *Body and Language: Intercultural Learning through Drama*, edited by Gerd Bräuer, 183–231. Westport, CT: Greenwood Publishing, 2002.

Spolin, Viola. *Improvisation for the Theater*. 3rd ed. Evanston, IL: Northwestern University Press, 1999.

———. *Theater Games for the Classroom: A Teacher's Handbook*. Evanston, IL: Northwestern University Press, 1986.

———. *Theater Games for the Lone Actor*. Evanston, IL: Northwestern University Press, 2001.

van Lier, Leo. "The Semiotics and Ecology of Language Learning: Perception, Voice, Identity and Democracy." *Utbildning & Demokrati* 13, no. 3 (Fall 2004): 79–103.

Wagner, Betty Jane. *Educational Drama and Language Arts: What Research Shows*. Portsmouth, NH: Heinemann, 1998.

PART II

LITERATURE AND FILM

CHAPTER THREE

SOME BENEFITS TO GOING
NARROW INSTEAD OF BROAD.
Rethinking Cultural Instruction in the French Language Classroom: Andrée Maillet as a Case Study

Rebecca Josephy, Oakland University

In 1996, the *Standards for Foreign Language Learning in the 21st Century* listed culture as one of the five goals of learning foreign language, with the term "culture" being generally understood to include "the philosophical perspectives, the behavioral practices, and the products—both tangible and intangible—of a society."[1] But what society? In the context of French language instruction, the question of society is particularly complex. Should instructors be focusing on societies within the *Hexagone*?[2] the Maghreb? sub-Saharan Africa? the French Caribbean? Islands in the Indian and Pacific Ocean? Southern Asia? or North America: Quebec, Northern Ontario, Cajun, and Créole regions? This, of course, is further complicated by growing immigration, shifts in identity, and globalization.

In order to address these complexities, in the past twenty years—and especially the last decade—there has been a move toward the internationalization of curricula across almost all cross-sections of French-language learning.[3] With very few exceptions, beginner-level French-language textbooks include cultural sections on francophone countries. Writing and composition textbooks have undergone major revisions with an eye toward inclusion. The newest edition of *Tâches d'encre*,[4] for example, includes several new example texts by authors such as Nathacha Appanah and Dai Sijie. In earlier editions, excerpts by Jean-Marie Gustave Le Clézio and Michel Tournier were used, thus moving from a set of writers who write about "La Francophonie" to a set of writers who are part of "La Francophonie." Even intermediate and advanced grammar textbooks tend to include reading excerpts from varied francophone regions and diverse voices within the *Hexagone*. The new *En super forme*[5] by Simone Renaud and Jean-Luc Desalvo—a follow-up of the very successful *En bonne forme*—includes a greater variety of texts from writers such as Maryse Condé, Roch Carrier, Azouz Begag, and Nancy Huston. Other textbooks such as *Controverses* seek to incorporate authentic documents including speeches, interviews, and political articles on debatable issues such as immigration, the status of the French language globally, and Islamophobia. These endeavors ultimately contribute to canon creation, introduce students to a larger vision of culture, and place the study of French language in a global context.

However, despite these improvements, the integration of francophone culture(s) within foreign language instruction is, of course, not without its challenges. In the study of different cultures, there is a danger, as Michael Guest notes, of misrepresenting foreign cultures "as monolithic, static 'Others' rather than dynamic, fluid entities."[6] Language textbooks have generally replaced "culture capsules" with more integrated cultural commentary, but there is still an inclination to rely on trivia, famous personalities, heroes, major festivals and celebrations, national foods, and so forth that can appear both disconnected and stereotypical.[7] In addition to these difficulties, there can also be the expectation, as John Guillory notes, that authors are supposed to stand for certain social groups, thus opening up the syllabus to "demographic demand, the demand of representation."[8] In other words, that the cultural components of a language class, particularly upper-year language classes that tend to use reading passages, shift from a list of culturally rich texts to a "list of representative [minority] authors or social identities."[9] The question thus becomes, How do instructors integrate culture while not glossing over the intricacies of a culture and without reducing culture to a series of authors who seem to be chosen specifically for their social identities? What exciting and innovative ways are there to incorporate a deep and sustained understanding of culture, and especially francophone cultures, into the foreign language (FL) classroom?

One possible solution is to design a language class around noncanonical literature,[10] thus creating a project-based cultural exploration centered on the texts of a single francophone author. At first glance, this may seem to be the stuff of literature classes, but, in this chapter, I am advocating for its use in language-based curriculum. In this way, the study of an author becomes the springboard from which both culture and language skills are acquired. In the following pages, I will outline my experience integrating cultural content in a French Grammar Review (FRH 3140) class through the use of a series of short stories by the little-known francophone Québécois author Andrée Maillet. I'll begin by summarizing the theoretical and pedagogical framework for using noncanonical literature in an intermediate language class. In the next part of the chapter, I will explain why I chose Andrée Maillet's writings and how that criteria could be applied to other noncanonical authors. I will then delve in the details of the class with sample activities, assignments, and course outlines.

The class explored in this chapter does not intend to cover all the different facets of francophone experience but rather attempts to show some of the benefits of focusing on a single noncanonical francophone author through a sustained and concentrated project-based study of culture and language. This model could then be applied to other second language (L2) classes using a wide range of lesser-known authors from any number of francophone regions.

THE CASE FOR CULTURAL INSTRUCTION THROUGH LITERATURE IN A GRAMMAR REVIEW CLASS

Incorporating culture into an upper-year language class may not seem like it would be immediately necessary. The catalogue description for the class (FRH 3140: French Grammar Review) simply states, "Review of French grammar through a variety of approaches such as reading, translation and composition. Conducted in French."[11] Cultural competence is not listed as a requirement nor is it, in fact, part of the class objectives, yet its importance in language-based curriculum is both necessary and germane to today's language instruction. The 2007 Modern Language Association report "Foreign Languages and Higher Education: New Structures for a Changed World" emphasized the need for the development of cultural competencies and identified it as "one of the five imperative needs to which higher education must respond if it is to remain relevant."[12] More specifically, research has shown that language and culture are inseparable and that "the acquisition of a second language, except for specialized, instrumental acquisition ... , is also the acquisition of a second culture."[13]

There seems, therefore, to be little doubt within the academic community and FL guidelines as to the importance and validity of teaching culture in language-orientated curriculum. The question then shifts from "Should culture be integrated in a predominantly linguistic or grammar-based course?" to "How can culture be integrated?" or, to borrow the title of an essay in Zena Moore's *Foreign*

Language Education, "How Do Teachers Teach It?"[14] In an upper-year grammar review class, literature may not seem like the obvious choice, but its ability to provide concrete examples of grammar usage, while also generating culturally rich topics of discussion, has the potential to create a uniquely rich project-based course.

The use of literature in language-based curriculum is, of course, not new. Literature has historically nourished students' understanding of language (word choice, syntax, etc.) and vice versa, although, as Daniel Shanahan writes, there has been an increasing separation between the two: "[T]wo camps have developed, one basing its emphasis on communicative competence, the other on the importance of exposure to culture, and especially, literature."[15] In their article, "The Avatars of Literature in Language Study," Claire Kramsch and Olivier Kramsch further explore this rift, documenting the particular pressures the study of foreign literature has faced over the last century and its progressive movement out of language departments:

> [T]he teaching of foreign literatures in the original has been more vulnerable to geopolitical swings of fortune than other aspects of language study. It has remained fragmented into national language groups and professional bodies, where language teachers and literature scholars occupy distinct positions in the academic hierarchy. Literary scholarship has forged alliances with history, political science, sociology, critical theory, and anthropology and found an enriched raison d'être in Cultural Studies (e.g. Berman, 1994; Daniel & Peck, 1996). But its link to the study of language itself has gradually waned since the demise of philology and the onset of the communicative turn in language learning and teaching.[16]

Indeed, the trend over the last decades has been a steady erosion of literature within language instruction, so much so that incorporating literature and literariness into language-based curriculum can seem almost radical, which begs the question: Why use literature, and specifically obscure noncanonical literature, in a grammar review class when the pedagogical tendency so clearly favors communicative language teaching rooted in real-life situations rather than fictional literary universes?

The reason resides in the immense benefits it yields, in regard not only to language acquisition but also to culture. Literature, as Kramsch noted in her study *Context and Culture in Language Teaching*, has an incredible capacity to contextualize students' understanding of language and to "represent the particular voice of a writer among the many voices of his or her community and thus to appeal to the particular in the reader."[17] Shanahan emphasized literature's ability to grab the emotional interest of students, thus promoting the learning of culture through empathy,[18] and James Davidheiser noted how useful literature could be in the learning and retention of new vocabulary.[19] More specifically, the idea of centering an entire class around an obscure author and her texts creates a project-based exploration in which students are able to gradually discover a new author and specific area of francophone culture—in this case, Québécois. While using anthologies and a wide array of texts and authors from various francophone regions has numerous benefits, it can also lead to confusion and superficial cultural awareness and knowledge. In this class model, with each new piece of information and each new short story, students gain a greater familiarity with the topic,[20] build on previously acquired information, and develop an expertise that culminates in a final project. In this way, cultural competency is acquired in layers, with each aspect of an activity contributing to a deeper understanding of both language and culture.

WHY ANDRÉE MAILLET?

I chose to focus on Andrée Maillet for a number of reasons, which could be used as a tool for choosing other francophone authors, regions, and periods for a similar class model. The criteria that I used are as follows:

1. Texts needed to be at an intermediate level for a third-year[21] French language class. The importance of ascertaining the level of text difficulty in both vocabulary learning and comprehension in L2 learning has been amply studied.[22] Overly simplistic language could lead to disengagement, whereas overly complex or advanced language could overwhelm students and impede metamemory accuracy. Maillet's short stories provided the appropriate level of difficulty. In some limited cases, vocabulary exceeded a B1–B2 level, but with vocabulary lists and activities designed around these lists, students were able to learn the more difficult words and use them appropriately.

2. Readings needed to be brief in order to allow an adequate amount of time for analysis of vocabulary, comprehension, grammar, and culture. Brevity also had the added benefit of fostering students' learning. While research has long revealed that narrative texts are easier for students to understand than expository texts,[23] length also plays a role in student retention, engagement, and motivation,[24] although as J. Charles Alderson notes, "text length is a surprisingly under researched area."[25] Practically speaking, Maillet's short stories are appropriately short, ranging from three to twelve pages and rarely exceeding 5,000 words. In a literature class, the short stories would need to be supplemented by longer novels or other material, but in a grammar review class, the succinctness of these stories are ideal, allowing time to analyze the grammar of the texts alongside content.

3. Readings were chosen to cover a range of subjects, genres, and styles, since variability has also been shown to play a role in student engagement.[26] Maillet's short stories vary in

tone, writing style, and genre, running the gamut of more avant-garde and experimental stories ("Ici, Léon Duranceau" or "Le Lendemain n'est pas sans amour"), to quaint or touching stories depicting snapshots of life in Montreal ("Pleure, pleure," "L'Écœurant," "Un Noël pour Chouchou"), to stories that play with magic realism, illusion, and the fantastic ("Les Doigts extravagants," "Le Lendemain n'est pas sans amour," "Le Plat des chats").

4. It was important that the readings provide a window into a specific francophone experience, allowing for both the passive or incidental absorption of culture as well as active reflection and critical thinking about culture. The majority of Andrée Maillet's short stories that were studied were started in the 1940s yet published in the early 1960s during Quebec's *Révolution tranquille*—a period of intense social and political upheaval. Thus, the texts provided a fascinating glimpse into a changing period of time in Canadian history when culture itself had become a subject of conversation. Additionally, a number of Maillet's short stories contain language unique to Quebec. These examples of Québécois French provided opportunities for students to engage in a deeper understanding of culture, wherein culture is not merely an abstract notion but a phenomenon with tangible, physical manifestations that could be parsed and analyzed in the use of grammar, syntax, and word choice. This allowed students to move beyond standardized conjugations and vocabulary lists and to appreciate how language is used in different regions and contexts, thus enabling them to gain an important metalinguistic awareness or, to use Jan Blommaert and Ben Rampton's terminology, a "metapragmatic reflexivity."[27]

5. While the aim of the class was to delve into the writings of

a single noncanonical author in order to provide students with a deep, multifaceted, complex, and layered appreciation of culture and language, it was important that readings resonated with students in an era of globalization in which French is not simply the linguistic product of a nation-state but the result of shifting and dynamic interactions.[28] Maillet's short stories, of course, predate globalization generally viewed as beginning in the 1980s as well as terminology such as interculturalism, trans-culturalism, or even diversity as it applies to race and culture. However, her life and work nonetheless provided a good jumping-off point from which to explore the diversity of the francophone experience. In addition to writing fiction, Andrée Maillet was a journalist in post–World War II Germany and an accomplished opera singer who studied music in New York in 1943. These experiences become important influences in her writing and showcase a rich, varied, and complex cultural panorama. More specifically, the short stories were pulled from two volumes: *Les Montréalais* and *Le Lendemain n'est pas sans amour*. Both volumes were published within one year of each other, in 1962 and 1963 respectively, yet provided vastly different windows into French and francophone culture. As the title suggests, *Les Montréalais* is focused on life in Montreal. Every short story captures a facet of life in the Canadian city with references to local newspapers, local parks, local pastimes, and so forth. Conversely, *Le Lendemain n'est pas sans amour* is international in flavor. The majority of the short stories in this collection take place in New York with numerous references to large European cities such as Berlin and Paris.

6. Finally, it was important that the author be considered noncanonical for a project-based class in which students were able to not only discuss how culture relates to canon-

icity and curriculum development but also contribute to the understanding of a lesser-known voice within Québécois culture through their own research and study. Canon formation is, of course, a complex process resulting from multiple factors.[29] However, it is clear that the maintenance of tradition plays a significant role in what and who is studied, particularly in the context of French language instruction in which metropolitan French writers overwhelmingly dominate. Andrée Maillet's status as a noncanonical author, both within Québécois literature and more widely in the French language publishing world,[30] allowed students to feel that they were discovering and contributing to a new, exciting, and underappreciated area of study.

In this sense, the danger of falling into stereotypes or glossing over culture was largely avoided as students increased their cultural awareness through readings, discussions, and other project-based inquiries. While the class remained focused on the improvement of language skills through the study of grammar, reading, communication, and so forth, the specific nature of the texts and Maillet's status as a noncanonical author, which encouraged exploration and independent research into her writings, allowed for students to develop a deeper and more nuanced understanding of culture, more common in upper-level literature classes or graduate seminars.

More generally, the principles and criteria above could be used as a template for instructors who wish to develop a language class around the writings of a different noncanonical francophone writer or region. In 2018, for example, Christl Verduyn, Andrea Cabajsky, Andrea Beverley, and Kirsty Bell listed Andrée Maillet among a long list of lesser-known Canadian female authors solicited in a call for papers for their book project titled *Refaire surface: écrivaines canadiennes des années 1970*. The list included authors such as Suzanne Paradis, Claire Martin, Louise Maheux-Forcier, Madeleine

Gagnon, Solange Chaput-Rolland, Adrienne Choquette, Denise Boucher, and Monique Bosco. Other possibilities include the study of more contemporary authors who have yet to benefit from the time needed for canon formation. Outside of Quebec, the list of excellent noncanonical authors multiplies, and there are numerous resources available to find these authors. For example, Patti M. Marxsen established a list of ten Haitian authors[31] who could benefit from wider study, of which only Dany Laferrière could be considered mainstream.[32] To highlight another possible source of material, there are several short story collections with useful editorial information. For example, in 2010, Magellan & Cie published a collection of short stories, *Nouvelles du Sénégal*, that could be used as a resource to find a specific Senegalese author on which to base a similar type course. Fortunately, there is a significant amount of research today devoted to discovering new and underappreciated voices. Each francophone region and author would, of course, have its own specificity and would lead to a uniquely rich cultural exploration. Indeed, the most important aspect of this type of course is that there is a void in the research on the author chosen so that students can participate in the discovery of a new area of knowledge, combining the acquisition of language expertise with cultural depth.

COURSE DESIGN: INTEGRATING CULTURE IN A GRAMMAR REVIEW CLASS

These, then, were the general criteria and goals for the class. In practice, however, the use of a noncanonical author presented a number of challenges. As noncanonical works, many of Maillet's texts were out of print. Recently, there has been some renewed interest in her writing,[33] and, in 2018, there was a re-edition of her most well-known novel, *Les Remparts du Québec*[34]; however, the short story collections *Le Lendemain n'est pas sans amour* and *Les Montréalais* have yet to be reprinted. This presented some initial, but not insurmountable, difficulties.[35] Maillet's minority status also posed a challenge when students had specific questions, and the information was not readily or widely available. This, however, was easily made into a positive when questions were integrated into project-based activities, and students could then actively search for answers through online and library research. Another challenge involved the design and layout of the class. Unlike a literature course in which culture is often explicitly listed as one of the objectives and is usually inherent in the course material, in the French Grammar Review class, cultural content and instruction had to be woven more subtly into each class.

Since the course's main objective was the review of French grammar, the class was structured around weekly grammatical units (le présent, l'impératif, les temps du passé, and so on and so forth) that aligned with a specific short story. For example, the opening units on the present and imperative tenses were paired with Maillet's short story "Pleure, pleure," which provided numerous examples of both of these verb conjugations; the chapter on negations and interrogatives was paired with "Ici, Léon Duranceau," a short story constructed almost entirely of questions and negations. This was repeated over the entirety of the semester, with each short story specifically chosen for the prevalence of that particular grammatical construction. In total, students read six short stories—"Pleure, pleure," "Les Doigts extravagants," "Un Noël pour Chouchou," "La Fête," "L'Écoeurant," "Ici Léon Duranceau"—and could choose as a seventh short story for their final project either "Le Plat du chat" or "Le Lendemain n'est pas sans amour."

In addition to the short stories listed in Table 1, a grammar textbook—Michèle Boularès and Jean-Louis Frérot's *Grammaire progressive du français, niveau B1–B2*—was required for the class.[36] Over the course of the semester, students were assigned grammar exercises from the textbook as well as numerous Andrée Maillet assignments called "Devoirs de lecture." These assignments generally began with a vocabulary list generated from the assigned short story and were followed by a series of comprehension reading questions.³⁷ In this way, I ensured that students had completed both an introductory exploration into the grammar chapter for that unit and the Andrée Maillet readings before coming to class. A typical outline of the division between class and home assignments is listed in Table 2.

Generally, a class would then begin with a brief outline and review of the grammatical chapter and the correction of the textbook exercises. This opening grammar presentation would then be followed by an Andrée Maillet activity called "activité" that students would complete in pairs (often over several classes), followed by either a "dictée" or composition designed to require students to use the vocabulary from the Andrée Maillet homework.³⁸ In this way, Andrée Maillet's short stories became the thread linking the various aspects of the class together—grammar, vocabulary acquisition and retention, communication, and culture.³⁹

Table 1.

« Pleure, pleure »	Présent Impératif Passé composé Imparfait Plus-que-parfait
« Les Doigts extravagants »	Passé simple Futur Conditionnel
« Un Noël pour Chouchou »	Subjonctif présent Les pronoms relatifs
« La Fête »	Les adjectifs Les pronoms personnels (C.O.D et C.O.I)
« L'Écœurant »	Les verbes pronominaux
« Ici, Léon Duranceau »	La négation L'interrogation
« Le Plat du chat » ou « Le Lendemain n'est pas sans amour »	Projet final : la phrase complexe

Table 2. Semaine 3 : L'impératif

En classe ou à la maison ?	Activités et devoirs :	Date :
En classe	Discussion sur l'impératif et corrections des exercices sur l'impératif. Activité n.1 (« Pleure, pleure ») Dictée et/ou rédaction	Le 14 et le 16 septembre
Chez vous **Andrée Maillet** Lisez p. **24 à 30** de "Pleure, pleure" sur Moodle. **Grammaire** Lisez p. 36 et 38 dans le manuel de grammaire.	**Faites « Devoirs de lecture (semaine 3) »** **Faites les exercices 1,2 p. 37.** **Faites les exercices 1,2,3,4,5,6 p. 39**	Le 20 septembre

The in-class Andrée Maillet activities, in particular, served to combine the above competencies. The first section of the activity usually focused on the analysis of a particular grammar structure in one of Maillet's short stories. For example, for the opening unit on the present and imperative conjugations, students were asked to underline the present tenses and circle the imperative tenses in the short story "Pleure, pleure," thus distinguishing between the two. In groups they would then replace each imperative verb with a verb of their choosing, thus changing the meaning of Maillet's short story and ultimately generating new texts. For example, one group chose to replace the verb "pleure, pleure" (cry, cry) with "regarde, regarde" (look, look). The story is about a young woman whose fiancé breaks off their engagement. Her parents first try to figure out what she must have done to elicit the breakup but ultimately support her and encourage her to "pleure, pleure" in order to get over her former fiancé. By changing the verb to "regarde, regarde" as well as replacing a number of other imperative verbs throughout the story, the group was able to create a hilarious new narrative, in which every time there is a heavy emotional moment in the story, a character points to something in the distance, saying "regarde, regarde." The exercise allowed students to properly identify and distinguish different verb tenses, understand the meaning of these verbs in the story, and then use new imperative conjugations in a creative and contextualized way, thus developing creative higher thinking skills in line with Bloom's taxonomy.

The next part of each Andrée Maillet in-class activity was often aimed at encouraging students to practice the assigned grammar difficulty in pairs in a communicative way. For example, in the "Pleure, pleure" activity, students were asked to imagine that their group partner had just received some bad news (similar to Réjane in the Maillet story) and asked to come up with a series of commands for their partner to follow in order to feel better. They were then asked to imagine that their partner received some very good news and to repeat the activity, alternating between each partner. In this way, students could use the short story as a model while also creating new discussions on new topics using the particular grammatical construction (in this case the imperative form).

Either the final section of the Andrée Maillet activity or the Andrée Maillet homework was designed to focus students' attention on the historical, political, and cultural context of the short stories. Many of the texts studied during the semester were originally written in the 1940s, yet published in the 1960s, and it is difficult to know precisely when each was completed during this twenty-year period. What is clear, however, is that, while many of the short stories deal with universal and relatable human themes—a young woman whose fiancé has broken off their engagement ("Pleure, pleure"), a man looking for a job ("Ici, Léon Duranceau"), a group of impoverished girls who are trying to celebrate the holidays ("La Fête")—in the background of almost all of the short stories are underlying tensions indicative of the period of *La Révolution tranquille* (the Quiet Revolution). For example, in the first assigned short story, "Pleure, pleure," when the narrator, Réjane, comes home after the breakup, her father is reading

Le Devoir and is preoccupied with the mistreatment of minority French-Canadian citizens in the western provinces of Canada.[40] As the short story continues, other issues rise to the surface. He reads about a man who is angry about not being spoken to in French on the Canadian national railway[41] as well as a controversy regarding the singing of the British hymn "God Save the Queen": Should one stay seated out of nationalism or stand out of politeness?[42] These concerns also become motivating factors in the character's personality and actions. When, for example, Réjane's father learns of the broken engagement, the narrator intimates that perhaps he is angry that her daughter's former fiancé is French-Canadian and that he can't blame the breakup on the English: "Sans-doute enrage-t-il de ne pouvoir blâmer un Anglais, en cette déplaisante occurrence."[43] Beneath the surface of this short story—like many others—there is concern over the status of the French language, over the treatment of francophone citizens in and outside of Quebec, and a yearning for the preservation of Québécois culture and lifestyle.

In order to foster in students an appreciation for this context, Andrée Maillet in-class activities and/or homework often included a number of culture-based questions. These often involved small research quests. In this way, instead of being lectured to on the history of Quebec, students were encouraged to discover this history on their own through a series of project-based activities.[44] The cultural questions from the "Pleure, pleure" homework are in Table 3.[45]

The two final speculative questions (n. 6 and n. 7) led to a dynamic debate during subsequent class discussions, in which students were naturally split between two positions: Should one be more respectful and polite and accept that one has a minority language and culture or should one fight for the preservation and expansion of that language and culture? Numerous students also saw links between Maillet's short story and current events and were especially interested in the connection between Réjane's father's dilemma of what to do during the singing of "God Save the Queen" and the 2017 NFL national anthem debate. At the time, Colin Kaepernick's refusal to stand during the US national anthem was still fresh in many people's minds. In this way, what could be considered obscure and distant culture—Quebec in the 1940s to the early 1960s—took on new relevance and poignancy.

Table 3. Devoirs de lecture

Où se déroule la nouvelle « Pleure, pleure » d'Andrée Maillet ?
Combien de provinces y a-t-il au Canada ? Combien sont anglophones et francophones ? Où parle-t-on le français et l'anglais au Canada ? Quelle sont les langues officielles du Canada ?
Quel journal le père de Réjane lit-il ? Quels types de sujets sont abordés dans ce journal ? Existe-t-il toujours aujourd'hui ?
En faisant des recherches en ligne, décrivez La Révolution tranquille. De quoi s'agit-il ? Quand a-t-elle eu lieu ? Quels sont les éléments clés et les débats principaux ? Voyons-nous des traces ou une anticipation de cet évènement politique et historique dans la nouvelle « Pleure, pleure » ?
Faites une analyse du titre « La Révolution tranquille ». Pourquoi, selon vous, appelle-t-on cette période La Révolution tranquille ?
Imaginez que l'anglais soit une langue minoritaire aux États-Unis et que le français soit la langue officielle. En tant qu'anglophone, comment vous sentiriez-vous ? Comment votre vie quotidienne changerait-elle ? Croyez-vous qu'il soit important de lutter pour la protection de la langue anglaise, et si oui, pourquoi et comment ?
Voyez-vous des liens entre les débats qu'écoute le père de Réjane dans le journal et à la radio et des évènements actuels ?

With each cultural question, students would thus build upon their knowledge of Quebec and of Andrée Maillet. Each one of Maillet's short stories also showcases different facets of Québécois culture. Texts with religious undertones such as "La Fête" offer a window into a more traditional society on the cusp of change and usher in a dialogue on religion in Quebec before and during *La Révolution tranquille*. Conversely, "Les Doigts extravagants" creates a portrait of a Quebecer who is radical, liberal, and international in aptitude. The fantastic tale rife with references to lesbian film and culture is set in New York after World War II and follows a female narrator who discovers five male fingers in a coat. The fingers come alive, climb up the wall of her apartment, and set out to write a masterpiece on the kitchen table. Despite the fingers' success, the narrator demonstrates incredible hate for the fingers—symbols of patriarchy—and attempts to break free from them. The short story, like many others by Maillet, exhibits a fierce sense of feminism[46] and opened the door to a cultural activity in which students were asked to compare Maillet's narrator to Maillet herself.[47] Hints in the story (such as when Maillet writes "chez-nous on dit les coquerelles"[48] when describing the narrator's insect-infested apartment) also suggest that the narrator was Québécoise. This led to an exploration into the regional and national linguistic differences in the French language.

For the final Andrée Maillet activity, called "Activité de synthèse," students were tasked with studying a scathing 1963 book review of *Les Montréalais* by the famous critic Jacques Godbout.[49] The book review made reference to a number of stories that the students had read during the semester and was ruthless in its criticism of Maillet, with allusions to specific journals and intellectuals of the period. The ensuing study of Godbout's review encouraged students to evaluate all of Maillet's short stories together and to consider whether they agreed or disagreed with Godbout. The review also gave way to an important discussion on how political positions, gender, and perceived alliances could influence the success of a work and how these might have lasting consequences on whether a work becomes part of the literary canon.

Finally, students were assigned an end-of-semester project. For this assignment, students worked individually on a new short story by Andrée Maillet and completed a number of tasks that required a systematic analysis of both grammar and culture.[50] By the end of the course, students had thus read a total of seven short stories by Maillet, completed a vast number of grammatical analyses (first from the textbook and then supplemented by a close examination of Maillet's writing), learned new vocabulary derived from Maillet's short stories (assigned as homework and then tested using *dictées* and short compositions), and completed several activities that required research and critical thinking about Quebec. Indeed, with each new short story and each new activity, students developed a deeper appreciation and understanding not only of grammar but also of the politics, history, and culture of Quebec.

While the tendency among instructors might be to want to rectify years of academic bias by introducing students to a variety of French and francophone cultures and a wide array of texts, the emphasis on one noncanonical author and one francophone region created a cohesive and intellectually stimulating project-based focus for the course. This approach came, of course, with some challenges. Creating vocabulary lists and reading comprehension questions as well as in-class activities and a final project derived from Maillet's short stories was labor intensive; so too was making sure there was a good balance between grammar, communication, and cultural content. The material also demanded considerable interest in Maillet and a willingness to explore different aspects of this author along with students. As Annette Kolodny writes, since canonization is based on prior readings and expertise, "radical breaks are tiring, demanding, uncomfortable, and sometimes wholly beyond our comprehension."[51] However, despite these challenges, the benefits of centering the class on a lesser-known, non-canonical francophone author were immense. By the end of the class, not only did students gain grammatical expertise and considerable knowledge of Québécois culture, but they joined only a small handful of people in the world who could consider themselves experts in Andrée Maillet.

NOTES

1. National Standards in Foreign Language Education Project, American Council on the Teaching of Foreign Languages (ACTFL), *Standards for Foreign Language Learning in the 21st Century*, 3rd ed. (Yonkers, NY: National Standards in Foreign Language Education Project, 2006), 47.
2. Continental France.

3. For information on language instruction within a global context, see Arjun Appadurai, *Modernity at Large: Cultural Dimensions of Globalization* (Minneapolis: University of Minnesota Press, 1996); Celeste Kinginger, "Alice Doesn't Live Here Anymore: Foreign Language Learning and Identity Reconstruction," in *Negotiation of Identities in Multilingual Contexts*, ed. Aneta Pavlenko and Adrian Blackledge (Clevedon, UK: Multilingual Matters, 2004), 219–242; and Claire Kramsch, "Teaching Foreign Languages in an Era of Globalization: Introduction," *Modern Language Journal* 98, no. 1 (2014): 296–311.
4. H. Jay Siskin, Cheryl Krueger, and Maryse Fauvel, *Tâches d'encre: French Composition*, 4th ed. (Boston: Cengage Learning, 2016).
5. Simone Renaud and Jean-Luc Desalvo, *En super forme* (Toronto: Canadian Scholars, 2018).
6. Michael Guest, "A Critical 'Checkbook' for Culture Teaching and Learning," *ELT Journal* 56, no. 2 (2002): 154.
7. The following researchers have all noted this tendency: Paula R. Heusinkveld, "The Foreign Language Classroom: A Forum for Understanding Cultural Stereotypes," *Foreign Language Annals* 18, no. 4 (1985): 321–325; Renate A. Schulz, "The Challenge of Assessing Cultural Understanding in the Context of Foreign Language Instruction," *Foreign Language Annals* 40, no. 1 (2007): 9–26; Erin Kearney, "Cultural Immersion in the Foreign Language Classroom: Some Narrative Possibilities," *Modern Language Journal* 94, no. 2 (2010): 332–336; Gwendolyn Barnes-Karol and Maggie A. Broner, "Using Images as Spring Boards to Teach Cultural Perspectives in Light of the Ideals of the MLA Report," *Foreign Language Annals* 43, no. 3 (2010): 422–445; Isabelle Drewelow, "American Learners of French and Their Stereotypes of the French Language and People: A Survey and Its Implications for Teaching," *French Review* 84, no. 4 (2011): 748–762; and Oxana Dema and Aleidine J. Moeller, "Teaching Culture in the 21st Century Language Classroom," in *Touch the World: Selected Papers from the 2012 Central States Conference on the Teaching of Foreign Languages*, ed. Tatiana Sildus (Eau Claire, WI: Crown Prints, 2012), 75–91.
8. John Guillory, "Canon, Syllabus, List: A Note on the Pedagogic Imaginary," *Transition*, no. 52 (1991): 52.
9. Guillory, 52.
10. In this chapter, I am referring to authors who could be considered obscure or unknown both within the francophone community and the wider literary establishment.
11. See the Oakland University catalogue: http://catalog.oakland.edu/preview_course_nopop.php?catoid=29&coid=59117

12. Modern Language Association Ad Hoc Committee on Foreign Languages, "Foreign Languages and Higher Education: New Structures for a Changed World," *Profession* (2007): 235.
13. H. Douglas Brown, *Principles of Language Learning and Teaching* (New York: Pearson, 2007), 189–190.
14. Zena Moore, "Culture: How Do Teachers Teach It?," in *Foreign Language Teacher Education: Multiple Perspectives*, ed. Zena Moore (Lanham, MD: University Press of America, 1996), 269–288.
15. Daniel Shanahan, "Articulating the Relationship between Language, Literature, and Culture: Toward a New Agenda for Foreign Language Teaching and Research," *Modern Language Journal* 81, no. 2 (1997): 164.
16. Claire Kramsch and Olivier Kramsch, "The Avatars of Literature in Language Study," in "A Century of Language Teaching and Research: Looking Back and Looking Ahead, Part 1," ed. James P. Lantolf, special issue, *Modern Language Journal* 84, no. 4 (2000): 568–569.
17. Claire Kramsch, *Context and Culture in Language Teaching* (Oxford: Oxford University Press, 1993), 131.
18. Shanahan, "Articulating the Relationship."
19. See James C. Davidheiser, "Fairy Tales and Foreign Languages: Ever the Twain Shall Meet," *Foreign Language Annals* 40, no. 2 (2007): 222.
20. Topic familiarity has been shown to increase textual understanding. As Yukie Horiba and Keiko Fukaya's research shows, "when the effects of language proficiency and vocabulary knowledge were statistically controlled, students with high topic-familiarity outperformed students with low topic-familiarity, suggesting that topic-familiarity facilitated learning the content of the text." Yukie Horiba and Keiko Fukaya, "Reading and Learning from L2 Text: Effects of Reading Goal, Topic Familiarity, and Language Proficiency," *Reading in a Foreign Language* 27, no. 1 (2015): 34.
21. Oakland University is on a four credit/per course model. This FRH 3140 course is offered at a point when students have had a minimum of sixteen French credits or four semesters of French.
22. See, for example, Charles Weaver and Deborah Bryant, "Monitoring of Comprehension: The Role of Text Difficulty in Metamemory for Narrative and Expository Text," *Memory & Cognition* 23, no. 1 (1995): 12–22; Aiping Zhao et al., "Exploring Learner Factors in Second Language (L2) Incidental Vocabulary Acquisition through Reading," *Reading in a Foreign Language* 28, no. 2 (2016): 224–245; Yasukata Yano, Michael H. Long, and Steven Ross, "The Effect of Simplified and Elaborated Texts on Foreign Language Reading Comprehension," *Language Learning* 44, no. 2 (1994): 189–219; and Marcella Hu

Hsueh-chao and Paul Nation, "Unknown Vocabulary Density and Reading Comprehension," *Reading in a Foreign Language* 13, no. 1 (2000): 403–430.

23. See Weaver and Bryant, "Monitoring of Comprehension"; Laura M. Sáenz and Lynn S. Fuchs, "Examining the Reading Difficulty of Secondary Students with Learning Disabilities: Expository Versus Narrative Text," *Remedial and Special Education* 23, no. 1 (2002): 31–41; S. J. Berkowitz and B. M. Taylor, "The Effects of Text Type and Familiarity on the Nature of Information Recalled by Readers," in *Directions in Reading: Reading and Instruction*, ed. Michael L. Kamil (Washington, DC: National Reading Conference, 1981), 157–167; Arthur Graesser, Jonathan M. Golding, and Debra L. Long, "Narrative Representation and Comprehension," in *Handbook of Reading Research*, ed. Rebecca Barr, Michael L. Kamil, Peter B. Mosenthal, and P. David Pearson (New York: Longman, 1991), 2:171–204; and Lauren Leslie and JoAnne Caldwell, *Qualitative Reading Inventory*, 4th ed. (Upper Saddle River, NJ: Pearson, 1993).

24. See, for example, Saeed Mehrpour and Abdolmehdi Riazi, "The Impact of Text Length on EFL Students' Reading Comprehension," *Asian EFL Journal* (2004); R. S. Newsom and A. J. H. Gaite, "Prose Learning: Effects of Pretesting and Reduction of Passage Length," *Psychological Reports* 28, no. 1 (1971): 123–129; or William Grabe, "Research on Teaching Reading," *Annual Review of Applied Linguistics* 24 (2004): 44–69.

25. J. Charles Alderson, *Assessing Reading* (Cambridge: Cambridge University Press, 2000), 108.

26. See, for example, the section "Variability in Text" in chapter 3 of Catherine Snow's *Reading for Understanding: Toward an R&D Program in Reading Comprehension* (Santa Monica, CA: RAND, 2002).

27. Jan Blommaert and Ben Rampton, "Language and Superdiversity," *Diversities* 13, no. 2 (2011): 8.

28. For a definition of "globalization" as it applies to the L2 classroom, see page 13 of Jan Blommaert, *The Sociolinguistics of Globalization* (Cambridge: Cambridge University Press, 2010), as cited in Kramsch, "Teaching Foreign Languages," 296.

29. For an excellent overview of these factors, see Joan L. Brown's "Constructing Our Pedagogical Canons," *Pedagogy* 10, no. 3 (2010): 537.

30. During her lifetime, Maillet won a number of prestigious awards (she was named a member of the Académie Canadienne-française in 1974, Officer of the Order of Canada in 1978, and received the Athanase-David prize in 1990). However, despite these accolades, her writing is not widely known today, and she is rarely studied.

31. Eight of the ten write in French.

32. See Patti M. Marxsen, "Public Places, Silent Voices? Modern Haitian Literature in American Public Libraries," *Journal of Haitian Studies* 17, no. 1 (2011): 59–86.
33. In 2018, I consulted Andrée Maillet's personal writings (journals, rough drafts, etc.) at the Bibliothèque et Archives nationales du Québec (BAnQ) in Montreal. I have also given numerous talks and published several articles on Maillet. See Rebecca Josephy, "Une traversée en théorie intertextuelle : la 'seconde main' dans 'Les doigts extravagants' d'Andrée Maillet," @nalyses 6, no. 3 (2011): 167–191; and "Mains (in)visibles : intertextualité, intratextualité et autoréflexivité dans 'Les doigts extravagants' d'Andrée Maillet," *Voix plurielles* 7, no. 1 (2010): 52–78. However, there is still much to discover about this author.
34. Andrée Maillet, *Les Remparts de Québec*, ed. Pascale Ryan (Montréal: Bibliothèque Québécoise, 2018).
35. Companies such as XanEdu will often seek copyrights and create course packs for out-of-print material.
36. While there is no shortage of good grammar textbooks, I chose this particular textbook because it did not include vocabulary and cultural content, which would be covered by activities based on Andrée Maillet's short stories. In this way, there was no confusion over which vocabulary and which readings students should learn. This also ensured that students were only paying for what they needed and that the textbook in the class was cost effective.
37. For a sample Andrée Maillet assignment, please see Appendix 3.2 on Fulcrum. As the course was conducted in French, these assignments were called "Devoirs de lecture" on the course syllabus.
38. For a sample dictée, see Appendix 3.4 on Fulcrum.
39. See Appendix 3.1 on Fulcrum for the full syllabus schedule.
40. "Il tient Le Devoir à la main. La venue de sa fille l'arrache, le front encore tout refrogné, à la lecture d'un éditorial sur les minorités canadiennes-françaises des provinces de l'Ouest, à qui on fait subir, selon la coutume, toute sorte de sévices moraux." Andrée Maillet, "Pleure, pleure," in *Les Montréalais* (1962 ; Reprint, Montréal: Hexagone, 1987), 17.
41. "...on ne lui parle qu'en anglaise sur les chemins de fer nationaux." Maillet, 19.
42. "Le billet de Zadig traite avec ironie la question de l'Union Jack et de God Save the Queen : doit-on rester assis, par nationalisme, quand on joue l'hymne britannique ou bien se lever par politesse ?" Maillet, 18.
43. Maillet, 19.
44. For an overview of the benefits of using a constructivist approach to teaching culture, see Linda Quinn Allen, "Implementing a Culture Portfolio Project

within a Constructivist Paradigm," *Foreign Language Annals* 37, no. 2 (2004): 232–239.
45. Sample Andrée Maillet activities can be found in Appendix 3.3 on Fulcrum.
46. See Josephy, "Mains (in)visibles."
47. While there are many differences, there are also a number of similarities. Maillet had lived in New York and had worked in Germany post WWII—a significant influence in the text.
48. Andrée Maillet, "Les doigts extravagants," in *Le Lendemain n'est pas sans amour* (Montréal: Beauchemin, 1963), 12.
49. Jacques Godbout, "Les Montréalais (Andrée Maillet)," *Liberté* 5, no. 1 (1963): 67–68.
50. Please see the Appendix 3.5 on Fulcrum for the final project.
51. Annette Kolodny, "Dancing through the Minefield: Some Observations on the Theory, Practice, and Politics of Feminist Literary Criticism," *Feminist Studies* 6, no. 1 (1980): 12.

REFERENCES

Alderson, J. Charles. *Assessing Reading*. Cambridge: Cambridge University Press, 2000.

Allen, Linda Quinn. "Implementing a Culture Portfolio Project within a Constructivist Paradigm." *Foreign Language Annals* 37, no. 2 (2004): 232–239.

Appadurai, Arjun. *Modernity at Large: Cultural Dimensions of Globalization*. Minneapolis: University of Minnesota Press, 1996.

Barnes-Karol, Gwendolyn, and Maggie A. Broner. "Using Images as Spring Boards to Teach Cultural Perspectives in Light of the Ideals of the MLA Report." *Foreign Language Annals* 43, no. 3 (2010): 422–445.

Berkowitz, S. J., and B. M. Taylor. "The Effects of Text Type and Familiarity on the Nature of Information Recalled by Readers." In *Directions in Reading: Reading and Instruction*, edited by Michael L. Kamil, 157–167. Washington, DC: National Reading Conference, 1981.

Block, David, and Deborah Cameron, eds. *Globalization and Language Teaching*. London: Routledge, 2002.

Blommaert, Jan, and Ben Rampton. "Language and Superdiversity." *Diversities* 13, no. 2 (2011): 1–21.

———. *The Sociolinguistics of Globalization*. Cambridge: Cambridge University Press, 2010.

Boularès, Michèle, and Jean-Louis Frérot. *Grammaire progressive du français, niveau B1–B2*. Paris: CLE, 2019.

Brown, H. Douglas. *Principles of Language Learning and Teaching.* New York: Pearson, 2007.

Brown, Joan L. "Constructing Our Pedagogical Canons." *Pedagogy* 10, no. 3 (2010): 535–553.

Davidheiser, James, C. "Fairy Tales and Foreign Languages: Ever the Twain Shall Meet." *Foreign Language Annals* 40, no. 2 (2007): 215–225.

Dema, Oxana, and Aleidine J. Moeller. "Teaching Culture in the 21st Century Language Classroom." In *Touch the World: Selected Papers from the 2012 Central States Conference on the Teaching of Foreign Languages,* edited by Tatiana Sildus, 75–91. Eau Claire, WI: Crown Prints, 2012.

Drewelow, Isabelle. "American Learners of French and Their Stereotypes of the French Language and People: A Survey and Its Implications for Teaching." *French Review* 84, no. 4 (2011): 748–762.

Godbout, Jacques. "*Les Montréalais* (Andrée Maillet)." *Liberté* 5, no. 1 (1963): 67–68.

Grabe, William. "Research on Teaching Reading." *Annual Review of Applied Linguistics* 24 (2004): 44–69.

Graesser, Arthur, Jonathan M. Golding, and Debra L. Long. "Narrative Representation and Comprehension." In *Handbook of Reading Research,* vol. 2, edited by Rebecca Barr, Michael L. Kamil, Peter B. Mosenthal, and P. David Pearson, 171–204. New York: Longman, 1991.

Guest, Michael. "A Critical 'Checkbook' for Culture Teaching and Learning." *ELT Journal* 56, no. 2 (2002): 154–161.

Guillory, John. "Canon, Syllabus, List: A Note on the Pedagogic Imaginary." *Transition,* no. 52 (1991): 36–54.

Heusinkveld, Paula R. "The Foreign Language Classroom: A Forum for Understanding Cultural Stereotypes." *Foreign Language Annals* 18, no. 4 (1985): 321–325.

Horiba, Yukie, and Keiko Fukaya. "Reading and Learning from L2 Text: Effects of Reading Goal, Topic Familiarity, and Language Proficiency." *Reading in a Foreign Language* 27, no. 1 (2015): 22–46.

Hsueh-chao, Marcella Hu, and Paul Nation. "Unknown Vocabulary Density and Reading Comprehension." *Reading in a Foreign Language* 13, no. 1 (2000): 403–430.

Josephy, Rebecca. "Mains (in)visibles : intertextualité, intratextualité et autoréflexivité dans 'Les doigts extravagants' d'Andrée Maillet." *Voix plurielles* 7, no. 1 (2010): 52–78.

———. "Une traversée en théorie intertextuelle : la 'seconde main' dans 'Les doigts extravagants' d'Andrée Maillet." *@nalyses* 6, no. 3 (2011): 167–191.

Kearney, Erin. "Cultural Immersion in the Foreign Language Classroom: Some Narrative Possibilities." *Modern Language Journal* 94, no. 2 (2010): 332–336.

Kinginger, Celeste. "Alice Doesn't Live Here Anymore: Foreign Language Learning and Identity Reconstruction." In *Negotiation of Identities in Multilingual Contexts*, edited by Aneta Pavlenko and Adrian Blackledge, 219–242. Clevedon, UK: Multilingual Matters, 2004.

Kolodny, Annette. "Dancing through the Minefield: Some Observations on the Theory, Practice, and Politics of Feminist Literary Criticism." *Feminist Studies* 6, no. 1 (1980): 1–25.

Kramsch, Claire. *Context and Culture in Language Teaching.* Oxford: Oxford University Press, 1993.

———. "Teaching Foreign Languages in an Era of Globalization: Introduction." *Modern Language Journal* 98, no. 1 (2014): 296–311.

Kramsch, Claire, and Olivier Kramsch. "The Avatars of Literature in Language Study." In "A Century of Language Teaching and Research: Looking Back and Looking Ahead, Part 1," edited by James P. Lantolf, special issue, *Modern Language Journal* 84, no. 4 (2000): 553–573.

Leslie, Lauren, and JoAnne Caldwell. *Qualitative Reading Inventory.* 4th ed. Upper Saddle River, NJ: Pearson, 1993.

Maillet, Andrée. *Le Lendemain n'est pas sans amour.* Montréal: Beauchemin, 1963.

———. *Les Montréalais.* 1962. Reprint, Montréal: Hexagone, 1987.

———. *Les Remparts de Québec.* Edited by Pascale Ryan. Montréal: Bibliothèque Québécoise, 2018.

Marxsen, Patti M. "Public Places, Silent Voices? Modern Haitian Literature in American Public Libraries." *Journal of Haitian Studies* 17, no. 1 (2011): 59–86.

Mehrpour, Saeed, and Abdolmehdi Riazi. "The Impact of Text Length on EFL Students' Reading Comprehension." *Asian EFL Journal* (2004).

Modern Language Association Ad Hoc Committee on Foreign Languages. "Foreign Languages and Higher Education: New Structures for a Changed World." *Profession* (2007): 234–245.

Moore, Zena. "Culture: How Do Teachers Teach It?" In *Foreign Language Teacher Education: Multiple Perspectives*, edited by Zena Moore, 269–288. Lanham, MD: University Press of America, 1996.

National Standards in Foreign Language Education Project, American Council on the Teaching of Foreign Languages (ACTFL). *Standards for Foreign Language Learning: Preparing for the 21st Century.* Yonkers, NY: National Standards in Foreign Language Education Project, 1996.

———. *Standards for Foreign Language Learning in the 21st Century.* 3rd ed. Yonkers, NY: National Standards in Foreign Language Education Project, 2006.

Newsom, R. S., and A. J. H. Gaite. "Prose Learning: Effects of Pretesting and Reduction of Passage Length." *Psychological Reports* 28, no. 1 (1971): 123–129.

Renaud, Simone, and Jean-Luc Desalvo. *En super forme*. Toronto: Canadian Scholars, 2018.

Sáenz, Laura M., and Lynn S. Fuchs. "Examining the Reading Difficulty of Secondary Students with Learning Disabilities: Expository Versus Narrative Text." *Remedial and Special Education* 23, no. 1 (2002): 31–41.

Schulz, Renate A. "The Challenge of Assessing Cultural Understanding in the Context of Foreign Language Instruction." *Foreign Language Annals* 40, no. 1 (2007): 9–26.

Shanahan, Daniel. "Articulating the Relationship between Language, Literature, and Culture: Toward a New Agenda for Foreign Language Teaching and Research." *Modern Language Journal* 81, no. 2 (1997): 164–174.

Siskin, H. Jay, Cheryl Krueger, and Maryse Fauvel. *Tâches d'encre: French Composition*. 4th ed. Boston: Cengage Learning, 2016.

Snow, Catherine. *Reading for Understanding: Toward an R&D Program in Reading Comprehension*. Santa Monica, CA: RAND, 2002.

Weaver, Charles, and Deborah Bryant. "Monitoring of Comprehension: The Role of Text Difficulty in Metamemory for Narrative and Expository Text." *Memory & Cognition* 23, no. 1 (1995): 12–22.

Yano, Yasukata, Michael H. Long, and Steven Ross. "The Effect of Simplified and Elaborated Texts on Foreign Language Reading Comprehension." *Language Learning* 44, no. 2 (1994): 189–219.

Zhao, Aiping, Ying Guo, Carrie Biales, and Arnold Olszewski. "Exploring Learner Factors in Second Language (L2) Incidental Vocabulary Acquisition through Reading." *Reading in a Foreign Language* 28, no. 2 (2016): 224–245.

CHAPTER FOUR

LA CHANSON ENGAGÉE: WAGING WAR ON WAR!

Using Songs to Teach French Language and Culture

Christophe Corbin, Haverford College

Everything is said to end with a song in France.[1] To sing about love, for a person or for a region, to praise or to ridicule a political regime or a statesman, to fuel patriotism or to call for peace, to denounce social hardships or urban despair, songs have long played a central role in popular culture. As such, they often belong to individual and collective memory and may be regarded as "a defining characteristic of French culture."[2]

Regardless of whether songs in general should be worthy of scholarly attention—a question to which the Swedish Academy may have brought an answer by awarding the 2016 Nobel Prize in Literature to American folk singer Bob Dylan "for having created new poetic expressions within the great American song tradition"[3]—thanks to their exceptional evocative power, songs certainly constitute most valuable material for the pedagogue. Whether for a class in which culture is the main focus or for one in which culture is an integrated component toward language acquisition, songs can indeed provide stimulating entry points to topics under study as well as an opportunity to delve into cultural specificities.

The recent celebration of the centennial of the end of World War I triggered renewed interest in what iconic French songwriter and singer Georges Brassens considered (sardonically) to be his "favorite war." Such an interest has led numerous scholars and journalists to revisit the cultural production about the war, including the many songs it generated during and after the Great War. This study offers suggestions about how to use songs in a French course, particularly songs belonging to a tradition of *chanson engagée*, songs written not only to entertain but also to bring awareness and to take a stand, a genre that should appeal to students and that lends itself rather well to a final creative and performative project.

The theme of war is chosen for this chapter for what it reveals about the society and the time at which the selected songs were composed. The first song discussed in this chapter is "La Chanson de Craonne" (the Song of Craonne), which was popular among soldiers during the Great War and reverberates topics illustrated in iconic war novels such as Henri Barbusse's *Under Fire* (1916). Georges Brassens's "La Guerre de 14-18" (The War of 1914–1918) and finally Boris Vian's and Renaud's versions of "Le Déserteur" (The Deserter) are other examples of popular (anti-war) songs that exemplify the pacifist trend of the 1960s and the resulting emergence of the figure of a new breed of hero, or anti-hero (depending on one's perspective of the matter): that of men refusing to fight in wars regarded as unjust and absurd.

Conceived as a series to be used over several days of instruction, these songs may also be used individually to complement a lesson on World War I (songs 1 and 2), or on the rise of pacifism in the second half of the twentieth century (songs 2, 3, and 4). The activities found in this chapter are designed to promote cultural awareness and to improve linguistical competences at any level beyond intermediate. The former is achieved by introducing learners to both particular historical events and iconic figures of the twentieth-century French cultural landscape and by inviting them to reflect upon the world around them by establishing a meaningful relation to the subject matter, thereby fostering critical thinking as well. The latter is achieved by developing comprehension through the listening and the analysis of complex lyrics in a second language (L2); oral and written production skills will develop through group discussions and the creation and performance of a final group project, whose outcomes will be explained in the last part of this chapter.

Depending on the type of curriculum in which they appear, the suggested activities may be used differently: traditional language classes are indeed likely to focus largely on the form (register, lexicon, syntax, grammar) while including cultural references and historical perspectives necessary to the understanding of the intended message of the song under study. Content-based classes are more likely to concentrate on ideas expressed in a given framework, reflecting inclinations of a social group at a particular point in time, and follow up on notions evoked in the song in question. This said, one certainly does not exclude the other, and both approaches should be used in each setting. Given the abundance of resources available about World War I, the proposed activities are unequal in length (which certainly does indicate a preference given to one song over the others) and in the number of possible additional activities.

SONGS AS TIME-SENSITIVE BAROMETERS

If everything ends with a song in French literature, everything also begins with a song (about war): the first French poetic compositions about war were indeed meant to be sung. Among the earliest texts still available to us today is a "chanson de geste" (from Latin *gesta*, meaning "deeds, actions accomplished"), an epic poem meant to be performed. Composed between around 1040 and 1115, "The Song of Roland" depicts the heroic deeds of Roland, nephew of Charlemagne, leading the rear guard of the French forces against the Saracens. In spite of notable exceptions (major authors such as Rabelais, Voltaire, Stendhal, Maupassant, or Céline forcefully denounced the absurdity of war), for centuries, literary fictional representations of war continued to glorify war and to praise "heroic deeds." Songs, too, long served a practical purpose: to encourage men to fight for the motherland; the songs written and sung during World War I were no exception. However, as the war was unfolding, songs signaled a shift in the collective perception of the war and in its representation.

The different stages of World War I can almost be understood through the songs sung at the time. As the *poilus*, the civilians drafted into the infantry who paid the highest toll during the war, started to understand that the war was going to last much longer than they had first thought, their songs started to reflect a growing sense of resignation, if not despair. Whereas the songs sung early on in the war were largely patriotic ("Ils ne passeront pas," "Valmy," and, of course, the national anthem, "La Marseillaise") and fiercely anti-German ("Corbeaux d'Allemagne" and "Les Boches c'est comme des rats"), "La Chanson de Craonne" indeed testifies to the prevailing sentiment among the *poilus* of hopelessness and illustrates the grievances shared by most men on the front line. Songs sung during the war can indeed be regarded as oral documents of the daily life of these soldiers.

Some of these wartime songs were performed by professionals, some were created for propaganda purposes, and many others were written by soldiers themselves: "Ma P'tite Mimi" is a rowdy conversation between a soldier and his rifle. "Le Pinard," "fait du bien par où ce que ça passe," shows the importance of (cheap) wine in surviving life in the trenches. "La Roulante" expresses soldiers' disgruntlement with food as well as their frustration with war profiteers: "Les nouveaux riches dînent chez Paillard, les profiteurs y-z-ont un bar, mais le Poilu lui se sustente à la roulante [wheeled food cart]." And "Pan pan l'Arbi" reminds us of the racism tainted with a form of paternalism that existed toward colonial troops engaged in the conflict to save the "motherland." If these songs offer small vignettes about life in the trenches, they are also a way to forget about life in these trenches: "La Madelon" tells the story of soldiers flirting with a young waitress in a tavern in the country. Though not strictly speaking about the war, the song quickly acquired a patriotic status and long remained the most popular French World War 1 song. Finally, although songs cover almost every aspect of soldiers' experiences on the front line, the subject matter of songs about the war is not limited to them: "Les Tricoteuses" (The Knitters) elevates knitting woolens to a sacred duty, whereas "Les Tourneuses d'obus" (The Shell Makers) reminds us of the role played by women in replacing men in various capacities, notably in machining shell casings. While crediting women's contribution to the war effort, the song "Pour remplacer les hommes" (To replace men) also reminds us of the prevalent sexism, if not overt misogyny, of the time: "Il leur manquera toujours quelque chose, Pour nous remplacer totalement" ("They will always be missing something to replace us completely").

Songs are also a sensitive time barometer of the mood of the troops. They may be used to relieve stress during wartime but also to contest situations of war, as is the case with "La Chanson de Craonne," one of the two songs (with "La Madelon") to have survived the test of time and to have been passed on to us in part thanks to films set during the Great War. An important song in the collective memory and a historical document in itself, "La Chanson de Craonne" lends itself particularly well to a scaffolding activity in an L2 class following a introductory presentation of World War 1 songs.

"LA CHANSON DE CRAONNE": GODDAMN THIS WAR!

"Good-bye to life, good-bye to love / Good-bye to all the women / It's all over now, we've had it for good / With this awful war." So goes the well-known refrain of the "La Chanson de Craonne," which expressed soldiers' weariness due to the seemingly endless war and alluded to mass disobedience months before the mutinies of 1917.

The following activity is designed to be conducted entirely in the target language (French) in class to meet the learning objectives as defined earlier in this chapter. Instructors may first want to offer some historical background by offering a summary of World War I, including its causes, its actors, its impact, a timeline, and to initiate the conversation, to invite learners to make sense of the expression associated with it: "La Der des Ders." Sometimes used as an equivalent to "the very last time" today, the expression indeed points to the belief in 1914 that the war not only was going to be brief but also would end all wars ("the war to end all wars"). Given the war's length (from 1914 to 1918), the magnitude of the destruction it caused (including 40 million casualties), and its aftereffects (notably World War II), the expression is now used essentially sardonically.

Attesting to the song's popularity and longevity, several performances of "La Chanson de Craonne" are available online, including on the website of the Memorial Museum of the Chemin des Dames, which offers three different interpretations in the same video.[4] Instructors may, however, choose to play the 2003 version by Maxime Le Forestier.[5] This choice first constitutes an opportunity to present the author of two songs that might be considered for an activity similar to one proposed here, and by the same token to introduce the theme of pacifism illustrated by the songs selected for this chapter, and characteristic of the epoch in which they occurred. Another reason for selecting Le Forestier's version of the "La Chanson de Craonne" is his somewhat problematic choice to occult a paragraph of the original lyrics, an omission that will be discussed in class after students answer a series of questions presented later in this section (and in French in appendix 4.1 on Fulcrum).

In this optional warm-up sequence, the instructor shows the cover of Le Forestier's immensely popular album at the time of its release in 1972 and invites students to make sense of the cultural signs it contains: the folk singer can be seen in his twenties, next to a rose, and wearing a beard and long hair that may indeed be viewed as an indication of his political stance, or at least of the spirit of the time. If students are unable to identify the cultural signs of the image in question, instructors may remind their class of the emergence of the counterculture particular to the 1960s and 1970s in most of the Western world and of one of the well-known lasting slogans invoked in anti-war contexts around the world: "Make love, not war" ("Faites l'amour, pas la guerre"). The instructor may point out that Le Forestier is still known today for his anthemic song "San Francisco," where he lived in 1971 in a hippie commune in now iconic "blue house." The album in which the song appears, "Mon frère," includes another iconic anti-military song considered for this chapter, "Parachutiste," written after the author had completed his military service in a paratroopers' unit, a decade after the end of the Algerian War (to which paratroopers are automatically associated in the collective memory).[6] Le Forestier, however, also paid homage to fallen World War I soldiers by singing a series of letters written by a conscript to his wife between 1912 and 1916 in "Les lettres" (1975). This song might also be used as a case study in conjunction with the collection of letters written by infantrymen: *Paroles de poilus : Lettres et carnets du front 1914–1918*.[7]

To facilitate understanding while listening to the song, instructors provide students a version of the (full) lyrics with blanks (corresponding to key words underlined in the version provided later in this chapter) to be filled in as the song is being played. Students are then asked to share their impressions of the song and how much they understood. They will probably pick up on two cognates, "condamnés" and "sacrifiés," as well as on "Adieu la vie": these can be used to trigger interest for the topic and to resume the conversation about World War I.

To (re)activate background knowledge, students are invited to share what they know about World War I, a topic with which most college students are usually familiar. Either orally or in "snowball" manner (by jotting down on a piece of paper to be crumpled and thrown on the floor to preserve anonymity in the target language, or in English if they lack the vocabulary), students are asked share notions they immediately associate with the Great War (trench warfare, barbed wire, shell shock, Triple Alliance, etc.). Results may be shared orally and written up on the board.

At this point, the instructor may discuss the history of the song, possibly with a PowerPoint presentation including visual aids and maps, explaining how the lyrics morphed during the war. Based on a popular song from 1911, "Bonsoir M'amour," the first version of "La Chanson de Craonne" appeared in 1915. At the time, it was known as the "Chanson de Lorette." Now the site of the largest French military necropolis, Notre Dame de Lorette was the focal point of three battles that took the lives of 100,000 men between October 1914 and October 1915. Other versions of the song appeared in different places at different times as it was adapted by infantrymen as it circulated from one battleground to the next. In 1916, "La Chanson de Vaux" referred to Verdun, which would come to signify, more than any other battle, the grinding and bloody nature of warfare on the Western Front. The same year, another version, "Les Misères de la Somme," referred explicitly to the Battle of the Somme, which lasted 140 days and resulted in over one million casualties. It is around that time that the refrain changed from past to present tense: "We were / are all condemned, we were / are the sacrificed ones."

The version of "La Chanson de Craonne" that we know today dates back to the time of the 1917 Nivelle Offensive on the Chemin des Dames (literally, "Ladies' path"), "a very desirable real estate"[8]

100 miles northeast of Paris. The ridge was ferociously contested for its strategical value. The failure of the offensive and the high number of casualties (over 100,000 in the first week of fighting, ten times the number anticipated for the whole offensive) resulted in mutinies. Philippe Petain, who replaced Nivelle as commander in chief, ordered the execution of forty-nine men refusing to fight. Craonne, a village (in ruins since 1914) on the Chemin des Dames, would thus be forever associated with a distressing episode of World War I.

A considerable reward is said to have been offered to identify the author of the song (though there clearly were several of them), unsuccessfully. According to Bertrand Dicale,[9] the different versions of the song are known to have been sung in no fewer than 68 of the 110 divisions of the French army, a number that testifies to the extent of the anger and despair of infantrymen who refused to be used as "chair à canon" (cannon fodder), some of whom put their rifle-grips up ("crosse en l'air") to signify their refusal to follow orders deemed absurd and irresponsible. "La Chanson de Craonne" first appeared in print in Paul Vaillant-Couturier's *La Guerre des Soldats*, published in 1919, and in *La Saignée* by Georges Bonnamy, in 1920, about the Chemin des Dames. It was first recorded in 1963 but remained censored until 1974 and was not mentioned in textbooks until the late 1970s.

Throughout this brief presentation, whose length may vary with the instructor's level of comfort and with the intended objectives of the lesson, instructors may show the different places mentioned on a map of France (on Google Maps or using the remarkable website of the Chemin de Dames memorial museum, presented in more detail later) to their students and invite students to react to the exorbitant number of causalities. In the same spirit of promoting multiliteracy, instructors may want to show clips of "The Battle of the Somme,"[10] considered to be the very first war movie ever made (in 1916 for propagandistic purposes), as well as sketches made by François Flameng on the front line, offering visual renderings of some aspects of the war discussed in introduction to the song and more (battlefields, no man's lands, scenes of destruction, portraits of colonial troops, etc.[11]).

Students are now ready to engage in the close reading of the lyrics. Key words have been underlined, and students are invited to make sense of these words and to either explain what they mean or to offer synonyms. Simplified equivalents likely to be understood even for students with minimal command of the target language, or explanations, are provided in a separate column to be kept hidden during the first reading of the lyrics (either by keeping it covered or by folding their handout in half).

In small groups, students now discuss the questions below (provided in L2 in the classroom: see appendix 4.1 on Fulcrum) and take notes to prepare the conversation with the rest of the class. The whole activity should be conducted in the target language. Students should be encouraged to cite from the lyrics to support their answers.

1. What are the infantrymen's grievances? What aspects of the war and of society do they reveal?
2. What mood transpires from the lyrics?
3. What did the change of tense in the last two lines of the refrain from past to present change?
4. Note the dissident words of the lyrics. How would you qualify this song?
5. Why can "La Chanson de Craonne" be regarded as a palimpsest and a manifest?[12]
6. What part of the song is omitted in the version performed by Maxime Le Forestier, and what does it change? (The part omitted is "Ceux qu'ont l'pognon, ceux là r'viendront / Car c'est pour eux qu'on crève / Mais c'est fini, car les troufions / Vont tous se mettre en grève.")
7. How do you explain the relative longevity of the song?

"La Chanson de Craonne" (1917)

Quand au bout d'huit jours le r'pos terminé	repos (ou permission)
On va reprendre les <u>tranchées</u>,	emblématique de la Grande Guerre
Notre place est si utile	
Que sans nous on <u>prend la pile</u>	argot militaire: subir une défaite
***	
Mais c'est bien fini, <u>on en a assez</u>	en avoir assez = être fatigué de
Personne ne veut plus marcher	
Et le <u>cœur bien gros</u>, comm' dans un sanglot	avoir le cœur gros = être triste
On dit adieu aux civ'lots	civils
***	
Même sans tambours, même sans trompettes	référence à la musique militaire des cérémonies
On s'en va <u>là-haut</u> en <u>baissant la tête</u>	"là-haut," car on "monte" au front, mais la tête basse en signe de découragement
***	
<u>Adieu</u> la vie, adieu l'amour,	adieu = au revoir final
Adieu toutes les femmes	
C'est bien fini, c'est pour toujours	
De cette guerre <u>infâme</u>	infâme = abjecte
***	
C'est à Craonne sur le plateau	
Qu'on doit <u>laisser sa peau</u>	= mourir
Car nous sommes tous condamnés	
Nous sommes les sacrifiés	
***	
Huit jours de tranchée, huit jours de souffrance	
Pourtant on a l'espérance	
Que ce soir viendra la <u>r'lève</u>	la relève = changements de soldats
Que nous attendons <u>sans trêve</u>	Sans perte de temps. Jeu de mots [truce]
***	
Soudain dans la nuit et dans le silence	
On voit quelqu'un qui s'avance	
C'est un officier de <u>chasseurs à pied</u>	de l'infanterie
Qui vient pour nous remplacer	
***	
Doucement dans l'ombre sous la pluie qui tombe,	
C'est à Craonne sur le plateau	
Qu'on doit laisser sa peau	

Car nous sommes tous condamnés	
Nous sommes les sacrifiés	
***	
C'est malheureux d'voir sur <u>les grands boulevards</u>	là où on s'amuse à Paris
Tous ces gros qui <u>font la foire</u>	ceux qui mangent bien et font la fête/s'amusent [fat cats]
Si pour eux la vie est rose	
Pour nous c'est pas la même chose	
***	
Au lieu d'se cacher tous ces <u>embusqués</u>	ceux qui se cachent à l'arrière/qui ne veulent pas faire la guerre [shirkers]
F'raient mieux d'monter aux tranchées	
Pour défendre leur bien, car nous n'avons rien	
Nous autres les pauv' <u>purotins</u>	qui vivent dans la misère
***	
Tous les camarades sont enterrés là	
Pour défendr' <u>les biens</u> de ces messieurs là	les possessions
***	
Ceux qu'ont l'<u>pognon</u>, ceux-là r'viendront	pognon = argent (argot)
Car c'est pour eux qu'on <u>crève</u>	mourir
Mais c'est fini, car les <u>trouffions</u>	argot militaire = soldat
Vont tous se mettre <u>en grève</u>	= mutinerie pour les soldats
***	
Ce s'ra votre tour, messieurs <u>les gros</u>	ceux qui ont de l'argent et mangent à leur faim/bourgeois
De monter sur le plateau	Le Plateau de Craonne
Car si vous voulez faire la guerre	
<u>Payez-la de votre peau</u>	avec votre vie / expression = faire la peau de quelqu'un = tuer

Other cultural mediums may be used to enhance the presentation of the song. For example, a sequence of the film *A Very Long Engagement* shows one of the characters (Six-Sous) accused of self-mutilation and condemned to face near-certain death in a no man's land between French and German trench lines singing "La Chanson de Craonne." Another example of valuable pedagogical tools that students should be encouraged to explore includes using a storyboard from Jacques Tardi's graphic novel *Goddamn*

This War! The storyboard in question presents the story of François Paulet, a soldier sentenced to death for having sung "La Chanson de Craonne" (and for refusing to snitch on those who had taught it to him) and for refusing to fight.

Figure 1. Excerpt from *Putain de Guerre!* Jacques Tardi © Casterman. Courtesy of the author and Casterman Publishing.

If time permits, instructors can expand the activity to include the story of Paulet told from the perspective of his pregnant wife in a song written and performed by Tardi's wife, Dominique Grange, whose closing line echoes the title of Tardi's graphic novel: "Executioners who rob him of his life / Butchers who tear my heart out / I will tell our child / Who will be born in the spring / That he can be proud of his father / Goddamn this war."[13] Grange's "Laisse-moi passer, sentinelle" ("Let me through, sentry") is indeed a rare reminder that women are often collateral and quickly forgotten victims in military conflicts traditionally almost exclusively remembered and depicted from the perspective of male soldiers.

Instructors may also consider including reproductions of handwritten versions of "La Chanson de Craonne" in cursive letters most of us would be unable to reproduce today as to accentuate the tragic dimension of the stories or trajectories of young individuals caught in the meshes of History ("L'Histoire avec sa grande hache," as Georges Perec put it: "History, spelt with a capital H as in hatchet or horror"). Students may put themselves in an imagined position of the writer and draft a short creative piece of correspondence with a partner. They should determine who that person is, where they are, and why they are writing the lyrics or the letter.

In a possible extension of the activity, depending on the level of the class and its objectives, students choose a topic pertinent to the historical points associated with the song and with the discussion leading up to it, first of which is the physical site of the Chemin des Dames and the mutinies during the war, life in the trenches but also life in the chalk mines below the Chemin des Dames to which the "La Chanson to Craonne" is associated, historical figures such as Philippe Pétain or African American Eugene Bullard (who would become the world's first Black fighter pilot), among other topics. Students research the topic of their choice and present it during the next class or classes following a set of guidelines and assessment criteria that may vary from one instructor to the next depending on the type of curriculum in which they appear.

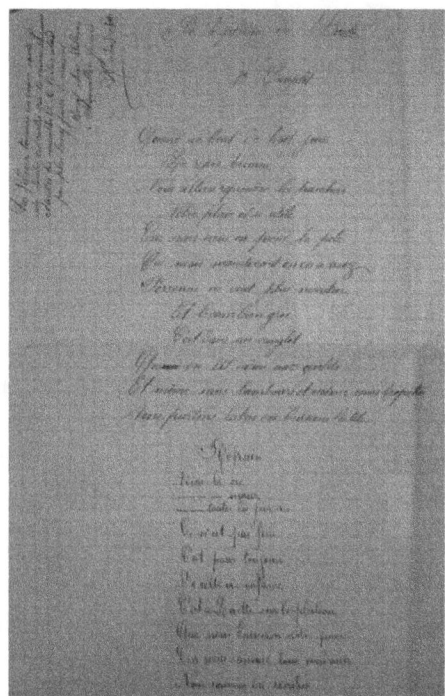

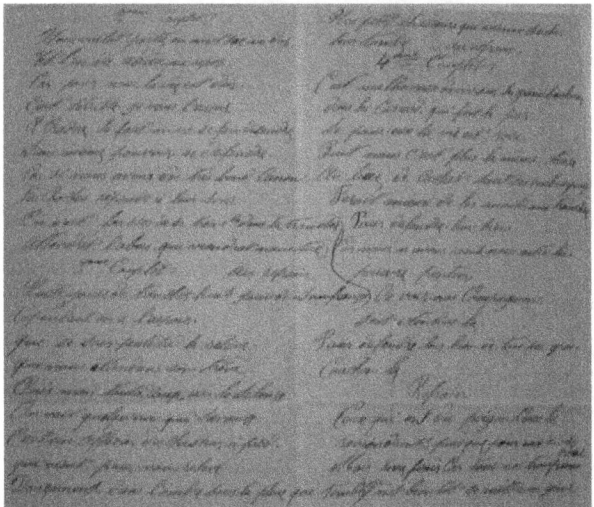

Figures 2 and 3. Anonymous handwritten manuscripts of "La Chanson de Craonne." From the archives of Service Historique de la Défense (SHDT 16N1552). Available at https://www.crid1418.org/espace_pedagogique/documents/ch_craonne.htm.

Students should be encouraged to visit Le Chemin des Dames memorial's website,[15] a valuable (sometimes interactive) resource that may inspire students for their own final project. The website includes virtual exhibits; photos of Dragon's Cave where artifacts and graffities left by French, German, and American soldiers who lived in it at one time or another left behind can be seen; maps of trenches; aerial photos from the war and from today; pedagogical activities; and photos and locations of the numerous military cemeteries, not only French but also American, British, Danish, German, and Italian. For students willing to explore beyond the realm of Le Chemin des Dames, another most valuable resource is the website of the centennial of World War I available in French, German, and English.[16]

Finally, students are encouraged to start thinking about a collaborative and creative project reproducing the style of "La Chanson de Craonne" with new lyrics, or creating an entirely new song about war, denouncing it, or glorifying it, or offering a more balanced view on the question of war. In this project, learners therefore assume a new and more active role, that of the militant artist, reflecting further upon the subject under study.

"LA GUERRE DE 14-18." THE BEST ONE!

We now turn to one of the most illustrious *chansonniers* of the twentieth century. As one of the most easily recognizable voices of the French *chanson* repertoire, Georges Brassens has long held a particular place in the collective memory and can be regarded as somewhat of a national icon. Laureate of the 1967 poetry prize of the prestigious Académie française founded in 1634, Brassens has inspired several doctoral dissertations and monographs, attesting to the literary credentials of his songs. His brilliant manipulation of the French language and usage of erudite rich cultural references certainly make his lyrics difficult to (fully) enjoy for an audience with limited command of French. However, students should be reminded that it is precisely this richness that makes Brassens's songs so unique and exciting to study and that few native speakers of French can pride themselves in being able to follow his songs without an open dictionary at their side. If his bawdy and dark humor may at times puzzle or even make uncomfortable a contemporary, younger audience, his natural disposition to satirize social conformity, moral hypocrisy, and bigotry and his contempt for authority figures will certainly appeal to students as it has to millions of his fans.

One of many contemporary singers greatly influenced by Brassens, Maxime Le Forestier recorded *Le Forestier chante Brassens* (2005), an album of the 171 (yes, 171) songs Brassens had played in his concerts over the years. Attesting to his own fascination of Brassens, Renaud, whose song will be discussed in the next section, also pays tribute to, in his words, the "poet-rebel against all institutions" by covering 23 of Brassens's songs in the album *Renaud chante Brassens* (1996). Brassens's simple melodies and spare accompaniment (from a bass or a second guitar, in addition to himself) make the song under discussion here, "La Guerre de 14-18," easily reproducible for students wishing to use it for their final project.

Students can listen to the song first without the lyrics and jot down key elements they pick up on. They can then listen to the song a second time while reading the lyrics. The third time, the whole class engages in a close reading activity and is invited to explain the lyrics using their own words, before an equivalent of complex sentences as well as brief explanations of cultural references made in the song are provided to them in a simplified form (as in the right-hand side column in the accompanying table).

"La Guerre de 14-18" (1962)

Depuis que l'homme écrit l'Histoire, Depuis qu'il bataille à cœur joie Entre mille et une guerres notoires, Si j'étais tenu de faire un choix,	= depuis Hérodote (Grèce ancienne) = avec grand plaisir = si je devais choisir une guerre parmi les milliers de guerres (qui ont ensanglanté l'humanité).

A l'encontre du vieil <u>Homère</u>,	qui considérait celle de Troie comme fondatrice
Je déclarerais tout de suite: Moi, mon colon, celle que j'préfère, C'est la guerre de quatorze-dix-huit!" Est-ce à dire que je méprise Les nobles guerres de jadis, <u>Que je me soucie comme d'une cerise</u> De celle de <u>soixante-dix</u> ?	colon = colonel. = La Grande Guerre (1914-1918) = je respecte les guerres qui ont précédé ("nobles": ironique) Expression idiomatique: se soucier de quelque chose comme de la "guigne." La cerise → reference to "Le temps des cerises", a song associated with the Franco-Prussian War of 1870.
Au contraire, je la révère Et lui donne un <u>satisfecit</u>, Mais, mon colon, celle que j'préfère, C'est la guerre de quatorze-dix-huit Je sais que les guerriers de <u>Sparte</u>	Second highest reward given to pupils in class (the first one being the "grand prix," which for Brassens goes to WWI, "La Grande guerre") Military city-state in Ancient Greece. The association of Sparta and Bonaparte is a reference to a well-known poem by Victor Hugo: "Ce siècle avait deux ans! Rome remplaçait Sparte, Déjà Napoléon perçait sous Bonarparte."
<u>Plantaient pas leurs épées dans l'eau,</u> Que les <u>grognards de Bonaparte</u> <u>Tiraient pas leur poudre aux moineaux...</u> Leurs faits d'armes sont légendaires, Au <u>garde-à-vous</u>, j'les félicite, Mais mon colon, celle que j'préfère, C'est la guerre de quatorze-dix-huit! Bien sûr, celle de <u>l'an quarante</u> Ne m'a pas tout à fait déçu, Elle fut longue et massacrante Et je ne crache pas dessus, Mais à mon sens, elle ne <u>vaut guère</u>, Guère plus qu'un premier <u>accessit</u>, Mais mon colon, celle que j'préfère, C'est la guerre de quatorze-dix-huit!	Donner des coups d'épées dans l'eau = inutile Old soldiers from Napoleon's Imperial Guard Idiomatic expression for a superfluous action At attention WWII (France was defeated in 1940). Also a reference to an idiomatic expression: "Se ficher de quelque chose comme de l'an quarante" = ne pas être concerné par = ne mérite pas plus que An honorable mention in a contest.

Mon but n'est pas de <u>chercher noise</u> Aux guérillas, non, fichtre! non, Guerres saintes, <u>guerres sournoises</u> <u>Qui n'osent pas dire leur nom</u>, Chacune a quelque chose pour plaire, <u>Chacune a son petit mérite</u>,	créer des problèmes guerre sans nom = Guerre d'Algérie (for many years officials refused to talk about a "war") chaque guerre a quelque chose de bon
Mais mon colon, celle que j'préfère, C'est la guerre de quatorze-dix-huit! Du fond de <u>son sac à malices</u>, <u>Mars</u> va sans doute, à l'occasion, En sortir une - un vrai délice! - Qui me fera grosse impression... En attendant, je persévère A dire que ma guerre favorite Celle, mon colon, que j'voudrais faire, C'est la guerre de quatorze-dix-huit !	bag of tricks. dieu de la guerre romain pulled a sweet one [a trick] out = il y aura peut-être une nouvelle grande guerre

After having analyzed the song, students form small groups to discuss the following questions in the target language (questions in French can be found in appendix 4.2 on Fulcrum):

1. What impression is created by the long enumeration of conflicts in the song?
2. Released in 1962, "La Guerre de 14-18" caused much ink to spill. How do you understand accusations that Brassens's song was disrespectful of those who had fought for their country, notably during the Great War ("14-18") and who were in their sixties at the time?
3. Watch a short sequence from 1978 of Brassens's response to these accusations on TV.[17] A moment of television history in itself, what does it show about Brassens's personality? Do you agree with Brassens's affirmation that his song was misunderstood and with his explanation that it suggests "Long live peace" ("Vive la paix," in French) and that it is not against those who fought for their country ("My intention never was to insult those who fought in the Great War, especially those who died")?

4. What does the title of another song by Georges Brassens inspire in you: "Mourir pour des idées, d'accord, mais de mort lente" ("To die for an idea, fine with me, but slowly")?
5. Can patriotism be blind?

Figure 4. Still image of film of Georges Brassens (center) with Jean-Pierre Elkabbach in 1978. Image courtesy of the Institut national de l'audiovisuel.

The last two questions may be used to organize a debate by dividing the class into two groups supporting opposing views, in preparation for a paper to be written individually.

Two groups are formed. One will prepare arguments supporting the position that it is worth dying for an idea, and the other will argue that it is not. Following the same principle, new groups are formed to discuss common expressions and the beliefs attached to them, such as "tombé(s) au champ d'honneur" or "mort(s) pour la nation," "fallen in the line of duty" or "to die for one's country," and argue for or against them. Students will then write an outline for a paper on a topic of their choice pertinent to the questions discussed, with a title capturing its "spirit" to trigger readers' interest. Once the outline has been discussed in small groups, students proceed to write their papers.

"LE DÉSERTEUR": NOT ANTI-MILITARIST, PRO-CIVILIAN!

The next case study provides an example of a song re-accenting an existing song, with contemporary inflections. In this activity, students work on one of the most famous anti-war songs, Boris Vian's "Le Déserteur," and on its cover thirty years later by an equally colorful character of the French cultural landscape, Renaud. Instructors may wish to provide some biographical information about the two artists and about the time periods when they performed the song.

An iconic figure of the Parisian intellectual and artistic scene of Saint-Germain-des-Prés, though remembered today mostly for his novel *L'Écume des jours* (*Froth on a Daydream*), Boris Vian was a man of many talents: writer, poet, musician, singer, translator, critic, actor, inventor, and engineer. Here instructors may choose to explain the role Saint-Germain played in France's intellectual scene at the time, with its famous *cafés littéraires* such as Les Deux Magots or Le Café de Flore, "headquarters" of the existentialist couple Simone de Beauvoir and Jean-Paul Sartre.

Written in February 1954, "Le Déserteur" was first performed by Marcel Mouloudji (who also performed "La Chanson de Craonne") toward the end of the First Indochina War (1946–1954) when French paratroopers were defeated in Dien Bien Phu. At this point students share what they know about that war, which countries made up Indochina, and why and whom the French army was fighting, which can establish a link to a war better known to American students: the Second Indochina War, or Vietnam War. As students may not know much about the nature of the First Indochina War, instructors may use this as an opportunity to point to its particular nature and to present the colonial past of France.

Punishable by death at the time, deserting was regarded by many as a lack of respect for men who had fought in previous wars or who were currently fighting for their country and was thus (and probably still is) a very sensitive subject to sing about.

"Le Déserteur" was almost immediately censored and quickly forgotten until it found a second life across the Atlantic during the Vietnam War. The American folk group Peter, Paul and Mary and singer-songwriter-activist Joan Baez indeed sang it (in French)[18] to protest (against) conscription and a war they deemed unjust and unnecessary (it should be noted that Baez also sang Le Forestier's song "Parachutiste" shortly after its release, also in French). It has since become one of the most famous anti-war songs across the world. Judging the original last lines to be against the message of pacifism conveyed by the song, Mouloudji suggested changing them, thereby ending the song on a less rebellious and more compliant note. If the first lines of the song show the humility of its narrator and expose his rationale for refusing war, his call for disobedience is indeed followed by resignation (he is ready to die for his plea of nonviolence). Interestingly, the song was slightly ahead of its time as conscripts were not required to fight in Indochina, whereas the subsequent decolonization war, the Algerian War (1954–1962), involved the extensive use of conscripts (about two-thirds of army troops at the height of the conflict in 1957).

Following this brief contextualization of the song, students listen to it first without reading its lyrics and then listen to it again to fill out missing words in an incomplete version of the lyrics of the song (see full activity in appendix 4.3 on Fulcrum). The review of this activity will allow instructors to walk their students through the song, probably the most accessible of the songs presented in this chapter.

"Le Déserteur" (Boris Vian, 1954)	"Le Déserteur" (Renaud, 1983)
Monsieur le Président	Monsieur le président
Je vous fais une lettre	Je vous fais une bafouille [= lettre]
Que vous lirez peut-être	Que vous lirez sûrement
Si vous avez le temps	Si vous avez des couilles [= avez du courage (vulgaire)]
Je viens de recevoir	Je viens de recevoir
Mes papiers militaires	Un coup de fil [de téléphone] de mes vieux [= parents]
Pour partir à la guerre	
Avant mercredi soir	

Monsieur le Président Je ne veux pas la faire Je ne suis pas sur terre Pour tuer des pauvres gens C'est pas pour vous fâcher Il faut que je vous dise Ma décision est prise Je m'en vais déserter [Variant: C'est pas pour vous fâcher, Il faut que je vous dise Les guerres sont des bêtises, Le monde en a assez.] Depuis que je suis né J'ai vu mourir mon père J'ai vu partir mes frères Et pleurer mes enfants Ma mère a tant souffert Elle est dedans sa tombe Et se moque des bombes Et se moque des vers Quand j'étais prisonnier On m'a volé ma femme On m'a volé mon âme Et tout mon cher passé Demain de bon matin Je fermerai ma porte Au nez des années mortes J'irai sur les chemins Je mendierai ma vie Sur les routes de France De Bretagne en Provence Et je dirai aux gens: Refusez d'obéir Refusez de la faire N'allez pas à la guerre Refusez de partir S'il faut donner son sang Allez donner le vôtre Vous êtes bon apôtre Monsieur le Président Si vous me poursuivez Prévenez vos gendarmes Que je n'aurai pas d'armes	Pour me prévenir que les gendarmes [= police] S'étaient pointés [= allés] chez eux J'ose pas imaginer Ce que leur a dit mon père Lui, les flics [= policiers], les curés Et pis les militaires Les a vraiment dans le nez [= il les déteste] Peut-être encore plus que moi Dès qu'il peut en bouffer [s'il peut les confronter] Le vieil anare [= anarchiste] y se gêne pas Le vieil anare y se gêne pas Alors y parait qu'on me cherche Que la France a besoin moi C'est con [= dommage], je suis en Ardèche [= associé dans la mémoire collective aux hippies des années 70] Y fait beau, tu crois pas Je suis là avec des potes [= des amis] Des écolos marrants [=militant écologistes] On a une vieille bicoque [= maison] On la retape tranquillement On fait pousser des chèvres On fabrique des bijoux On peut pas dire qu'on se crève [= qu'on travaille dur] Le travail, c'est pas pour nous On a des plantations Pas énormes, trois hectares D'une herbe qui rend moins con [= marijuana] Non, c'est pas du Ricard [= boisson alcoolisée un temps associée à la classe ouvrière] Non, c'est pas du Ricard Monsieur le président Je suis un déserteur De ton armée de glands [= d'imbéciles] De ton troupeau de branleurs [= de fainéants] Ils auront pas ma peau

Et qu'ils pourront tirer [Variant: Si vous me condamnez, Prévenez vos gendarmes, Que j'emporte des armes Et que je sais tirer.]	Toucheront pas à mes cheveux Je saluerai pas le drapeau Je marcherai pas comme les bœufs [= suivre] J'irai pas en Allemagne Faire le con [= perdre mon temps] pendant douze mois [la durée du service militaire obligatoire à l'époque] Dans une caserne infâme Avec des plus cons [= idiot] que moi J'aime pas recevoir des ordres J'aime pas me lever tôt J'aime pas étrangler le borgne [= se masturber (vulgaire)] Plus souvent qu'il ne faut Plus souvent qu'il ne faut Puis surtout ce qui me déplaît C'est que j'aime pas la guerre Et qui c'est qui la fait Ben c'est les militaires Ils sont nuls, ils sont moches [= pas beaux] Et pis ils sont teigneux [= agressifs] Maintenant je vais te dire pourquoi Je veux jamais être comme eux Quand les Russes, les Ricains Feront péter [= exploser] la planète Moi, j'aurais l'air malin [= stupide] Avec ma bicyclette Mon pantalon trop court Mon fusil, mon calot [= couvre-chef militaire] Ma ration de topinambour [= légume, associé à la Seconde Guerre mondiale dans la mémoire collective] Et ma ligne Maginot [= défense militaire inutile pendant la Seconde Guerre mondiale] Et ma ligne Maginot Alors me gonfle pas [= ne m'énerve pas] Ni moi, ni tous mes potes Je serai jamais soldat J'aime pas les bruits de bottes [des militaires] T'as plus qu'à pas t'en faire [s'en faire = s'inquiéter]

> Et construire tranquilos [tranquille, sans être inquiété]
> Tes centrales nucléaires
> Tes sous-marins craignos [= inutiles]
> Mais va pas t'imaginer
> Monsieur le président
> Que je suis manipulé
> Par les rouges ou les blancs
> Je ne suis qu'un militant
> Du parti des oiseaux
> Des baleines, des enfants
> De la terre et de l'eau
> De la terre et de l'eau
> Monsieur le Président
> Pour finir ma bafouille
> Je voulais te dire simplement
> A la ferme c'est le panard [= c'est le pied = super]
> Si tu veux, viens bouffer [= manger]
> On fumera un pétard [= un joint]
> Et on pourra causer [= discuter]
> On fumera un pétard
> Et on pourra causer

Once students have listened to the song at least three times, small groups are formed to answer the following questions (in French):

1. To whom is the letter addressed? To one or more persons?
2. Why write a letter to the president?
3. What information is given about the author at the beginning of the song? And why does he remain anonymous?
4. What parts are, to you, the most subversive?
5. What parts were most likely to cause the song to be censored?
6. Comment on the variants at the end of the song (found in brackets)?
7. Comment on the artist's plea against censorship: "My song is not anti-militarist, but I admit it is violently pro-

civilian. To die for your country, fine, as long as not everybody dies for it, otherwise there would be no country left. A country is not a land; people make a country. Soldiers are not the ones who need to be defended; civilians are the ones who need to be defended. And soldiers can't wait to be civilians again since when they are that means that the war is over."

After having discussed these questions, which may inspire composition topics to prolong the discussion, class participants watch a video of Renaud singing his 1983 rendition of "Le Déserteur."[19] A colorful, left-wing radical, Renaud is known for his very innovativeuse of French, making his lyrics particularly difficult to translate in other languages. The son of an intellectual anarchist ("Le vieil anare" in the song), Renaud was sixteen at the time of the May 1968 events in France (civil unrests that, at their height, almost brought France's economy to a halt) and quickly adopted the attitude of working-class youth of the 1970s (he wore a black leather jacket, a bandana, had long hair, etc.). Recurrent themes of his songs include social inequalities, his abhorrence of petit bourgeois, authority in general, and the military and the police in particular.

As are most of his songs, Renaud's "Le Déserteur" is laden with street-smart slang and is almost incomprehensible without extensive knowledge of French. Consequently, equivalents in French of key words in slang are provided between brackets throughout the lyrics in the table above. After having walked students through the song by rephrasing certain parts in a more accessible language, the instructor gives them a list of questions (in French; see appendix 4.3 on Fulcrum) to first discuss in small groups in the target language before engaging a conversation with the rest of the class. Some of the answers are provided in brackets.

1. How does Renaud address the president throughout the song?
2. Make a list of the adjectives used to describe the military. What do they reflect?
3. How do you imagine the narrator and his friends? To what trend does the following passage refer: "On a une vieille bicoque ... On fait pousser des chèvres"? [→ Back to nature]
4. To what war is Renaud alluding when he says, "J'veux jamais être comme eux, quand les Russes, les Ricains feront péter la planète," and what do you know about it (and how is the Vietnam War linked to it)? [→ The Cold War]
5. To what nascent movement is Renaud referring when he says, "Je n'suis qu'un militant du parti des oiseaux, des baleines, des enfants, de la terre et de l'eau"? [→ environment]
6. Compare the two versions of "Le Déserteur": What elements are present in both songs, and what elements are not? Compare the style, register, and tone of the two songs. Can the differences be regarded as indicators of the time periods in which the songs appeared?
7. Which song do you prefer and why?
8. Have these songs changed your position on the subject matter?
9. What threats are we facing today?
10. Are there battles worth fighting for today?

FINAL COLLABORATIVE PROJECT

As everything is said to end with a song in France, students are invited to present their own song following a presentation of its subject matter. Students may use an existing song (in French or not) to use with their own lyrics (in L2) or create their own. They may do so in several ways: by either adapting their own lyrics to the melody of one of the songs studied, respecting its style and tone as well as language register, or by creating a whole new song about an issue about which they wish to protest or to bring awareness.

"La musique adoucit les moeurs" ("Music softens morals") is another French saying based on ancient beliefs. Music is thought to soften the soul, to appease the mind as it entertains and educates. Students will be expected to do just that. They may thus choose to expand on the theme of war to fighting for a cause deemed right (war on racism, war for more diversity and inclusion in college, fighting for the environment, etc.). They may write a song from their own perspective or by assuming the position of groups or movements in France (such as the "Yellow Jackets"). As Erin Kearney reminds us, intercultural learning is indeed "very much about learning to perform, create and reframe meanings and, in a broader way, to possibly reconsider oneself and one's perspectives. . . . At least part of language learning is a process of finding one's voice in another language."[20]

The final project's preparation should follow the following steps: groups are constituted by affinity but with the help of the instructor to ensure that they are somewhat balanced in terms of proficiency in L2. Ideally, each group should include at least one musician. Once each group is formed, students brainstorm to determine the topic of their song. Students research the topic in question and submit the first draft of their presentation for a peer-editing activity. They then revise their draft and submit a new one to their instructor. Students repeat this step with the lyrics of their song. As far as the music of the created song, students may either create their own, reproduce an existing melody, or use an existing song and sing over its lyrics using the free software GarageBand (which allows one to keep the music of an existing song while adding one's own lyrics). The final product will be delivered using the VoiceThread program, with a voice-over (in L2) contextualizing the topic of the song as slides including visual and written explanations are being played, before moving to the recording of the song in question, unless the group of students/musicians/militants decides to perform it live. Projects should be assessed on both their content and their delivery. The whole class's written production (presentations and song's lyrics) should be combined and bound in one album to be titled collectively (for instance "French Rocks"). Each participant will receive a hard copy of the album to keep as souvenir of the class.

Finally, to the question of why singers such as Georges Brassens or Renaud, revered in France, enjoyed a limited audience internationally, Peter Hawkins argues that their very "Frenchness" makes their songs inaccessible to the "non-initiate," that their textual subtleties make them very dependent on refined awareness of the nuances of the French language and culture, by the same token creating a sense of complicity among French speakers, the most likely audience to be in a position to best understand and therefore fully enjoy their songs.[21] We hope, however, that the activities suggested in this example project will promote students' engagement thanks to the linguistic and literary richness of these cultural products to enlarge the circle of initiates. If songs by Brassens, Renaud, or Vian do illustrate the social prestige attached to literature in French society, and of the social status associated with a mastery of the French language,[22] they should also remind us of the power of music not only in creating communities but in gaining access to them as well.

NOTES

1. Another saying, probably also stemming from the very last line of Beaumarchais's play *Le Mariage de Figaro*, goes "Tout commence et tout finit par des chansons." A nod to Beaumarchais is also found at the end of René Goscinny's *Asterix and the Normans* (1966) when Asterix declares that the Vikings (who fled for their lives after hearing the unbearable singing of the village bard Cacofonix) shall now know that in Gaul everything ends with a song.

2. Peter Hawkins, *Chanson: The French Singer-Songwriter from Aristide Bruant to the Present Day* (Burlington, VT: Ashgate, 2000), 6.
3. "All Noble Prizes in Literature," https://www.nobelprize.org/prizes/lists/all-nobel-prizes-in-literature. In 2018, rapper Kendrick Lamar also won the Pulitzer Prize for music, becoming the first nonclassical or jazz artist to collect the award.
4. Former president François Hollande can be seen assisting one of the live performances during his visit to Le Chemin des Dames, where he delivered a historical (and arguably political) speech that instructors may choose to study with their class. See https://www.centenaire.org/fr/en-france/picardie/aisne/discours-du-president-de-la-republique-francois-hollande-cerny-en-laonnois. The three versions of the song are available at https://www.chemindesdames.fr/fr/ressources/en-images/videos/16-avril-2017-la-chanson-de-craonne-3-versions.
5. Ministère de l'Education nationale, "Chanson de Craonne," https://eduscol.education.fr/chansonsquifontlhistoire/Chanson-de-Craonne.
6. Pacifist and social activist singer Joan Baez sang "Parachutiste" in 1973.
7. Yves Laplume and Jean-Pierre Guéno, *Paroles de poilus : lettres et carnets du front 1914–1918* (Paris: Librio, 2001).
8. Richard Rubin, in the PBS program *The American Experience*: https://www.pbs.org/wgbh/americanexperience/features/great-war-le-chemin-des-dames/.
9. Bertrand Dicale is the author of a remarkable series on Radio France about war songs and of an equally valuable and beautifully illustrated book, *La Fleur au fusil* (Paris: Acropole, 2014).
10. The film is available online. A version is accessible on YouTube through a useful article from *The Guardian*. Richard Nelsson, "Battle of the Somme Film—Archive," *The Guardian*, June 30, 2016, https://www.theguardian.com/world/from-the-archive-blog/2016/jun/30/battle-of-the-somme-film-1916-archive.
11. Compiled in François Flameng's *Croquis de guerre* (Paris: L'Illustration, 1916), https://recherche.archives.somme.fr/ark:/58483/a011350474799OIHUFV.
12. To use the words of Guy Marival, author of *La Chanson de Craonne : enquête sur une chanson mythique* (Orléans, France: Regain de lecture, 2014).
13. "*Bourreaux qui lui lui volez sa vie / Bouchers qui m'arrachez le cœur / Moi, je dirai à notre enfant/Qui verra le jour au printemps / Qu'il peut être fier de son père / Putain de guerre !*"
14. Available on Dailymotion, https://www.dailymotion.com/video/x288gtt.
15. Chemin des Dames, https://www.chemindesDames.fr/fr.
16. Mission Centenaire 14-18, https://centenaire.org/fr.

17. In this short clip available on the Institut national de l'audiovisuel's website, Georges Brassens can be seen discussing the misunderstanding concerning the interpretation of his song on the war of 1914–1918 with TV host Jean-Pierre Elkabbach in a most candid manner during an evening dedicated to peace. "Georges Brassens parle de sa chanson sur la guerre de 14-18," December 18, 1978, https://www.ina.fr/video/I04076281.
18. "Joan Baez -le déserteur - Paris 80," YouTube video, https://www.youtube.com/watch?v=WOl9XfmNDDo.
19. Renaud 'Le Déserteur,' YouTube video, https://www.youtube.com/watch?v=vvolGwaMOUs.
20. Erin Kearney, *Intercultural Learning in Modern Language Education: Expanding Meaning-Making Potentials* (Bristol, UK: Multilingual Matters, 2016), 146–147.
21. Hawkins, *Chanson*, 61.
22. Hawkins, 59. In *La distinction* (1979), Pierre Bourdieu also discusses musical preferences as social markers.

REFERENCES

Dicale, Bertrand. *La Fleur au fusil*. Paris: Acropole, 2014.

Hawkins, Peter. Chanson: The French Singer-Songwriter from Aristide Bruant to the Present Day. Burlington, VT: Ashgate, 2000.

Haworth, Rachel. "French *chanson*." *French Studies: A Quarterly Review* 72, no. 1 (2018): 87–96.

Kearney, Erin. Intercultural Learning in Modern Language Education: Expanding Meaning-Making Potentials. Bristol, UK: Multilingual Matters 2016.

Laplume, Yves, and Jean-Pierre Guéno. *Paroles de poilus : lettres et carnets du front 1914–1918*. Paris: Librio, 2001.

Looseley, David L. Popular Music in Contemporary France: Authenticity, Politics, Debate. Oxford: Berg, 2003.

Marival, Guy. La Chanson de Craonne : enquête sur une chanson mythique. Orléans, France: Regain de lecture, 2014.

Nelsson, Richard. "Battle of the Somme Film—Archive." *The Guardian*, June 30, 2016, https://www.theguardian.com/world/from-the-archive-blog/2016/jun/30/battle-of-the-somme-film-1916-archive.

Rearick, Charles. "Madelon and the Men—in War and Memory." *French Historical Studies* 17, no. 4 (1992): 1001–1034.

CHAPTER FIVE

TEACHING FRANCOPHONE AND FRENCH CULTURES THROUGH PROJECT-BASED LEARNING

Eliza Jane Smith, University of San Diego

INTRODUCTION

In her article, "The Cultural Component of Language Learning," Claire Kramsch defines culture in both a historical and an ethnographic sense, positioning it from the perspective of the humanities that concerns "the way a social group represents itself and others through its material productions, be they works of art, literature, social institutions, or artifacts of everyday life" as well as from the perspective of the social sciences that encompasses "the attitudes and beliefs, ways of thinking, behaving and remembering shared by members of that community."[1] In addition to material products and values, culture can also refer to the collective memories of specific communities.[2] With these definitions in mind, in addition to the complex and hegemonic dynamic between "high" versus "low" and dominant versus dominated cultures, the incorporation of culture into language courses in a globalized context becomes increasingly challenging to foreign language (FL) instructors at the university level who are constrained by national standards for curriculum content and language proficiency, institutionalized trends on pedagogical methodologies, and the most valuable commodity of all—time.

At present, the landscape of language learning at the college level in the United States includes an accelerated curriculum that generally spans ten to sixteen weeks (depending on the structure of the institution's academic calendar). In the quest for communicative competence and eventually symbolic competence,[3] language instructors face the dilemma of covering the adequate number of chapters in a short amount of time, often utilizing textbooks that resemble "tourist brochures" that inadequately capture semiotic variation and/or promote skills for navigating symbolic systems of meaning.[4] The time constraints placed on instructors and language learners means that certain aspects of communicative competence, mainly intercultural competence and pragmatics, must be sacrificed to a large extent.[5] As Kramsch writes, instructors deprioritize and generally treat culture as a "fifth skill" due to the academic division between lower-level language courses and upper-division content courses, a hierarchy that still pervades in spite of formal appeals to dismantle it by the 2007 Modern Language Association (MLA) report.[6]

Nowadays, with globalization informing FL teaching practices, the degree to which one is linguistically competent relies on their intercultural competence as well. Knowing what, when, and how to say things within the target culture makes the difference between a novice and an advanced speaker and is the main idea behind the study of pragmatics, that is, "the place where language and culture meet."[7] Additionally, as Kramsch has recently argued, the communicative approach of the 1970s and 1980s, in addition to institutionalized pedagogical norms such as *The Standards for Foreign Language Learning* (2006) and the MLA report, do not necessarily create a space for the analysis of collective memory and history, politics, religion, and society across cultures nor does it enhance students' awareness of diversity and their role as active participants in an interconnected world.[8] And although the 5 C's of the *Standards* explicitly includes "cultures," Heidi Byrnes reminds us that there is a notable silence on the precise curricular implementations that would fulfill this standard.[9]

Furthermore, fast-paced language instruction means that students do not receive the luxury of working with grammatical and lexical structures for weeks at a time. Rather, instructors cover a new grammar point every day or every other day, leaving students little time to process and digest each structure, which results in a kind of sink-or-swim learning environment. Consequently, the adoption of a predominately communicative approach favors auditory learners while leaving visual or kinesthetic learners by the wayside, and it does not accommodate the increasingly globalized world in which learners live.[10] Byrnes also notes that pedagogical conventions like the *Standards* prioritize listening and speaking over reading and writing, which often leaves these proficiencies underdeveloped in language learners.[11] The widening disparities between the grammar-heavy focus of language courses and the writing- and reading-intensive upper-division courses result in a disconnect between the development of skills as well as in the breadth and depth of intercultural competence acquired. In fact, Erin Kearney reminds us that language learning in the United States constitutes a "linear process," one that begins with structural linguistic forms (grammar and lexicon) and makes its way "from the concrete, immediate and referential to the abstract and symbolic."[12] In reality, this idealistic approach in which language acquisition begets intercultural competence places students at a disadvantage since they often do not possess intercultural skills, which includes "the ability to interpret and make meaning and to exercise agency in using language,"[13] by the time they matriculate into advanced cultural and literary courses. The gap in skills, Kate Paesani, Heather Willis Allen, and Beatrice Dupuy remark, can ultimately harm students' motivation and ability to learn.[14]

Although university instructors have little control over the speedy reality of beginner language courses, they do have the ability to reflect on the ways in which the primarily neglected aspects of communicative competence in first-year language classrooms can be prioritized in a way that accommodates various learning styles and simultaneously encourages grammar acquisition and the development of the four skills (listening, reading, writing, and speaking) in order to better prepare learners for upper-division courses. While institutionalized pedagogical conventions serve an important role in structuring language curriculum and learning objectives, it would also behoove FL instructors to expose learners to cultural products, perspectives, and memories in order to practice what Kramsch calls a "postmodernist relational pedagogy [that] practices translations of all kinds across codes, modes, modalities, genres, and points of view and encourages the learner to adopt an alien speakers' perspective."[15] As Adriana Raquel Diaz and Maria Dasli note, if the linguistic point-of-reference changed from that of native speaker to that of "intercultural speaker" instead, students could acquire a cultural, discursive, and linguistic fluidity earlier on in their academic careers.

With these objectives in mind, this chapter seeks to analyze the incorporation of multimodal project-based learning using film and literature in beginner language courses as a means of effectively exposing students to various aspects of francophone and French culture while still adhering to a rigid curriculum standard with regard to grammar and the four skills. Unlike communicative language teaching (CLT), which "focuses on language usage," that is, a perfect understanding and output of the foreign language structures, adopting a full or partial multiliteracies pedagogy[16] that "focuses on language use," or the ability to use and view the foreign language structures as makers of meaning, transforms the role of the student from mere producer to interactive interpreter.[17]

In addition to strengthening students' overall communicative competence, the use of project-based learning (PBL) in the language classroom ultimately seeks to bridge the intercultural content gap between language courses and advanced courses through a targeted interaction with literary texts and films beginning in the first semester. Incorporating authentic texts and films in the context of PBL differs from a traditional CLT approach, in which materials simply provide a launching point for grammar and vocabulary practice: "Instead, [authentic materials] function as a vehicle for communicative language use and cultural inquiry as students analyze, interpret, and transform discourse and relate the world of the FL culture to their experience and thinking."[18] Finally, as Kramsch states, the objective of FL instructors "is not just to expose students to a diversity of accents and registers but [to] have them critically engage with the social and political differences that they index."[19] Through implementation of PBL as means of deepening student understanding of culture and pragmatics, students can begin to dissect and reflect on outside perspectives in addition to their own, a pivotal step in developing symbolic competence.

PROJECT-BASED LEARNING DEFINITION AND BENEFITS

In his overview of PBL,[20] John Thomas defines project-based learning according to five characteristics:

1. *PBL projects are central, not peripheral, to the curriculum.*
2. *PBL projects are focused on questions or problems that "drive" students to encounter (and struggle with) the central concepts and principles of a discipline.*
3. *Projects involve students in a constructive investigation.*
4. *Projects are student- driven to some significant degree.*
5. *Projects are realistic, not school-like.*[21]

Upon reading these criteria, it becomes apparent that Thomas's rubric for what counts as PBL disproportionately favors STEM disciplines. A more thorough investigation of the research at hand reveals that the majority of studies center on projects related to environmental studies, mathematics, and science.[22]

The multimodal projects that I created for first-year French courses at the University of Colorado (CU) Boulder were designed to better incorporate culture into the curriculum while also improving students' reading, writing, listening, and speaking skills. According to Thomas's standards, these projects do not qualify as PBL. First, students were not driven by a specific problem or inquiry; their objective was to gain an in-depth exposure to aspects of francophone and French culture that might otherwise be reduced to a one-page reading in the textbook (and perhaps a twenty-minute conversation). In addition to this exposure, the design of the projects themselves facilitated the development of students' capacity to analyze simple literary texts and film and to express their interpretations through speaking, writing, and visuals. Additionally, when considering culture as collective memory, the use of narrative-based projects incites reflection on "stories about the past real or imagined."[23] The idea of reducing interpretation to a single inquiry is inherently at odds with the nature of humanities courses, which seek to promote multiple analyses of our representations of the world. Second, students at CU Boulder did not engage in a "constructive investigation," which Thomas defines as "a goal-directed process that involves inquiry, knowledge building, and resolution."[24] Similarly to the question-focus criterion, the notion of an investigation aligns strongly with the setup of STEM courses but is incompatible with that of humanities courses, which grant a looser definition to the term "investigation."

Finally, the criterion asserting that projects must be "realistic" relates to the second criterion on a problem-driven inquiry. By implementing projects with a literary and cinematic focus in order to prepare students for upper-division French courses and to provide a discursive catalyst that develops students' intercultural competence, the term "realistic" does not apply. When it comes to creative output, the "real-life challenges" that Thomas mentions cannot be identified in black-and-white terms; when it comes to the visual arts, literary texts, and critical thought, in addition to cultural interaction, points of view, and memory, these "real-life challenges" remain in constant flux as a result of dominant versus dominated representations and cultural, ethnic, gender, racial, and sexual subjectivities. Again, notions of applicable and concrete projects more closely align with the STEM disciplines.

From this perspective, Thomas's criteria possess a bias toward certain subject matters and discriminate against others. For the purposes of this chapter, I will offer up a modified version of Thomas's PBL criteria in order to align them more closely with learning objectives in humanities courses so that they may be applied to a beginner language course.

1. *PBL projects are included in the curriculum.*
   The extent to which projects can be "central" to a university-level curriculum is relative to the department. CU Boulder students cover Units 1–6 in French 1010 and Units 7–13 in French 1020 with the textbook *Promenades*.[25] The idea of a curriculum that revolves mainly around projects for beginner French courses is unrealistic given the national standards for second-language proficiency at the college level. In an ideal setting, students would have more time to work on fewer structures in order to better absorb and retain the material. Unfortunately, students only have several weeks, and the tenet that PBL projects must be central to the curriculum in order to count might discourage PBL from entering less advanced language courses or humanities courses in gen-

eral. Therefore, I have modified this tenet to simply state that PBL projects be included.

2. *PBL projects are focused on the execution of tasks that "drive" students to encounter (and struggle with) the concepts and principles of a discipline.*

   In language courses, there are several benefits to adopting a task-based approach. David Nunan defines a task as "any classroom work, which involves learners in comprehending, manipulating, producing, or interacting in the target language while their attention is principally focused on meaning rather than form."[26] In terms of PBL, designing projects composed of several tasks not only ensures adequate intake of the input on the part of students but also ensures adequate output. Although I agree that PBL projects should revolve around "execution of tasks that 'drive' students," the definition of "the central concepts and principles of a discipline" may be more relative to each instructor's learning objectives in a beginner language course. Therefore, I have modified the tenet by eliminating the term "central."

3. *Projects involve students in a constructive analysis and critical thought.*

   By introducing PBL projects in first-year language courses one wonders to what extent students can engage in "constructive analysis and critical investigation" given the introductory nature of the material coupled with students' abilities. However, even projects that challenge students to write simple, descriptive narratives and/or to give descriptive presentations in the target language forcibly engage their ability to constructively analyze and think critically about the task at hand. The solution is not to exclude PBL from beginner language courses but to exchange the term "investigation" for "thought."

4. *Projects are student driven in terms of the process and the final interpretation.*

   When designing projects, it may not always be best practice to leave problems fully in the hands of the students but to offer some limitations around the content of the students' exploration. In Thomas's research regarding scientific PBL projects, he determined that when students were left to decide which questions they would pursue, "[they] tended to pursue questions without examining the merits of the question, they tended to pursue questions that were based on personal preference rather than questions that were warranted by the scientific content of the project, they had difficulty understanding the concept of controlled environments, [and] they created research designs that were inadequate given their research questions."[27] In this sense, placing restrictions around the students' task objectives may not hinder but rather enhance the benefits of PBL. The inclusion of PBL projects that are student driven may happen to the extent that students choose their own analysis and interpretation around a particular topic, as well as their own process for arriving at certain conclusions.

5. *Projects are designed to encourage analysis and open interpretation of various representations.*

   Rather than focusing on the "realistic" nature of PBL projects, we should shift the focus back to analysis and the development of critical thinking skills. In order for students to adequately develop the four skills in preparation for upper-division courses and learn to shift their subjective perceptions as foreign language learners in a globalized society, we need to swap out the "realistic" requirement for one that encourages creativity, original thought, community, and continual questioning of the status quo.

With these new tenets in mind, PBL projects now have their place in humanities and especially language courses. This raises the question: Why use PBL in these courses? In his book, *Project-Based Learning Using Information Technology*, David Moursund outlines the ways in which PBL favors different pedagogical approaches such as a constructivist approach, inquiry-based learning, problem-based learning, and cooperative learning.[28] He states that "one of the defining characteristics of PBL is a focus on students challenging problems and tasks and improving their higher-order thinking skills."[29] Furthermore, a study conducted by Phyllis Blumenfeld and colleagues emphasized the relationship between PBL and increased student motivation and ability to solve problems in addition to a deeper understanding of the concepts at hand.[30] In terms of learning styles, Moursund addresses the fact that PBL may cater to various learner abilities.[31] Since CLT disproportionately favors auditory learners, incorporation of PBL would better support the kinesthetic and visual learners whose educational needs are often neglected. In her 2003 study on the effects of PBL for low-achieving learners in a junior high in Israel, Yaron Doppelt found that designing scientific-technological projects that are "practical and relate to pupils' everyday life" increased these learners' motivation and bettered their self-image.[32] PBL also favors a student-centered classroom, a key component of the communicative approach adopted in language courses. Finally, instructors can design projects that are multimodal in nature, which target specific competencies and skills in relation to a language program. The multilayered aspect of PBL might assist university instructors who feel confined by time and the rigid textbook curriculum but who would like to give students a more comprehensive formation of skills that promote communicative and symbolic proficiencies and that ultimately prepare them for advanced courses.

PROJECT DESIGN

In terms of the design of the projects, there are several common elements that each project shares. First, for both first- and second-semester French, students complete two projects: one focused on literature and another focused on film. By the end of their first academic year, students complete four projects in total. This is intended to begin textual and visual analyses in the first year in order to assist students as they continue in their French and francophone studies.[33] Second, the projects contain aspects that work the three modes of communication: interpersonal, interpretive, and presentational.[34] Third, the projects simultaneously develop students' listening, reading, writing, and speaking skills. For each project, students receive aural, written, and visual input and must produce oral and written output. There is also a strong group component[35]; however, unlike CLT, in which group collaboration is rooted in the execution of grammatical structures via an "exchange of information about oneself," the group collaborations using PBL function similarly to those within a multiliteracies framework that "takes place through the interaction with texts and with others within a classroom community."[36] As Paesani, Allen, and Dupuy note, this kind of group work fosters meaning-making "as [group members] give and receive assistance in textual creation and interpretation."[37] Finally, Projects 1–3 revolve around the creation of a specific genre (children's story, travel narrative, and fable), whereas Project 4 centers on a specific literary device (personification). Genre in particular can be extremely useful in rendering students aware of the "logics" and the schematic structures that ultimately affect and create meaning.[38] At the heart of any genre, as Byrnes highlights, lies a narrative; narratives, whether literary or otherwise, are inherently tied to concepts of perspective, collective and individual identities, and memory, which also function as key components in the development of intercultural and symbolic competence.[39]

Although the choice in texts and films may prioritize big C culture and seem essentialist at first glance, it is important to remember that the cultural knowledge of first-year language students does not generally extend beyond the cliché. And while cultural hegemony should be challenged by instructors, it also extremely beneficial to work with, instead of against, students' content schemata as the launching point into more sophisticated analyses and conversations that challenge students' cultural biases. These projects seek to situate themselves within a familiar intercultural context in order to encourage a higher level of thought among students when interacting with aspects of the francophone and French world. The following explanations detail the overall design of each project.

PROJECT 1: *LE PETIT PRINCE* (CHILDREN'S STORY)

The first project of the first semester centers on the text *Le Petit Prince* by Antoine de Saint-Exupéry. This project takes place during Weeks 5 and 6 and focuses on the creation of a short children's story. In Week 5, over the course of one class period,[40] students begin by working on questions on the generic features of children's books and historical information about *Le Petit Prince* in small groups of two to three people.[41] Due to the limited nature of the students' French, the questions are in English, and students may respond in English when writing. However, the class discussion is in French and facilitated by the use of cognates, gesture, and key words written on the board (*Quelles sont les caractéristiques d'un livre pour enfants ? Avez-vous un livre pour enfants préféré ? Qui est l'auteur du Petit Prince ? En quelle année est-ce que le livre a été écrit ?*). Following this brief overview of the children's story genre, students watch a two-minute video clip in French from the 2015 film of the same title (dir. Mark Osborne). The clip does not include subtitles, and students must answer questions inductively based on what they see (the clip may be shown a few times). Again, students work together in their respective groups to answer the questions correctly, and although the questions are in English, the discussion on the video clip is also in French.

The final part of this analysis includes an excerpt in English from chapter 21 of *Le Petit Prince* that students must read together in order to answer question 7: "With your partner, read the excerpt from *The Little Prince*. Who are the characters? What kind of language and vocabulary is used? What is the moral at the end?" Discussion of question 7 occurs in French, in addition to a class discussion on the meaning of the final quote at the end of the excerpt: "On ne voit bien qu'avec le cœur. L'essentiel est invisible pour les yeux." Students attempt a collective translation, and once the meaning is pieced together, the students discuss the significance of the quote for them. These group questions and shared discussions rely on students' content schemata, a key component of textual or visual interpretation since learners must analyze the views of the characters, director, or writer in relation to their own perspectives and experiences.

At the end of the class period, students receive a copy of the project outline.[42] One week after the in-class analysis, at the beginning of Week 6, students bring a copy of a rough draft of an original 150- to 200-word children's story. Given their limited grammar and vocabulary, the story must utilize the structures and words that they know. The limitation on content has the additional benefit of discouraging the use of online translators (significantly lower grades are given to students who use structures not yet learned in class). During the first fifteen minutes of class, students exchange copies of their rough draft with a partner. They must read their partner's story and give positive and useful feedback (*Donnez des commentaires positifs et utiles*). They must not correct grammar.

However, the instructor may circulate around the room and answer any grammatical questions students may have. The rough draft is worth 25 percent of the final project grade.

At the end of Week 6, after students complete the peer review of their rough drafts, they must present their children's story in French to the class. Presentations are three minutes in length and must include a PowerPoint with visuals and little to no text.[43] Presentations make up one to two class periods, and while each student speaks, their peers must fill out presentation notes for a participation grade.[44] On the last day of presentations, students submit a final version of their story and must include a minimum of three images.

PROJECT 2: *LE FABULEUX DESTIN D'AMÉLIE POULAIN* (TRAVEL NARRATIVE)

The second project of the first semester centers on the popular French film *Le Fabuleux Destin d'Amélie Poulain* directed by Jean-Pierre Jeunet (*Amélie*, 2001). This project takes place in Weeks 14 and 15.[45] At the beginning of Week 14, students watch the film with English subtitles over the course of two and a half class periods. They receive a copy of the questions to review beforehand but are not encouraged to answer the questions during the course of the film.[46] Before watching the film, it is also recommended that the instructor give students a brief introduction to prepare the students (*C'est un film de 2001. Ce film est très populaire aux États-Unis. C'est un film surréaliste*). The instructor asks students to take notes on what they notice, but as the questions will be a collaborative effort, the main emphasis is on students enjoying and appreciating the film. The students are given time in class on the third day to start working on the questions together in small groups. The small group is intended to lessen the pressure to take all-encompassing notes on the film. By telling students that they will each notice different aspects of the film, they can relax more into the experience of analyzing the film itself. Following the final showing on the third day, students are given time to start their questions. The questions are comprehension questions to give students a better understanding of the story arc and to provide the first step into their eventual creation of a travel narrative.

The second component of the project involves the creation of a traveling gnome narrative, similar to the one in the film. In groups of two to three people, students are given a paper gnome attached to a Popsicle stick that resembles the one in the film. Students have one week to design their own travel narrative and must provide a minimum of six photos that document their gnome's journey. Each group presents their photos to the class in a PowerPoint slideshow at the end of Week 15. Group presentations take place over the course of one to two class periods, and each group member must speak for one to two minutes, relying very little on notes. While each group speaks, their peers must fill out presentation notes for a participation grade. Finally, students draft a collective travel narrative in which each group member contributes 100 words of the narrative that is handed in on one document. The entire narrative must be 200 to 300 words minimum and must make up a coherent narrative from start to finish.

PROJECT 3: "L'ARBRE NOURRICIER" (FABLE)

The first project of the second semester centers on the Senegalese fable "L'Arbre nourricier," which appears in the French textbook *Chez Nous*.[47] This project takes place during Weeks 4 and 5 and focuses on the creation of a fable. In Week 4, before reading the fable, students read the short preface (*Avant de lire*) and then engage in a short in-class discussion on the characteristics of the fable genre. Students read the fable at home and then take turns reading it aloud in class the next class period. The instructor acts as a guide, pausing students after each paragraph to ask them to summarize the plotline. Following this collective reading, students work together to answer analytical and comprehension questions on the fable, which they submit for a homework grade.[48] At the end of the class, the instructor distributes the project outline.[49] The first part of the project consists of a rough draft of a fable worth 25 percent of the final grade. The rough draft is due at the beginning of Week 5 and must include four parts: an original title, an introduction (to the setting, the characters, and the problem), the different scenes, and an ending (the resolution of the problem and the moral). Similar to the children's book project in French 1010, students must bring a copy of their rough draft to class for peer review. During this time, students exchange their draft with a partner, read the draft, and provide useful and positive comments; again, they do not correct grammar. The instructor circulates around the room to verify that everyone has a copy of their draft and to answer any grammar-related questions that the students have. Peer review can take a minimum of fifteen to twenty minutes of class time. At the end of Week 5, students give a three- to five-minute presentation of their fable to the class. They must include a PowerPoint slideshow with visuals (no text) and can have notecards but are prohibited from reading. Depending on the class size, presentations may last one or two class periods, and students must fill out presentation notes while their peers speak. On the last day of presentations, students submit the final version of their fable, which must be 200 to 300 words in length and must include at least four images.

PROJECT 4: *FERRAGUS* AND *LA HAINE* (PERSONIFICATION)

The second project of the second semester centers on the film *La Haine*, directed by Mathieu Kassovitz (1995), as well as on the novel *Ferragus*, by Honoré de Balzac (1833). This project takes place during Weeks 10, 11, and 12 and shifts away from genre to focus on the development of the literary device personification. At the end of Week 10, students begin with four preliminary questions on the famous French author Honoré de Balzac as well as on personification.[50] Working together in groups of two to three people, students may use the internet to respond to these questions, especially those that are historical in nature, such as biographical information about Balzac; students may also prefer to use online dictionaries to look up unfamiliar words. Once they have completed the preliminary questions, the instructor presents these questions to the class and a collective discussion takes place. Once the preliminary questions have been reviewed, a joint close reading takes place of an excerpt from chapter 1 of *Ferragus*, in which Balzac describes the streets of Paris using personification.[51] The instructor may call on different students to read aloud and then have everyone summarize together after each short reading. Since the passage is slightly above the comprehension level for second-semester students, the instructor must serve as a guide in order for students to adequately comprehend. Following the reading, students must work in their respective groups to answer the questions on the literary excerpt.

At the beginning of Week 11, the instructor may take the first ten to fifteen minutes to discuss the ways in which Balzac personifies Paris in the nineteenth century. As a natural segue into the film, the instructor can ask students to discuss with a partner words and/or images that they associate with Paris today. After about five minutes of discussion, the instructor can write all of the students' responses on the board (or even create a word cloud) for students to visualize their collective representation of the city. Generally speaking, student responses verge on the idealistic (*Paris est romantique*) while occasionally realistic (*Paris est sale; il y a beaucoup de bruit*), but students possess little to no knowledge of Parisian suburbs. Based on the words and expressions on the board, the instructor can launch a cultural discussion on the status of Parisian suburbs and of minorities in France. This mini-discussion provides a natural introduction to the film *La Haine* and the ways in which its depiction of Parisian suburbs still resonates nearly twenty-five years later. Similar to the *Amélie* project in French 1010, students receive the film questions in advance and may look through them beforehand but are encouraged to enjoy the film and take notes on what they notice since the questions will be a collaborative effort.[52] Given that the theme of this project is personification, the instructor may gently remind students to think about potential personifications that may exist in Kassovitz's respective portrayals of the suburbs and of Paris. The showing of the film takes about two and a half class periods. Following the film, the instructor may want to have a short ten-minute discussion with students about the ending as well as about their overall thoughts on the film.

Following this discussion, students receive a copy of the project outline.[53] The first part consists of the questions, to be discussed in small groups, on *Ferragus* and on *La Haine*, which are worth 25 percent of the final grade and are due two or three days following the showing of the film. The second part requires students to choose a city, district, road, or another place that they know well and to create a personification of this place. The personification, worth 45 percent of the final grade, must include an original title, a 200- to 250-word description, and three images. Students complete peer reviews of each other's rough drafts that are due the same day as the questions at the end of Week 11. The final version of the personification is due one week later on the last day of student presentations. The third and final part of the project consists of a visual interpretation of the personification, worth 30 percent of the final grade, that each student must present to the class one week following the peer review. Students are encouraged to utilize a variety of media (personal photos, personal illustrations, or video) in their interpretation. No text is allowed on the visual representation, and students must explain their personification for three to five minutes. During presentations, each student must fill out presentation notes for a participation grade.

STUDENT FEEDBACK

In fall 2018, anonymous student feedback surveys were distributed to forty-seven French 1010 students and thirty-one French 1020 students at CU Boulder. The surveys were designed to assess students' judgment of their intercultural competence, speaking skills, and writing skills, in addition to their knowledge of literary genre and literary techniques.[54] The results of the surveys are available in appendices 5.10 and 5.11 in the open access version of this volume on Fulcrum.

French 1010 (first semester)

Before taking this class, 34 percent of students felt that they had "little-to-no knowledge of the target culture," 49 percent felt that they had "general knowledge of the target culture," only 4 percent felt that they possessed "advanced knowledge of the target culture," 0 percent responded "superior knowledge of the target culture," and 13 percent of students did not respond. Eighty-five percent of students agreed that the instructor adequately taught francophone and French culture, and 96 percent of students were interested in learning more about francophone and French culture. Before working on *Le Petit Prince*, only 34 percent of students were familiar with the story, and only 45 percent of students felt that the story gave them greater insight into French culture and values. However, 77 percent of students felt that by writing their own children's story, their knowledge of the children's story genre improved, and 100 percent felt that their written French skills improved. In terms of speaking, 83 percent of students felt that their spoken French improved.

In terms of their familiarity with *Le Fabuleux Destin d'Amélie Poulain*, only 32 percent of students had previous knowledge of the film, and 85 percent felt that the viewing of and the questions on the film gave them greater insight into French culture and values. Seventy-seven percent of students believed that by writing their own travel narrative, their knowledge of the travel narrative genre improved, and 98 percent felt that their written French skills improved. Additionally, by presenting their travel narrative to the class, 91 percent of students felt that their spoken French skills improved. Finally, after taking the class, 4 percent of students felt that they had "little-to-no knowledge of the target culture," 68 percent felt that they had "general knowledge of the target culture," only 26 percent felt that they possessed "advanced knowledge of the target culture," and 2 percent responded "superior knowledge of the target culture."

Based on these results, the majority of students felt that their understanding of French culture had improved by the end of the course.[55] Regarding the importance of learning more about francophone and French culture, students often cited studying abroad, living abroad, and becoming more globally aware as reasons. In terms of the aspects of French culture and values that students gleaned from *Le Petit Prince* and *Le Fabuleux Destin d'Amélie Poulain*, students often cited French daily life, humor, storytelling, cinematography, and increased vocabulary and comprehension. Even though these works align more closely with students' cliched notions of French culture, students focused more on cultural perspectives following the completion of the projects, which suggests a paradigm shift that centers on more nuanced intercultural similarities and differences rather than simplistic stereotypical representations.

French 1020 (second semester)

Before taking this class, 16 percent of students felt that they had "little-to-no knowledge of the target culture," 61 percent felt that they had "general knowledge of the target culture," only 13 percent felt that they possessed "advanced knowledge of the target culture," 0 percent responded "superior knowledge of the target culture," and 10 percent of students did not respond. Seventy-four percent of students agreed that the instructor adequately taught francophone and French culture, and 94 percent of students were interested in learning more about francophone and French culture. Before working on "L'Arbre nourricier," 0 percent of students were familiar with the story, and only 35 percent of students felt that the story gave them greater insight into Senegalese culture and values. Similarly, 0 percent of students were familiar with Balzac's *Ferragus* before beginning the semester's second project, and only 10 percent of students were familiar with the film *La Haine*. Fifty-two percent of students felt that the reading and discussion of *Ferragus* gave them greater insight into French culture and values, while 87 percent of students felt that the viewing and discussion of *La Haine* gave them greater insight into French culture and values.

Regarding their writing, 74 percent of students felt that by writing their own personification of place, their understanding of the novelistic genre and the literary technique of personification improved. Furthermore, 87 percent of students felt that by writing their own personification, their written French skills improved. Regarding speaking, 81 percent of students felt that their speaking skills improved from their presentations. Finally, after taking the class, 0 percent of students felt that they had "little-to-no knowledge of the target culture," 74 percent felt that they had "general knowledge of the target culture," 23 percent felt that they possessed "advanced knowledge of the target culture," 0 percent responded "superior knowledge of the target culture," and 3 percent did not respond.

Based on these results, the majority of students felt that their understanding of francophone and French culture had improved by the end of the course. Regarding the importance of learning more about francophone and French culture, the 1020 students were more likely to explicitly acknowledge the relationship between language learning and culture.[56]

In terms of francophone values in the semester's first project, students were able to pinpoint the core principles of the Senegalese fable "L'Arbre nourricier," such as the negative consequences of greed, the importance of community, and the recognition of Senegal as a family-based culture that values sharing and generosity. With the second project, students expressed a deep appreciation of the historical aspect of Balzac's novel and the representation of Paris in the nineteenth century. Several students recognized Balzac's depiction as negative, while others felt that it granted a more realistic view of the city. Some students commented on the author's use of personification that helped them to understand the various "personalities" of the neighborhoods and, ultimately, made students more aware of their own romanticized ideas about Paris. This recognition of their stereotypical notions about the city provided the perfect segue into our analysis of *La Haine*, which provoked a more comparative train of thought in students regarding socioeconomic status and race. Students explicitly pointed out the lack of idealization in the film and admitted that the Paris depicted resembled a city that they never knew existed in France (several commented that the film's depiction seemed to parallel similar problems occurring in the United States). The director's portrayal of racial tensions and violence in addition to the severe socioeconomic issues that continue to affect France's minority populations even today helped to dismantle students' preconceived ideas and also expand their understanding of French culture and identity.

We see that over the course of one academic year, PBL projects centered on literature and cinema helped to expose beginner language students to meaningful elements of the francophone and French world. Engagement in these four projects introduced the learners to various literary genres and the literary device of personification, in addition to culturally significant films and texts. By using students' content schemata as the point of reference, which often exists in the realm of the cliché, both 1010 and 1020 courses participated in the early stages of intercultural analysis that improved the students' reading, writing, listening, and speaking skills, in addition to their critical thinking and analytical abilities.

Due to the extended time allotted to each project (between two to three weeks), the students at CU Boulder were able to work more closely with key cultural ideas and themes in order to gain a more extensive knowledge of popular culture, cultural values, literature, humor, and race relations. In their comments, students express an understanding of the main cultural ideas, and, in some cases, they also admit to a previous ignorance of these ideas. Their comments reveal the early onset of a cultural awareness that challenges and/or expands their own perspectives and symbolic value structures.

In the future, a study on the effectiveness of PBL to support a wider range of learning styles, improve the four skills, and foster communicative, intercultural, and symbolic competence could be enhanced with the addition of direct, indirect, and integrative assessments administered at the end of each term. Moreover, the first projects in 1010 and 1020, which involved literary texts, did not rate as high in terms of student perceptions of the cultural knowledge acquired.[57] Based on this feedback and the perceived effectiveness by learners of the film-based projects, it would be interesting to see how the addition of films to these projects, such as the movies *Le Petit Prince* (2015) for 1010 and *Kirikou et la sorcière* (1998) for 1020, would alter student responses. While I do not advocate eliminating literary texts as a valid modification, mainly because I believe that the majority of students in first-year language courses may not yet view literature as culturally relevant and perhaps prefer more contemporary, visual-heavy materials, I do feel that designing projects that incorporate both film and text would yield more positive reactions and help students to better understand the works' cultural significance.

Even though PBL may occur over the course of several weeks, by designing the projects in a way that work with, rather than against, the program curriculum, instructors can maximize students' communicative progress on a trimester or semester system. Furthermore, a partial or full adoption of a multiliteracies framework in beginner language courses can help bridge the transition from language to content courses. And while institutionalized pedagogical approaches and standards have value and should not necessarily be discarded, it is imperative for instructors to consider the educational needs of their students and to better cater to the various learning styles present in the classroom through a variety of approaches.

CONCLUSION

This chapter explores the use of project-based learning within novice-level language courses as a means of going beyond textbook grammar and content instruction to verse learners in skills that better prepare them for an intercultural reality and that are rooted in processes rather than "testable" knowledge, such as cognitive flexibility, linguistic and literary analysis, and semiotic and pragmatic variation.[58] Finally, by integrating culture with more intentionality, students begin to develop their intercultural and symbolic competence.

Overall, the 1010 and 1020 students polled at CU Boulder felt that the projects increased their cultural knowledge of France and the French-speaking world in addition to improving their writing and speaking skills. Although the surveys did not ask about listening and reading skills, some students in 1020 noted that their vocabulary and "comprehension" skills improved. The inclusion of film and texts functioned as aural, written, and visual input so that these more passive skills could be developed as well. In order to render the input comprehensible, several modifications were made, such as the use of vocabulary indexes, comprehension questions, guidance from the instructor, collective readings, and subtitles. These alterations aided students in their understanding of the input, which was otherwise very advanced for their level.

By designing multimodal projects that focus on a literary genre or device, students gain exposure to aspects of francophone and

French culture while also improving their interpersonal, interpretive, and presentational modes of communication, in addition to reading, writing, listening, and speaking skills. Although assessing and measuring intercultural competence can be tricky, by giving students the opportunity to self-assess, the instructor can see whether or not students focused on the correct material. One modification to these projects could be to require students to complete a self-assessment after every project and to even compare their progress from one project to the next. Using PBL projects in the beginner language classroom does not need to take away from valuable class time. In fact, if designed effectively, projects can enhance the curriculum material while remaining culturally focused. Furthermore, if each project contains writing and speaking components, students will have an easier transition to second- and third-year classes. The PBL projects challenge students linguistically and may also be more appealing to students who learn kinesthetically or visually. Devoting more quality time to culture in beginner language courses may help to motivate students who dream of working or studying abroad and seek a deeper understanding of francophone and French society. If instructors actively position themselves from the perspective of their students and continuously assess their needs and personal objectives, FL departments might better succeed in retaining more students for a longer portion of their academic career.

Finally, in order to encourage more PBL in humanities courses, we need to have modified standards for what constitutes PBL in the context of our disciplines. I have presented my own modifications of Thomas's five criteria, but depending on the content of a course, the duration, the learning objectives, and the students, these criteria could be altered as well. Given the expanding nature of disciplines and the nontraditional approaches being adopted in classrooms across college campuses in the United States, we as instructors must be flexible in our approach and methodology in order to better serve FL learners and to foster communicative flexibility in our students as well. A cookie-cutter, one-size-fits-all mindset to language teaching will inevitably result in frustrated and unmotivated students and will not encourage them to expand their intercultural perspectives and to think in creative and original ways. Utilizing PBL projects in the classroom to fulfill our particular learning objectives will not only cater to a wider student body in terms of interests, learning styles, and skills developed but also ultimately transform them into confident (and competent) culturally minded global citizens.

NOTES

1. Claire Kramsch, "The Cultural Component of Language Learning," *Language, Culture and Curriculum* 8, no. 2 (1995) 84.
2. Anne Freadman, "Fragmented Memory in a Global Age: The Place of Storytelling in Modern Language Curricula," *Modern Language Journal* 98, no. 1 (2014): 373–385.
3. Sociologist Dell Hymes defines "communicative competence" as the communicative umbrella that makes up discourse competence, grammatical competence, sociolinguistic competence, and strategic competence. The focus on "symbolic competence" in recent years refers to language users' ability to navigate symbolic systems and values, adopt new and diverse cultural perceptions and reframe one's role depending on the linguistic and cultural context, and, finally, negotiate symbolic power during linguistic interactions that considers "the various spatial and temporal resonances of these codes." See Claire Kramsch and Anne Whiteside, "Language Ecology in Multilingual Settings: Towards a Theory of Symbolic Competence," *Applied Linguistics* 29, no. 4 (2008): 664.
4. Claire Kramsch, "Teaching Foreign Languages in an Era of Globalization: Introduction," *Modern Language Journal* 98, no. 1 (2014): 302.
5. As Adriana Raquel Díaz and Maria Dasli note, intercultural competence (IC) is one of "four sub-competences" that make up intercultural communicative competence. They state that "IC is conceived as encompassing a set of practices that can be grouped under three dimensions: *cognitive* (knowledge), *behavioral* (skills) and *affective* (attitudes)." See Adriana Raquel Díaz and Maria Dasli, "Tracing the 'Critical' Trajectory of Language and Intercultural Communication Pedagogy," in *The Critical Turn in Language and Intercultural*

Communication Pedagogy: Theory, Research and Practice, ed. Maria Dasli and Adriana Raquel Díaz (New York: Routledge, 2017), 5.
6. Kramsch, "Cultural Component," 87.
7. Julie M. Sykes, "Technologies for Teaching and Learning Intercultural Competence and Interlanguage Pragmatics," in *The Handbook of Technology and Second Language Teaching and Learning*, ed. Carol A. Chapelle and Shannon Sauro (Chichester, UK: Wiley Blackwell, 2017), 118–133.
8. Claire Kramsch, "Teaching Foreign Languages," 305.
9. Heidi Byrnes, "Articulating a Foreign Language Sequence through Content: A Look at the Culture Standards," *Language Teaching* 41, no. 1 (2008): 107.
10. For more information on learning styles, see Howard Gardner's *Multiple Intelligences: The Theory in Practice* (New York: Basic Books, 1993).
11. Byrnes, "Articulating a Foreign Language," 107.
12. Erin Kearney, *Intercultural Learning in Modern Language Education: Expanding Meaning-Making Potentials* (Bristol, UK: Multilingual Matters, 2016), 11.
13. Kearney, 13–14.
14. Kate Paesani, Heather Willis Allen, and Beatrice Dupuy, *A Multiliteracies Framework for Collegiate Foreign Language Teaching* (Upper Saddle River, NJ: Pearson, 2016), 62.
15. Kramsch, "Teaching Foreign Languages," 305.
16. A multiliteracies approach revolves around texts starting at the introductory level: "The goals of this framework [are] to engage learners in the act of meaning design, the dynamic process of discovering form-meaning connections through the acts of interpreting and creating written, oral, visual, audiovisual, and digital texts." Paesani, Allen, and Dupuy, *Multiliteracies Framework*, 43.
17. Paesani, Allen, and Dupuy, 36.
18. Paesani, Allen, and Dupuy, 64.
19. Kramsch, "Teaching Foreign Languages," 306.
20. John W. Thomas, *A Review of Research on Project-Based Learning*, March 2000,
21. Thomas, 3–4.
22. See Jo Boaler, "Mathematics for the Moment, or the Millennium?," *Education Week* 17, no. 29 (1999). See also Thomas, *Review of Research*.
23. Freadman, "Fragmented Memory," 380.
24. Thomas, *Review of Research*, 3.
25. James G. Mitchell and Cheryl Tano, *Promenades : À Travers le Monde Francophone*, 3rd ed. (Boston: Vista Higher Learning, 2018).
26. David Nunan, *Designing Tasks for the Communicative Classroom* (Cambridge: Cambridge University Press, 1989), 10.

27. Thomas, *Review of Research*, 22–23.
28. David Moursund, *Project-Based Learning: Using Information Technology* (Eugene, OR: International Society for Technology in Education, 1999), 35–38.
29. Moursund, 39.
30. Phyllis C. Blumenfeld, Elliot Soloway, Ronald W. Marx, and Joseph S. Krajcik, "Motivating Project-Based Learning: Sustaining the Doing, Supporting the Learning," *Educational Psychologist* 26, no. 3–4 (1991).
31. "Solving problems and carrying out complex tasks requires having the necessary resources available and then using these resources effectively. One resource all individuals have is their own intelligence. Actually, it is much more accurate to speak of one's intelligences." Moursund, *Project-Based Learning*, 41.
32. Yaron Doppelt, "Implementation and Assessment of Project-Based Learning in a Flexible Environment," *International Journal of Technology and Design Education* 13 (2003): 259.
33. For more on the positive correlation between reading, writing, and second language acquisition, see Jean Marie Schultz, "The Gordian Knot: Language, Literature, and Critical Thinking," in *SLA and the Literature Classroom: Fostering Dialogues*, ed. Virginia M. Scott and Holly Tucker (Boston: Heinle and Heinle, 2001).
34. Klaus Brandl defines the "interpersonal mode of communication" as the act of "talking and listening, and when the communication breaks down, [interlocutors] have the opportunity to negotiate meaning"; the "interpretive mode of mode of communication does not allow for any kind of possibility of negotiation of meaning with the writer or speaker"; and the "presentational mode also constitutes one-way communication" in which the speaker or writer prepares content for an audience. See Klaus Brandl, *Communicative Language Teaching in Action* (Upper Saddle River, NJ: Pearson, 2008), 191.
35. Regarding the social aspect of language learning, we can look to the work of Russian psychologist Lev Vygotsky, who posited social interaction as a key component of the development of linguistic cognition.
36. Paesani, Allen, and Dupuy, *Multiliteracies Framework*, 36.
37. Paesani, Allen, and Dupuy, 36.
38. Paesani, Allen, and Dupuy, 65.
39. Byrnes, "Articulating a Foreign Language," 114.
40. Class periods for first-year French courses at CU Boulder meet five days a week and last fifty minutes.
41. See Appendix 5.1 on Fulcrum.
42. See Appendix 5.2 on Fulcrum.

43. Students could also use alternative presentation programs such as Google Slides or Prezi.
44. Please see Appendix 5.3 for a sample of the presentation notes. Notes may be adapted to each level.
45. See Appendix 5.4 on Fulcrum.
46. See Appendix 5.5 on Fulcrum.
47. Albert Valdman, Cathy Pons, and Mary Ellen Scullen, *Chez Nous : Branché sur le Monde Francophone* (Upper Saddle River, NJ: Pearson, 2014), 411–413.
48. See Appendix 5.6 on Fulcrum.
49. See Appendix 5.7 on Fulcrum.
50. See Appendix 5.8 on Fulcrum.
51. This literary excerpt can be found in the textbook *Réseau: Communication, Intégration, Intersections*, by Jean Marie Schultz and Marie-Paule Tranvouez (Upper Saddle River, NJ: Pearson, 2015), 92–94.
52. See Appendix 5.8 on Fulcrum.
53. See Appendix 5.9 on Fulcrum.
54. Please see Appendices 5.10 and 5.11 on Fulcrum for survey questions and results.
55. See Selected Student Feedback.
56. See Selected Student Feedback.
57. In French 1010, the response to the survey question "Did your class discussion on *Le Petit Prince*, the reading of the excerpt from the story, and viewing a clip from the film give you greater insight into French culture and values?" resulted in 45 percent of students stating "yes" and 55 percent of students stating "no." Similarly, in French 1020, the response to the survey question "Did your class discussion on 'L'Arbre nourricier' and the reading of the fable in French give you greater insight into Senegalese culture and values?" resulted in 35 percent of students stating "yes" and 61 percent of students stating "no."
58. Kramsch, "Teaching Foreign Languages," 306.

REFERENCES

Blumenfeld, Phyllis C., Elliot Soloway, Ronald W. Marx, and Joseph S. Krajcik, "Motivating Project-Based Learning: Sustaining the Doing, Supporting the Learning." *Educational Psychologist* 26, no. 3–4 (1991): 369–398.

Boaler, Jo. "Mathematics for the Moment, or the Millennium?" *Education Week* 17, no. 29 (1999). https://www.edweek.org/ew/articles/1999/03/31/29boaler.h18.html.

Brandl, Klaus. *Communicative Language Teaching in Action*. Upper Saddle River, NJ: Pearson, 2008.

Byrnes, Heidi. "Articulating a Foreign Language Sequence through Content: A Look at the Culture Standards." *Language Teaching* 41, no. 1 (2008): 103–118.

Díaz, Adriana Raquel, and Maria Dasli. "Tracing the 'Critical' Trajectory of Language and Intercultural Communication Pedagogy." In *The Critical Turn in Language and Intercultural Communication Pedagogy: Theory, Research and Practice*, edited by Maria Dasli and Adriana Raquel Díaz, 3–21. New York: Routledge, 2017.

Doppelt, Yaron. "Implementation and Assessment of Project-Based Learning in a Flexible Environment." *International Journal of Technology and Design Education* 13 (2003): 255–272.

Freadman, Anne. "Fragmented Memory in a Global Age: The Place of Storytelling in Modern Language Curricula." *Modern Language Journal* 98, no. 1 (2014): 373–385.

Gardner, Howard. Multiple Intelligences: The Theory in Practice. New York: Basic Books, 1993.

Kearney, Erin. Intercultural Learning in Modern Language Education: Expanding Meaning- Making Potentials. Bristol, UK: Multilingual Matters, 2016.

Kramsch, Claire. "The Cultural Component of Language Learning." *Language, Culture and Curriculum* 8, no. 2 (1995): 83–92.

———. "Teaching Foreign Languages in an Era of Globalization: Introduction." *Modern Language Journal* 98, no. 1 (2014): 296–311.

Kramsch, Claire, and Anne Whiteside. "Language Ecology in Multilingual Settings: Towards a Theory of Symbolic Competence." *Applied Linguistics* 29, no. 4 (2008): 645–671.

Mitchell, James G., and Cheryl Tano. *Promenades : À Travers le Monde Francophone*. 3rd ed. Boston: Vista Higher Learning, 2018.

Moursund, David. *Project-Based Learning: Using Information Technology*. Eugene, OR: International Society for Technology in Education, 1999.

Nunan, David. *Designing Tasks for the Communicative Classroom*. Cambridge: Cambridge University Press, 1989.

Paesani, Kate, Heather Willis Allen, and Beatrice Dupuy. *A Multiliteracies Framework for Collegiate Foreign Language Teaching*. Upper Saddle River, NJ: Pearson, 2016.

Schultz, Jean Marie. "The Gordian Knot: Language, Literature, and Critical Thinking." In *SLA and the Literature Classroom: Fostering Dialogues*, ed. Virginia M. Scott and Holly Tucker, 3–31. Boston: Heinle and Heinle, 2001.

Schultz, Jean Marie, and Marie-Paule Tranvouez. *Réseau: Communication, Intégration, Intersections*. Upper Saddle River, NJ: Pearson, 2015.

Sykes, Julie M. "Technologies for Teaching and Learning Intercultural Competence and Interlanguage Pragmatics." In *The Handbook of Technology and Second Language Teaching and Learning*, edited by Carol A. Chapelle and Shannon Sauro, 118–133. Chichester, UK: Wiley Blackwell, 2017.

PART III

VISUAL ARTS AND MASS MEDIA

CHAPTER SIX

THE FRENCH CLASSROOM AS A NEWSROOM

A Multiliteracies Framework

Kathryne Adair Corbin, Haverford College

Access to countless media outlets and the technology used to view video feeds, news articles, social media posts, and other cultural artifacts in real time allows students in French-language classrooms to become active and engaged participants in French and francophone culture on a daily basis. Indeed, as the daily newspaper once set the rhythm of daily life—picking up a copy of *le quotidien* went hand in hand with catching the 08h06 train or purchasing the daily baguette—the timestamp of today's breaking news, now accessible throughout the day via television, radio, mobile phone, or computer, and in dozens of forms, itself demonstrates the cultural changes in which we are the active participants.

In addition, because of the rapidity with which information is shared through online frameworks and in university courses focused on global perspectives, students today are more globally aware and as such seek to link their coursework from their language courses to that of other disciplines, leading to greater opportunities for intercultural contact. As Richard Kern and Jean Marie Schultz point out, the internet and news media introduce "new discourse structures, by opening up authorship to the masses, and by allowing users to form, choose, and maintain interactive learning communities that cross national boundaries," causing changes in the way that we learn and use languages.[1] Furthermore, Kern and Schultz called for a redefinition of literacy in this era of multicultural and multimodal communication, one that would better reflect changing social practices and identities: "Literacy redefined must encompass complex interactions among language, cognition, society, and culture."[2] A closer look at Michael Byram's definition of critical cultural awareness, or "an ability to evaluate critically and on the basis of explicit criteria, perspectives, practices and products in our own and other cultures and countries,"[3] points to the importance of cultural awareness for asserting the critique of our own societies, communities, and countries.

Successful students in the language classroom must, through reflective social practices, gain both cultural and linguistic awareness. In response to students' evolving multidisciplinary interests, and in order to foster critical cultural awareness, I looked to the changing landscape of mass media today. The informational and democratic exchange that defines the newspaper itself remains vital to understanding the world in which we live. In creating context for teaching French language, literature, and culture, it is essential to include contemporary popular culture alongside historical (and canonical) references in classroom exchanges, and perhaps no single authentic document incorporates politics, current events, fashion, theater, sports, and even the serialized novel as vividly as the newspaper.

Moreover, incorporating resources from and activities based on print, online, and televised media, which offers students access to multimodal materials, supports the educational paradigms of the Universal Design for Learning (UDL). The frameworks and tools that are often found in UDL-inspired courses provide diverse ways of engaging with and representing material and diverse ways of expression and also strive to render the classroom more inclusive and accessible for all learners, as Sheryl Burgstahler's work on the application of Universal Design has shown.[4] The basic principles of UDL may come as no surprise to foreign language (FL) instructors already familiar with the New London Group's call in 1994 for a multiliteracies framework, one that would reflect expanding cultural and linguistic diversity in the wake of globalization while also engaging with an array of text and tech to fully explore myriad possibilities in language, culture, and media.

In order to respond to the changing needs and tastes of an increasingly diverse group of learners, I redesigned an existing advanced grammar, conversation, and composition course, maintaining the course goals in respect to improving writing skills, grammar, and conversational fluidity while also integrating a framework of journalistic media and culture in order to stimulate fresh interest in language learning and writing. My objectives in so doing were threefold: First, by asking students to access and navigate the online press throughout the week, they would gain knowledge and (hopefully) increased interest in current events in the francophone world and also learn to identify the different aspects of a newspaper web page such as advertisements, blogs, and news articles. Second, by creating platforms such as class blogs and Twitter feeds that would allow information sharing, students would gain autonomy and agency in choosing course content, which would increase their engagement in and, ideally, appreciation for the course. Third, by gathering, reading, watching, or listening to the information and then discussing it from different angles in class, students would also be able to think critically about the dissemination of news across different cultures: from "fake news" and hoaxes to the question of what exactly *constitutes* news for a specific public—what is picked up and shared, or not, in a Western-centered mass media. Ultimately, developing one's language skills is also deeply cultural, for much meaning is embedded in structures and word choices. Journalists, therefore, are presented with the daily challenge of crafting concise new reference material for readers who sift through information based on their own cultural constructs. Students in this course would become aware of different cultural constructs and thereby their own as they explore and engage in the writing process.

THE COURSE: STRUCTURE AND FIRST DAYS

This course, Tous journalistes, includes discrete areas of study designed to engage and challenge students as learners of language and culture through discussion, process-based writing, grammar lessons, and critical inquiry. Students become journalists: they are required to consider actual potential breaches of ethics faced by contemporary journalists, to research current events in the francophone world and share findings via group Twitter, and to engage in genre-based writing assignments throughout the semester, each focusing on a specific point of grammar or stylistics. All student news articles, illustrations, and tweets are posted to our class news blog. In this chapter, I offer techniques and a course plan through which students develop critical cultural awareness by exploring the francophone media landscape and thereby cultivating the tools necessary for a critical evaluation of what makes a news story: angles, veracity, and objectivity. Students improve their techniques of composition writing by expressing themselves in a variety of genres and in rich, original syntax and structures and by contributing to peer review editing sessions.

In the first days of the course, students discover a range of sources for accessing the French and francophone written press, radio, and television, as well as internet portals. Certain web sites such as *Kiosko* or *Le Mur de la presse* allow students to familiarize themselves with the names of major news outlets and at a glance compare layouts, headlines, lead stories, and even angles of attack. Students can be asked to compare French national to local media or a French daily to a daily from Senegal or Canada thanks to online media guides featuring links to international news outlets.[5] After a few initial sessions in which students compare headlines, discuss and debate stories, and generally familiarize themselves with the francophone press, we establish a class Twitter feed to share articles among us and then create a widget for our course WordPress website. It is usually helpful to invite instructional technology staff to class, if possible, to show students how to use Twitter and how to post their final articles to the WordPress blog. Throughout the course of the semester, students will read or watch or listen to the news and then share stories of their choosing via unique Twitter hashtags that will be used only by our course, such as #HCFR-212reportage or #HCFR212chronique. Using Twitter and hashtags in this way, and then linking the Twitter feed to our web page via a widget, encourages students to contribute to the course content and also allows us to refer to a pre-selection of articles during class discussion as all students will have seen the tweets ahead of the class meeting time (see figure 1).

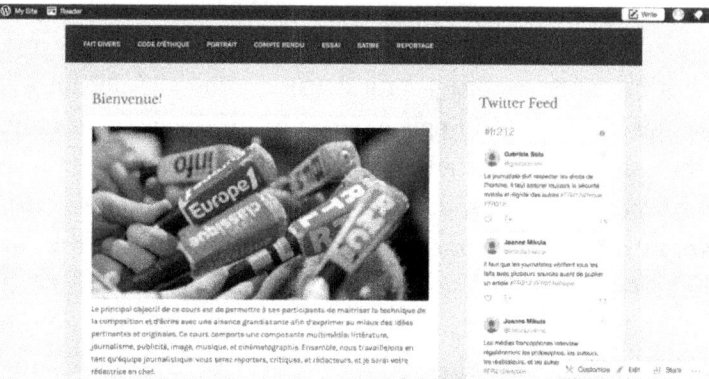

Figure 6.1. The main page of our course website, with the Twitter feed.

THE JOURNALISM CODE OF ETHICS

Once students have mastered the use of Twitter and the course website and have a feel for international media, we move toward the first and most important assignment: the journalistic code of ethics. With fake news, hoaxes, and the questioning of journalistic integrity on the rise given the current political climate, a section on ethics is fundamental to the positioning of accurate and comprehensive journalistic practices, even at the classroom level. Furthermore, students at Haverford College have defended their Honor Code for more than 100 years; according to the college's website, the Honor Code establishes "an environment based on mutual trust, concern, and respect" and influences personal relationships as deeply as academic principles.[6] Students at Haverford ratify the Honor Code every year. Because their engagement with ethics is already so visible in their daily lives, I wanted to shift some of this energy into questions of journalistic ethics by studying cases of ethics breaches, reading professional codes of ethics, and writing personal codes of ethics.

Perhaps one of the most comprehensive resources on journalistic ethics comes from the website of the Society of Professional Journalists (SPJ).[7] Not only does the SPJ offer printable posters and bookmarks of its ethics code (in case one should need an on-the-go reminder), but there are position papers, resources, an ethics hotline, and case studies for consideration and debate. While these resources are in English and most of the examples offered in the case studies pertain to the American press, the case studies can be translated into French or offer inspiration for similar cases in the francophone press (e.g., the coverage by the American press versus the French press of Dominique Strauss-Kahn's "perp walk" or the decision to publish caricatures of the Prophet Muhammad). Discussion of these cases in class leads to the broader cross-cultural examination of freedom of the press and interpretations of laws of slander, libel, and hate speech.[8] Having considered ethical case studies in the field, students are then asked to prepare close readings of codes of ethics, such as the "Charte d'éthique professionnelle des journalistes" of the Syndicat national des journalistes (France), the Code de déontologie journalistique of the Conseil de déontologie journalistique (Belgium), or even that of Mediapart, which serve as models for their own codes. Students then draft and share their codes on the course website as a pledge to uphold during the semester (figure 2). This activity, then, is at once linguistic—students recognize language, register, style in various codes—as well as culturally and socially pragmatic; students become civic-minded professionals and as such must consider potential breaches and adhere to their own codes.

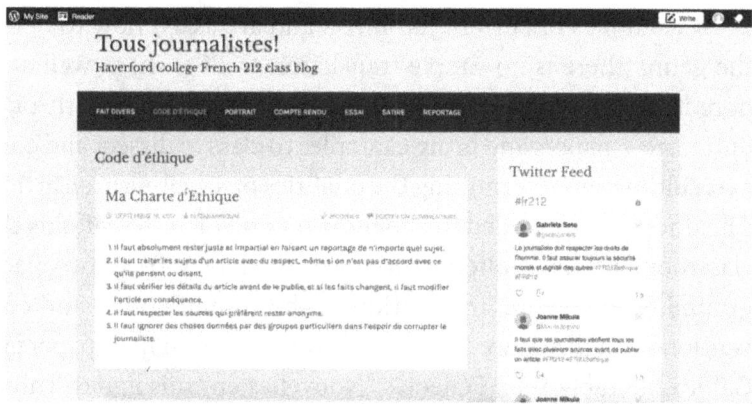

Figure 6.2. The Code of Ethics, as shown and shared on the course website.

WRITING ASSIGNMENTS: THE JOURNALISTIC GENRES

Each writing assignment takes place over the course of a few weeks and follows a process-based writing approach. Students begin by brainstorming reactions to a simple prompt, refine these ideas in a first draft, then present their work for editing among members of a "comité de redaction" (editorial board) before submitting a final draft to their professor. As the final editor of their work, I highlight grammatical, structural, syntactical, and stylistic errors and return the work to the student. They make any final changes before ultimately posting the work to our course news blog, along with any illustrations, and at that time I grade the work. The writing process is complemented by exercises to review grammar and stylistics according to students' needs or which grammar points best fit a genre unit (a review of the subjunctive pairs well with the unit on the essay, for example, while relating indirect discourse fits with the units on the portrait or the reportage).

Le Fait divers

The first journalistic genre under study is the *fait divers*, or the brief human interest/news item story. Students are presented with a few examples of current *fait divers* and are asked how to define the genre (there is no simple translation to English) as well as to note its characteristics and style markers. They also read through online newspapers and bring examples to class to dissect and compare, ultimately determining the qualities of a well-written article. The document provided in appendix 6.1 on Fulcrum scaffolds this classroom work and offers some playful nineteenth-century background on the genre. In addition to the contemporary and conventional *fait divers*, we also look through archival newspapers via Gallica,[9] notably Félix Fénéon's "Nouvelles en trois lignes" rubric, published in *Le Matin* beginning in 1906 (Figure 3).

While Fénéon's work is indeed factual, his "nouvelles" showcase a poetic quality that is rare in today's daily press. A quick read of a handful of "nouvelles" offers students the opportunity to pinpoint figures of style, concise vocabulary, rhythm, and notably the "chute" or rapid and witty conclusion to the "nouvelle." For example, "Trop de gens annoncent : 'Je vous couperai les oreilles!' Vasson, d'Issy, ne dit mot à Biluet, mais il l'essorilla bel et bien." (Too many people announce: "I will cut off your ears!" Vasson, from Issy, did not say a word to Biluet, but cropped his ears indeed). To culminate this unit, students experiment with their own creative writing of "nouvelles en trois lignes" based on campus events (real or fictional) and in a more contemporary 140 characters via tweets to the course Twitter feed.

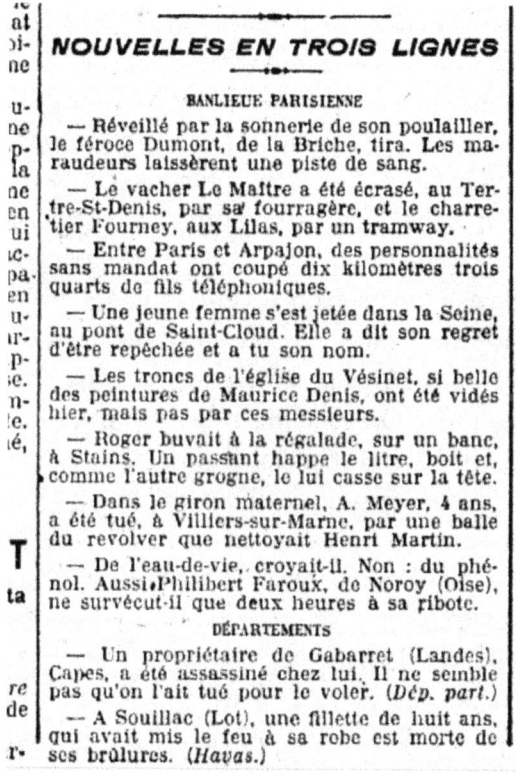

Figure 6.3. A clip of Félix Fénéon's "Nouvelles en trois lignes" rubric, published in Le Matin.

Le Portrait journalistique

For the journalistic portrait assignment, students will uncover ways to "raconter une personne comme on raconte un événement" (recount a person as one recounts an event).[10] Several initial activities guide students as they prepare to draft their portraits. First, students bring to class a few visual portraits that move them in some way. These can be paintings, photographs, or other mixed media portraits. We generally spend some time talking about the qualities and functions of an artistic portrait, and in-class freewrite exercises or group brainstorming activities that focus on a photograph or a painting furnish students with lexical fields and descriptive vocabulary adaptable to a written portrait.

Next, an initial sampling of portraits from *Le Monde* or *Libération*, for example, invites students to consider the following series of questions: Does the portrait follow a specific theme or series? What is this portrait about? Why is this person the object of the portrait? What is the question here? In which environment is the person described and why? What physical, psychological, moral, or intimate aspects of the person are presented? How does the journalist enhance these aspects? How much dialogue is used and to what effect? Is the journalist present in the portrait and how does that play into the reader's feeling about the portrait? As students discuss the stylistics and characteristics of the portraits they have found, they are learning more about the francophone mediatic tapestry—which types of people are chosen for the portraits and why but also what these people might mean to the readership and in the larger society.

While students prepare the cultural, textual, and stylistic aspects of the portrait they will write, they must also research the person and their activities in order to guide ideas and intuitions before preparing the interview. Students are strongly encouraged to find a French-speaking community member as the subject of their portrait for two main reasons: to conduct the interview in French and to get a glimpse into the life of a francophone or Francophile person in the local community. A peer editing workshop on the portrait can be held in class or exchanged among students (see appendix 6.2 on Fulcrum for a sampling of questions).

La Critique de film

To prepare for writing a film critique, students first study terms relevant to film studies (e.g., *gros plan, plan américain, le champ, la sequence*, etc.), and we view a *court métrage* in class in order to field questions about critique and discuss together. Using the online platform Hypotheses.is allows students to read one or two current critiques online, to comment, and to respond to fellow students' comments and questions. In so doing, we are able to quickly map the parts of a film critique, note the components: strong lede or hook ("l'attaque"), mention of actors, directors, title, genre, short summary, discussion of special technical or cinematographic qualities, global judgment—and not giving away the ending! I have also incorporated into lessons several activities based on clips from the Canal Plus tele-magazine *L'hebd'Hollywood* or *Cinéma sur Oreiller*, which offer critiques of films made for television.

Many of these writing assignments are linked as closely as possible to on-campus events, and I encourage students to read the master calendar at the college so they are aware of campuswide events. The film critique assignment generally coincides with one of the films our department screens during its annual film series. In so doing, as part of the critique, students can "report" on the event itself, interview members of the audience, and even ask questions of the guest speaker or moderator at the end of the film.

L'Essai

For the argumentative essay or opinion-editorial (op-ed) piece, students can once again work from current work found in newspapers or magazines of their choice, or the entire class can deconstruct the same essay chosen ahead of time by the instructor. In the latter case, I recommend chapter 4, "L'Essai," in *Tâches d'encre*[11] for its use of Albert Camus's article "La Contagion" taken from the newspaper *Combat* in 1947. In his essay, Camus composes a strong argument against racism using allegorical "signs" of a contagious disease, which is racism. The questions on content, structure, and style that follow this piece expose students to the intricacies and use of rhetorical figures necessary for drafting a strong argumentative essay. I ask students to work in reverse—that is, to create the outline for Camus's work by deconstructing the essay paragraph by paragraph—and they are able to see how the author proceeds in forming his argument; this outline serves them as they then craft their own argument surrounding a recent polemic in their community. Kern and Schultz underscore the importance of social and literary themes in multimodal courses and recommend that "students engage in an analysis of examples of French academic writing included in the course reader, comparing them to American rhetorical approaches to similar writing tasks, in an effort to understand better the culturally embedded intellectual processes behind specific types of writing."[12] This activity presents a strong argumentative essay as the end product by inviting students to consider issues of social justice on their campus or in their hometown that they will take up in their own op-ed. Rather than solely engaging in reader response criticism to an essay from the press, which, as Kern and Schultz note, risks leading students "to the misguided conclusion that other people and other cultures are in essence no different from themselves and their own cultures and that writing from a subjective point of view is always an acceptable form of the analytical,"[13] student journalists build a deep analysis from their lived experience and unique perspective.

Le Reportage

For the final writing assignment, I begin with a reportage by Colette, "Dans la foule," from *Le Matin* on May 2, 1912 (figure 4). In this article, Colette recounts what she witnessed as a woman journalist during the capture of the Bande à Bonnot gang outside of Paris earlier that week. Thanks to the digitized materials on Gallica, students compare the style, content, and layout of Colette's account, which appeared on page 4, with the *Le Matin* coverage of the shakedown from "la Une" on April 29 (slides and questions in appendix 6.3 on Fulcrum).[14] This initial comparison of reportages—which also introduces students to historical events, journalistic trends, and early women journalists—is then followed up with a brief history of the genre of reportage in France and a discussion of the goals of reportage. Excerpts of Yves Agnès's *Manuel de journalisme : écrire pour le journal* highlight characteristics of reportage and guide students in preparing their own. Alternatively, the resource 24 Heures dans une rédaction, a joint project of L'Agence française de développement médias and the École supérieure de journalisme de Lille is a thorough reference devised for the education of journalists according to international standards and as such offers practical printable dossiers relative to each step of the mediatic process, whether in press, web, radio, or television.[15] In the case of reportage, various dossiers on sources, investigations, and editing, for example, can be helpful in organizing lessons and "équipes de rédaction" for the editing process. In addition, the Centre pour l'éducation aux médias et à l'information (CLEMI) is a valuable resource with pedagogical dossiers and videos to guide students and teachers embarking on critical inquiry of the media. In the case of reportage, for example, one can find dossiers demonstrating how to verify information and sources as well as guides for how to write to inform. As students prepare to write their actual news report, I offer checklists and tip sheets; writing takes place over a couple weeks, which allows time to investigate a local story idea and work through processed drafts in editorial teams (see appendix 6.3 on Fulcrum).

Additional sites of inquiry for this unit on reportage are available through the pedagogical portals of TV5Monde and Radio France internationale (RFI), for example, and offer concrete culture-specific forms of news reports. One important activity for this course comes from Kiosque TV5Monde's *Les Médias à l'épreuve des faits alternatifs*. This roundtable news program was filmed just after the inauguration of Donald Trump, and the TV5 pedagogical dossier, complete with questionnaires for students, walks students through vocabulary related to fake news, hoaxes, and the like and presents perspectives from the French news media on relatively recent American news events that directly impact the field of journalism and free press. Engaging with this and other television news shows allows students to develop linguistic skills while becoming aware of cultural nuances.

Furthermore, working through news reportages from different francophone countries contributes to critical media literacy, which ultimately bolsters a participatory democracy, as Douglas Kellner and Jeff Share argue, "because new information communication technologies and a market-based media culture have fragmented, connected, converged, diversified, homogenized, flattened, broadened, and reshaped the world."[16] If material in a course can draw from different forms of mass communication and popular culture, accessed through a variety of technologies and from a diversity of cultures across power structures, a deeper understanding of the underpinnings of mass media and alternative media production will embolden students to critically analyze this literature and take a stance as they create their own material through written reports, satirical drawings, tweets, and video recordings. To further illustrate this point, students in my course met with and studied the reportages of recent Haverford alumna and freelance writer Allyn Gaestel, who is based in Lagos, Nigeria, and has published widely for top international news organizations. Gaestel's message for students, however, was one of decolonizing journalism in favor of shifting the narrative center of world news organizations away from traditional Western mediatic practices. Her challenge to students was to expand their engagement with media that seek to reproduce hegemonic representations and move to include media that open spaces to marginalized communities and cultures and present a vehicle for victimized others to tell their own stories. When built into the curriculum alongside a breadth of media analysis and continued creation, such a discussion with an expert from the field deepened both students' critical cultural awareness and critical media literacy.

Figure 6.4. Colette's "Dans la foule" from Le Matin, May 2, 1912.

VISUAL CULTURE: ADVERTISING, CARICATURE, AND PHOTOJOURNALISM

To fully negotiate students' engagement within a multiliteracies framework and encourage the appreciation of a breadth of journalistic genres and the characteristics that define them, we consider critical visual components in the periodic press as cultural artifacts as they are represented or debated in current events: advertising, caricature, and photojournalism. In advertising, for example, we take on advertisements that led to scandal or could be perceived as culturally offensive and debate reaction to such ads in the media and among the public, comparing these reactions in France, for example, to similar scandalous campaigns in the United States.[17]

I devote a few class periods to presenting and debating satire and caricature, notably since the attacks on the offices of *Charlie Hebdo* in January 2015. To offer important context for students, I begin with the historical importance of the satirical press and its deep connection to French politics, notably the laws of the July Monarchy that heavily censured the satirical press—as Honoré Daumier's series *Les Poires* (1831) and its textual evolution in the *Charivari* suggests (see figure 6.5). The January 2015 article by leading media scholars Marie-Ève Thérenty and Guillaume Pinson outlines the history of the French satirical press and is a great starting point for a discussion and comparison of contemporary use of satire and caricature in France and internationally; the collective work *La Caricature . . . et si c'était sérieux ? Décryptage de la violence satirique*, also published shortly after the Charlie Hebdo attacks, offers further context for studying French satirical responses to historical and cultural events.

Again, culture-specific forms of writing and expression provide essential links from which students can draw their own intercultural inquiries. One example is the use of the image of the Prophet Muhammad from the cover of the satirical weekly *Charlie Hebdo*. In the weeks following the attacks on the newspaper's offices,

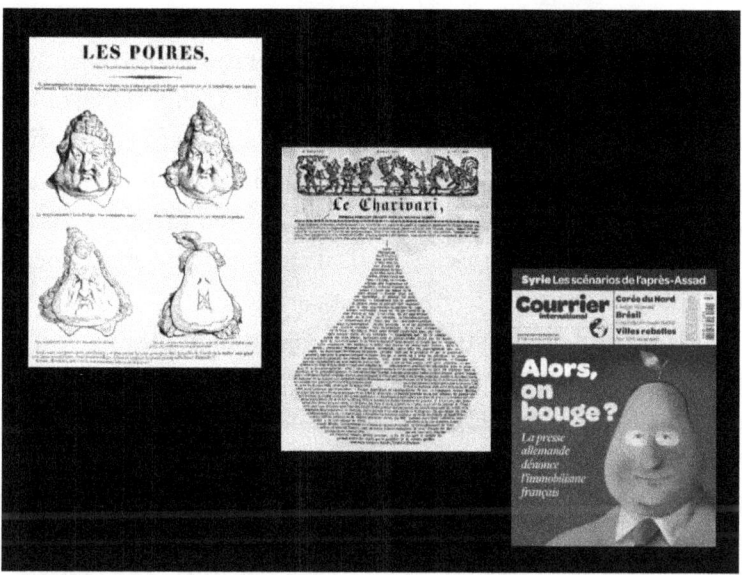

Figure 6.5. Slide showing evolution of Les Poires, by Honoré Daumier, 1831.

many American news outlets pixelated or censored the covers of *Charlie Hebdo* in illustrations on their sites, leaving Americans in the dark as to why the covers were problematic in the first place—but, perhaps, sparing potentially offensive content through editorial choice. A discussion about interpreting freedoms of the press, offensive speech, and self-censorship can be fruitful here, notably in comparing the way French and American media consider publishing portrayals of the Prophet Muhammad.[18]

The use of satirical cartoons and other multimodal frameworks allows us to focus on the images, metaphors, and symbols that can be recurrent in a culture across time (e.g., Marianne in Eugène Delacroix's *La Liberté guidant le peuple*) while also expanding learners' engagement with material and culture. Taking on a single subject in current events—immigration, for example—and exploring visual representations across cultures and languages support wider cultural perspectives and lead to enhanced critical analysis of one's own society and culture. Comparing photos that accompany news reports to the caricatural and satirical drawings that take on the same subject matter teases out the connotations and objectives of a satirical drawing, guiding students toward an emotional or ironic response that supports critical thinking. Finally, after some discussion and evaluation of caricature and satire in the press from both the United States and France, students—even the less artistically inclined—sketch their own satirical cartoons and share them on the course website.

A third and final visual component is that of photography and photojournalism. We begin by brainstorming and mapping concepts related to images and their role in the press before moving on to discussing students' selection of important images from the press. There are several good articles that treat questions of photography and "photoshopping" in the media: the case of the fake selfie of astronaut Thomas Pesquet[19] or the newsroom decision to make public photos of despots like that of Osama bin Laden.[20] In addition to ethical questions, students engage in debate surrounding what could be called the myth of objectivity in photojournalism as we consider the possible intentions, thoughts, and emotions of the photographer on assignment.

STRUCTURE AND SCAFFOLDING ASSIGNMENTS

Each class period begins with a rundown of the week's "revue de presse." If there is a student oral presentation slated for a given day, in which they present a topic, its controversy, and then open the floor to debate, this becomes the focus of discussion. If there is no oral presentation scheduled, students volunteer material they would like to discuss with classmates, generally taken from the course Twitter feed. Each week, students are responsible for tagging and tweeting at least two articles or videos to the course Twitter feed; hashtags vary per unit: #HCFR212cinema, #HCFR-212faitdivers, for example. As mentioned before, using specific hashtags in this way allows everyone to quickly share and find materials according to a genre unit, which then facilitates reading outside of class and in-class discussion (this also allows the instructor to easily search for assignments submitted as tweets). Examples of topics tagged for discussion range from current *fait divers* or reportages to current events in the field of journalism or the film industry.

The websites of media giants TV5Monde and RFI offer valuable video and audio clips in line with current news topics, and these are often available with added pedagogical materials for language learners: worksheets for vocabulary and grammar, essay prompts, and cultural explanations.[21] One example is an excerpt from an RFI program in which the invited guest tackles questions related to the cinema industry, notably the success of foreign films in the American market and their use—or not—of subtitles. Students complete some close listening activities, consider specific cases of French films screened in the United States (e.g., *Amélie, The Artist, Les Visiteurs*), and analyze the construction of the discourse of the specialist being interviewed. Finally, working in groups, students must create French subtitles for a two-minute clip of a well-known American film. This final task requires each student group to have access to the clip as well as paper and markers (or iMovie or Camtasia for the more tech-inclined students) so they can "try out" their subtitles at the end of the class period. This short but challenging and fun translation task forces students to think about which expressions are culturally American and how they can be translated in context. Additionally, this exercise serves students later in the semester as they prepare their final video projects for which they include French subtitles for any English interviews.

FINAL PROJECT

Having experimented with writing different news genres and explored publishing online and creating original content, students complete their own news magazine or televised news segment for their final project. In the former, students work alone and write then publish the original content, and in the latter they work in small groups or pairs. For those who choose the "journal télévisé" project, they work closely with the instructional technology department and learn how to use microphones, video recorders, and software such as Adobe Premiere Pro or Camtasia. Each five- to seven-minute video should include:

- an introduction by the anchor along with graphics, music, titles
- a detailed report on one particular subject
- a secondary feature, which can be "lighter" in content
- an interview with at least one expert (if the expert does not speak French, students create subtitles using Camtasia)

Those students who choose to create a news blog must write articles from different rubrics (opinion, news, culture, etc.) and should consider the layout as well as illustrations, widgets, advertising, and so on. Both final projects encourage students to engage with the visual and aesthetic practices they have considered during the semester while building their linguistic competence and moving beyond a curriculum based solely on language to one that also incorporates critical thinking in a multiliteracies framework.

Scaffolding the project is important as students must first write the content and then present it in a creative manner. Students first submit a collective project outline with answers to essential questions and show how tasks will be divided among members of a group. Class time is allotted for students to meet with instructional technology staff and learn about using cameras, microphones, software, and other resources, and weekly check-ins with groups and deadlines ensure that students are on task for completion. Along with the final product, which can be shared or screened on the last day of class, each student submits a short reflection paper about their own work, group work, and the overall process, ultimately evaluating themselves on the final product.[22]

TECHNICAL CONSIDERATIONS

Because of the various technologies accessed in this course and the ever-changing nature of technology, I offer an evaluation of what has been successful in my experience and what has posed barriers to a fluid learning environment. First, for any course that will use Twitter and have a widget or feed on a course website, it is paramount to open an account well in advance of the start of the semester and to test and experiment with tweeting to simulate as best as possible how it will be done with students. In the three years I have taught using Twitter, I have had three very different experiences and ways of incorporating it into the class because Twitter has changed its parameters and rules, mostly regarding group tweets to newly created websites. I am thankful to my supportive colleagues in instructional technology for creating my course WordPress blog and Twitter accounts and then finding the workarounds to make Twitter a successful component of my course. Once Twitter is up and running, it is important that students be held accountable and evaluated on their active and assiduous participation in this activity; otherwise, their participation lags and it falls apart.

The second, and perhaps most important, technological concern is at the core of the course: access to the francophone media. As international newspapers turn toward online media and more readers get their news from websites, social media, and podcasts, access to the news can be tricky to navigate for an entire class. Including podcasts and alternative media does allow for evaluation of style, voice, and form across cultures, and these sites should have their place among the more established media players, where access permits. Few college libraries subscribe to international daily newspapers. Newspaper sites such as *Le Monde* and *Libération* offer a limited number of free articles per month; beyond this, students must purchase a pricey subscription. As students click around the internet and read stories, it can be helpful to create a repository of articles (screenshots or PDF) in a course management system or on the course website. I subscribe to certain paid news sites and have provided PDFs of subscriber-only content to my students; unfortunately, this must be done ahead of time and still limits students to what they can choose to read on their own time.

CONCLUSION

Ultimately, the way we access the news media and what we are able to and choose to access across cultures and across borders generated fruitful discussion: Who determines newsworthiness and content in a Western-driven (and ostensibly democratic) global marketplace where access is not readily available to all? Whose story is told, and how is it told across the cultures and hemispheres?

In a classroom curriculum in which digital literacy is a tool as well as an outcome of the course, students learn to use digital media and technologies for critical inquiry and creation, leading to enhanced awareness and evaluation. With this as our aim, we as instructors must ensure curricula include a diversity of resources—in form, content, and origin—that shift focus from a Western-heavy mediatic landscape toward one that is more globally encompassing in order to rally against social othering and instead create communities of awareness and care. As the New London Group put forth in what has since become the model for theoretical overview of multiliteracies pedagogy, negotiating multicultural differences is a difficult but necessary component of education through which citizens, as "meaning-makers, become Designers of social futures."[23] As language educators, it is our responsibility to empower students to expand their critical reading and critical-making across myriad diverse international and intercultural sources and languages to make informed decisions that affect their own lives as well as the lives of others.

NOTES

1. Richard Kern and Jean Marie Schultz, "Beyond Orality: Investigating Literacy and the Literary in Second and Foreign Language Instruction," in "Methodology, Epistemology, and Ethics in Instructed SLA Research," ed. Lourdes Ortega, special issue, *Modern Language Journal* 89, no. 3 (Autumn 2005): 382.
2. Kern and Schultz, 382.
3. Michael Byram, *Teaching and Assessing Intercultural Communicative Competence* (Clevedon, UK: Multilingual Matters, 1997), 53.
4. Sheryl E. Burgstahler, ed., *Universal Design in Higher Education: From Principles to Practice*, 2nd ed. (Cambridge, MA: Harvard Education Press, 2015).
5. One such guide is Giga Presse: http://www.giga-presse.com. Previously, the Organisation internationale de la francophonie offered a "répertoire des médias" on its website, www.francophonie.org.
6. Honor Council, "What Is the Code?," Haverford College, https://www.haverford.edu/academics/honor-code.
7. Society of Professional Journalists, "Ethics," https://www.spj.org/ethics.asp.
8. James McAuley, "France Moves toward a Law Requiring Facebook to Delete Hate Speech within 24 Hours," *Washington Post*, July 9, 2019, https://www.washingtonpost.com/world/europe/france-moves-toward-a-law-requring-facebook-to-delete-hate-speech-within-24-hours/2019/07/09/d43b24c2-a25d-11e9-a767-d7ab84aef3e9_story.html?utm_term=.7bc47d394ef2.
9. The virtual exposition at the Bibliothèque nationale de France, "La Presse à la Une," is a gold mine of resources and includes not only historical archived images and text but also pedagogical resources and activities. See http://expositions.bnf.fr/presse/index.htm.
10. Yves Agnès, *Manuel de journalisme : écrire pour le journal*, new ed. (Paris: La Découverte, 2008).
11. H. Jay Siskin, Cheryl L. Krueger, and Maryse Fauvel, *Tâches d'encre: French Composition* (Boston: Cengage Learning, 2012).
12. Kern and Schultz, "Beyond Orality," 385.
13. Kern and Schultz, 384.
14. Because reading Colette's article in its original form on the screen via Gallica can be challenging, I suggest offering students printable copies of "Dans la foule" from the monograph of the same name, which appears in the Pléiade edition of Colette's *Œuvres*, tome II.

15. See www.24hdansuneredaction.com, an extensive resource for executing newsroom curricula. Materials are available in multiple languages in addition to English and French.
16. Douglas Kellner and Jeff Share, "Critical Media Literacy Is Not an Option," *Learning Inquiry* 1, no. 1 (April 2007): 59.
17. The website for GenrImages (www.genrimages.org), developed and created by the Centre audiovisuel Simone de Beauvoir, is an excellent resource for representations and stereotypes of gender in the media, including films and advertisements. A Google search for "publicités scandaleuses" also provides a solid bank of ads from which to choose. Students can do this work, finding ads from the United States and abroad and presenting their rationale for the injustice, or, to save time, the professor can provide a preselection from which to begin a broader classroom discussion.
18. Mark Memmott, "Why You're Not Seeing Those 'Charlie Hebdo' Cartoons," NPR, January 10, 2015, https://tinyurl.com/35k5e9a6.
19. Benjamin Hue, "Le Selfie de Thomas Pesquet dans l'espace était un fake," RTL, January 16, 2017, https://www.rtl.fr/actu/sciences-tech/le-selfie-de-thomas-pesquet-dans-l-espace-etait-un-fake-7786771357.
20. Luc Debraine, "Trophées de despotes," *L'Hebdo*, May 5, 2011.
21. In addition to the websites of news media companies, that of the Centre pour l'éducation aux médias et à l'information (CLEMI) offers numerous pedagogical tools and lesson inspirations for teachers at various levels.
22. See appendix for examples of students' final projects.
23. New London Group, "A Pedagogy of Multiliteracies: Designing Social Futures," *Harvard Educational Review* 66, no. 1 (1996): 65.

REFERENCES

Agnès, Yves. *Manuel de journalisme : écrire pour le journal*. New ed. Paris: La Découverte, 2008.

Bihl, Laurent, Christian Delporte, Pascal Ory, et al. La Caricature ... et si c'était sérieux ? Décryptage de la violence satirique. Paris: Nouveau Monde, 2015.

Burgstahler, Sheryl E. *Universal Design in Higher Education: From Principles to Practice*. 2nd ed. Cambridge, MA: Harvard Education Press, 2015.

Byram, Katra, and Claire Kramsch. "Why Is It So Difficult to Teach Language as Culture?" *German Quarterly* 81, no. 1 (2008): 20–34.

Byram, Michael. *Teaching and Assessing Intercultural Communicative Competence*. Clevedon, UK: Multilingual Matters, 1997.

Chun, Dorothy, Richard Kern, and Bryan Smith. "Technology in Language Use, Language Teaching, and Language Learning." *Modern Language Journal* 100 (2016): 64–80.

Colette and Claude Pichois. *Œuvres tome II*. Paris: Gallimard, 1991.

Debraine, Luc. "Trophées de despotes." *L'Hebdo*, May 5, 2011.

Duncum, Paul. "Visual Culture Isn't Just Visual: Multiliteracy, Multimodality and Meaning." *Studies in Art Education* 45, no. 3 (2004): 252–264.

Hue, Benjamin. "Le Selfie de Thomas Pesquet dans l'espace était un fake." RTL, January 16, 2017. https://www.rtl.fr/actu/sciences-tech/le-selfie-de-thomas-pesquet-dans-l-espace-etait-un-fake-7786771357.

Joffredo, Loïc. "Quand le reporter devient un mythe." Exposition 'La Presse à la Une.' Paris: Bibliothèque nationale de France, 2012. http://expositions.bnf.fr/presse/pedago/04.htm.

Kellner, Douglas, and Jeff Share. "Critical Media Literacy Is Not an Option." *Learning Inquiry* 1, no. 1 (April 2007): 59–69.

Kern, Richard, and Jean Marie Schultz. "Beyond Orality: Investigating Literacy and the Literary in Second and Foreign Language Instruction." In "Methodology, Epistemology, and Ethics in Instructed SLA Research," edited by Lourdes Ortega. Special issue, *Modern Language Journal* 89, no. 3 (Autumn 2005): 381–392.

McAuley, James. "France Moves toward a Law Requiring Facebook to Delete Hate Speech within 24 Hours." *Washington Post*, July 9, 2019. https://www.washingtonpost.com/world/europe/france-moves-toward-a-law-requring-facebook-to-delete-hate-speech-within-24-hours/2019/07/09/d43b24c2-a25d-11e9-a767-d7ab84aef3e9_story.html?utm_term=.7bc47d394ef2.

Memmott, Mark. "Why You're Not Seeing Those 'Charlie Hebdo' Cartoons." NPR, January 10, 2015. https://tinyurl.com/35k5e9a6.

New London Group. "A Pedagogy of Multiliteracies: Designing Social Futures." *Harvard Educational Review* 66, no. 1 (1996): 60–93.

Paesani, Kate, Heather Willis Allen, and Beatrice Dupuy. *A Multiliteracies Framework for Collegiate Foreign Language Teaching*. Upper Saddle River, NJ: Pearson, 2016.

Prinsloo, Mastin, and Jennifer Rowsell. "Digital Literacies as Placed Resources in the Globalised Periphery." *Language and Education* 26, no. 4 (July 2012): 271–277.

Rougemont, Elisabeth. *Série sequence didactique. Raconter et expliquer : le fait divers*. Département de l'instruction publique. Genève, 1993.

Schnedecker, Catherine. "Les chaînes de référence dans les portraits journalistiques : éléments de description." *Travaux de linguistique* 51, no. 2 (2005): 85–133.

Siskin, H. Jay, Cheryl L. Krueger, and Maryse Fauvel. *Tâches d'encre: French Composition*. Boston: Cengage Learning, 2012.

Syndicat national des journalistes. "Charte d'éthique professionnelle des journalistes." March 9, 2011. https://www.snj.fr/content/charte-d'éthique-professionnelle-des-journalistes.

Thérenty, Marie-Ève, and Guillaume Pinson. "D'où viens-tu, Charlie?" Mediapart, January 14, 2015. https://blogs.mediapart.fr/edition/bookclub/article/140115/d-ou-viens-tu-charlie.

Wallace, Catherine. "Local Literacies and Global Literacy." In *Globalization and Language Teaching*, ed. David Block and Deborah Cameron, 67–82. London: Routledge, 2002.

Warner, Chantelle, and Beatrice Dupuy. "Moving toward Multiliteracies in Foreign Language Teaching: Past and Present Perspectives ... and Beyond." *Foreign Language Annals* 51, no. 1 (2018): 116–128.

CHAPTER SEVEN

OF PRESIDENTS AND INTERNET MEMES

Fostering Student-Centered Learning, Cultural Competency, and Critical Thinking through the Use of Images

Heidi Holst-Knudsen, Columbia University

Working with pedagogical supports that embed language proficiency exercises within culturally relevant contexts is a central goal in a literacy-based foreign language curriculum.[1,2,3] Media images from the target culture offer an especially fertile means by which to introduce students to cultural material while stimulating intercultural reflection, critical thinking, and a sensitivity to the way in which different discursive systems function. Images also allow for more student-centered lessons because when students are asked to convert the visual into language by describing, deciphering, contextualizing, interpreting, analyzing, and comparing, the words are literally taken out of the instructor's mouth. In this chapter, I will share a variety of pedagogical sequences centered on a viral image of French president Emmanuel Macron. The sequences are composed of practical activities appropriate for secondary- and university-level classes. Although the Macron image in question refers to a specific sociopolitical moment, the activities and critical questions proposed could easily be adapted for use with another image featuring the French (or any other nation's) head of state, especially considering the fact that political figures are a prime subject of internet memes.[4] After discussing why the Macron image constitutes a particularly productive subject for use in the classroom, I will share a variety of activities developed within a multiliteracy framework[5], cycling through activities targeting communication, cultural analysis, discourse analysis, self-reflection, and lexical and grammatical competence.

The first part of the chapter features activities associated with the original photograph of Macron that inspired the meme, focusing in particular on the role of sports in society and on the mediatization of the presidential image. In part 2, I propose activities that take as their point of departure the internet memes inspired by the photograph. This section includes sequences whose goal is to attune students to an internet meme's discursive implications: How does this communicative device operate, and what are the implications of the form? I will conclude the chapter by sharing a selection of Macron memes whose social and political references lend themselves to addressing aspects of French culture and to teaching across the disciplines. The internet meme is a relatively simple unit of communication, at least at first glance, and students are familiar and conversant with the form; its exploitation as authentic cultural material thus offers an accessible point of entry for the consideration of progressively complex linguistic, social, and political questions.

PART I: MACRON GOES TO THE WORLD CUP: OF PRESIDENTS AND SOCCER CHAMPIONSHIPS

In 2018, French president Emmanuel Macron's jubilant reaction to the French soccer team's first goal against Croatia at the outset of the World Cup final in Moscow was captured by Russian

Figure 7.1. © ALEXEY NIKOLSKY / SPUTNIK / Kremlin Pool AP / Photo reproduced with the permission of the Associated Press.

photographer Alexeï Nikolsky (figure 7.1). This photograph was immediately and widely disseminated, garnering both praise and criticism and quickly becoming the object of myriad transformations as an internet meme. Several aspects of this image render it a propitious starting point for stimulating linguistic and cultural engagement. First, any image that features the president of the French Republic is a useful tool because (1) most students will recognize the individual and know something about them and so will be able to immediately engage with the image, and (2) the evocation of France's president automatically allows for comparisons with the American president, a subject with which students are certainly conversant.[6] Thus we can tap into students' existing knowledge to ensure that they will have something to say. Another beneficial aspect of this image is the sports context. Even if students know nothing about the particular sporting event or even much about the French president, they will be able to describe the scene, express personal opinions, and, eventually, formulate critical observations pertaining to sports and sporting events. The image's amalgamation of accessible cultural references renders it a fecund point of departure for a multifaceted exploration of culture.

Lexico-syntactic Exercises as Point of Entry

Although the exercises suggested in this chapter will focus primarily on stimulating communication pertaining to the analysis of culture, I wanted to begin by proposing a few exercises targeting vocabulary and grammar. These functional linguistic elements are, of course, crucial, and the room given here to more interpretive exercises is not intended to diminish their place in the lesson plan. A natural way to begin would be to engage students in the classic lexical exercise of describing, in pairs, what they see in the greatest detail possible (figure 7.2). Since the goal at this preliminary stage is the accumulation of key vocabulary, we could ask students to limit themselves to an objective description, refraining from identifying the specific context if they happen to recognize it. Students could begin by listing the discrete lexical items necessary to describe the scene (looking words up in the dictionary as necessary) before integrating them into the syntax of a descriptive paragraph. To review the vocabulary words generated in this describing phase, the instructor could indicate thematic rubrics on the board (or on a handout or on the internet application Padlet[7]) and ask students to organize the words they have found by category (figure 7.3), reinforcing retention through this cognitive ordering activity. We could then ask students to write a paragraph describing the scene and use their texts as the basis of a targeted review of specific grammar structures (figure 7.4).

Students' identification of the main character in the image—*C'est Emmanuel Macron*—will most likely generate a common grammatical error: the use of the pronoun "il" versus "ce" with the verb "être" followed by a noun. Review of this grammatical point

Description

Vocabulaire

Avec un partenaire, décrivez autant d'éléments de cette image que possible sans identifier le contexte spécifique (si vous le reconnaissez).

- Qui ?
- Où ?
- Quand ?
- Quoi ? (Qu'est-ce qu'il fait ?)
- Pourquoi ? (hypothèse)

Vocabulaire thématique

Vocabulaire du sport	
Un stade	Un terrain de foot
Être fan	Soutenir son équipe
Assister à	Marquer un but
Un match	Bourré de monde
Les tribunes	Les spectateurs
La Coupe du monde	

Vocabulaire des émotions et des sentiments	
S'exalter	Être passionné·e
Exploser de joie	Ressentir
(S')exprimer	Se sentir

Vocabulaire vestimentaire	Description physique	Vocabulaire du mouvement physique	
Être habillé·e	Jeune Dynamique	Faire un geste (d'exultation)	
- en costume	Mince	Lever les bras / les poings en l'air	
- en chemise-cravate	En forme	Se mettre debout	Frapper les mains
		Les poings serrés	Rester assis·e

Grammaire / Expression écrite

« TO SEEM » + ADJECTIF D'ÉMOTION

- Il a l'air joyeux.

TEMPS VERBAUX

- Il **lève** les bras.
- Son équipe **vient de marquer** un but.

EXPRIMER LA CAUSALITÉ (CONJONCTIONS DE CAUSE)

- parce que, car, puisque // à cause de

ÊTRE (+ ADJ. D'ÉMOTION) QUE + SUBJONCTIVE

- Il se réjouit que ...

Figures 7.2, 3, and 4

could allow for the integration of more cultural material, with different examples based on details about the president, his wife, and other French political figures. In the examples provided here (figures 7.5–8), students are asked to pool their knowledge about the French president by working in groups to finish sentences starting with "C'est" and "Il est," recording their completed sentences on the blackboard (or on a shared Google document) under the heading of the appropriate grammatical rubric (figure 7.6). To verify comprehension, follow-up exercises based on other associated political or cultural figures (here Macron's wife Brigitte) could be used (figures 7.7–8).

Grammaire

Reconnaissez-vous le personnage central dans cette image ?
Qui est-ce ?

C'EST EMMANUEL MACRON.

C'EST LE PRÉSIDENT DE LA FRANCE.

*~~IL~~ EST EMMANUEL MACRON.

C'est versus Il/Elle est

Que savez-vous d'Emmanuel Macron ?

Collaborez avec un partenaire pour indiquer vos connaissances sur le président français en utilisant les deux types de phrases ci-dessous et écrivez vos phrases au tableau.

C'est _____.	Il est _____.
C'est _____.	Il est _____.
C'est _____.	Il est _____.
+ noun	+ adjective

Figures 7.5 and 6

Verification

Qui est-ce ?

_C'_ est le président de la République française.

___ est un ancien banquier.

___ est le fondateur du parti politique « En Marche! ».

___ est marié.

___ est très intelligent et cultivé.

___ est un intello.

Qui est-ce ?

C'est Brigitte Macron.

____ est la Première Dame de France.

____ était prof de lettres avant de se consacrer à la carrière de son époux.

____ était l'ancienne prof de Macron.

____ est une militante pour les droits des personnes handicapées.

Figures 7.7 [8] and 8 [9]

CRITICAL CULTURAL AWARENESS THROUGH THE CONSIDERATION OF SOCCER AS SOCIETAL PRACTICE

Even in this initial phase, while students are developing lexical knowledge—learning the vocabulary of sporting events, physical appearance, emotional responses, physical gestures, and stadium seating—we can integrate cultural questions that target the higher-order thinking skills elaborated in Bloom's refined taxonomy.[10] We can push students to think more deeply about their descriptive assertations by asking them to reflect on the sociopolitical implications of what they are describing. We can start, for example, with lower-order "knowledge telling" discussion questions,[11] asking students whether they like attending sporting events, and, if so, how they dress when they go to see a game and why. We can ask where they prefer to sit and/or whether they prefer watching matches in the stadium, in a bar, or at home.[12] We could then ask students to analyze the photograph and consider the assumptions they might make regarding the main figure's socioeconomic status and social function based on where he is sitting and the way he is dressed for a sporting event: *Quelles hypothèses pouvons-nous émettre sur le statut socio-économique ou la fonction sociale d'une personne selon sa tenue vestimentaire ? Selon sa place dans le stade ?* What does attending a sporting event in a suit imply about a person's reasons for attending and their social status? Who gets access to VIP seating and why? Is access to the seating equitable? How is the sports fan's experience of the game affected by their seating? How is the experience of sitting in a private box different from sitting with the crowd? What aspects of the spectator experience might this type of seating enhance or diminish?[13] In this way, language proficiency and analysis are interwoven in a single sequence (figure 7.9). These critical reflections can be nourished by research and/or reading assignments.

For example, in 2007, a British sociologist published an article describing his study of soccer spectatorship and analysis of how watching a soccer match in a pub compares to watching in the stadium.[14] The article was reported on by the French newspaper *France Football* under the title "Voir ou vivre. Qu'est-ce être un spectateur d'un match de foot ?"[15] Another research resource can be found on the Collège de France's website under the rubric of "La Vie des idées," where the prestigious academic institution published a dossier titled "L'Empire du foot," bringing together a series of scholarly articles examining the planetary phenomenon that soccer represents.[16] Among the subjects examined are soccer and globalization, soccer as democratic institution, the organization and instrumentalization of fandom, the development (and encouragement) of imagined communities, the symbolic rivalry of nations, soccer and the colonial past, and so on. This sampling alone offers the stuff of myriad extension activities focused on critical thinking and critical cultural awareness.

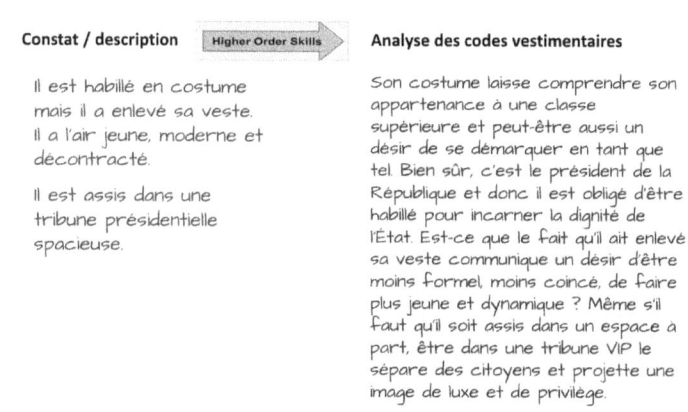

Figure 7.9

The Image of the President: Communication, Analysis, and Intercultural Comparisons

To return to our point of departure, the Macron image, once the students have objectively described and inventoried the elements in the photograph and worked on pertinent lexical and grammatical items, we can introduce one of the French media headlines that accompanied the image as a starting point for written work and discourse analysis (figure 7.10). As a preliminary assignment, students could be asked to imagine themselves in the role of a journalist tasked with reporting on this scene. In order to prepare them for the writing assignment, one could engage students in a whole-class discussion of how the modalities of newspaper journalism such as tone, perspective, length, and communicative objective (will this article offer judgment or simply present the facts?) would inform the redaction of their texts. Such a discussion would attune students to how different types of texts operate in different ways in the service of different communicative goals. After submitting their article (perhaps completed as an in-class writing assignment), students could research the news coverage of the event and compare their texts with authentic articles associated with the image.

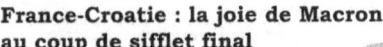
France-Croatie : la joie de Macron au coup de sifflet final

Rédigez un court article de journal pour accompagner cette image à partir des détails indiqués dans le titre.

Expression écrite
Analyse du discours

Figure 7.10 [17]

This expository writing assignment could be followed by a sequence dedicated to cultural analysis, providing another opportunity to progress from description to analysis. Immediately picked up by international media outlets, this image of the exuberant French president quickly went viral, first as a widely reported news item, then as an internet meme (more on this later).[18] The question of how this photograph reflects on the president and on the presidency necessarily imposes itself. How does this "spontaneous," "unguarded" moment make the sitting president look? Students can be asked to address this question in a variety of ways:

1) The most straightforward approach would be to ask students to discuss their opinions in small groups before sharing their views in a larger full-class discussion.

2) To enhance the critical thinking dimension of the exercise, one could exploit a modified jigsaw format and (A) divide the class into an even number of small groups and, irrespective of real opinions, assign a viewpoint to each group (asking groups to either defend or criticize the image of the president communicated by this photograph); group members would then collaboratively formulate arguments to defend their assigned point of view. (B) After the small groups have articulated their argument in a paragraph or as a list of bullet points, students could be "remixed" in new pairs so that students having worked on opposite viewpoints can compare arguments (each group = 1 "pro" + 1 "con"). Each student would need to explain to their partner (i.e., their new audience) the arguments they developed with their previous collaborators. The repetition/reformulation exercise and need to negotiate meaning in the new context would favor deeper learning. Students could then be asked to react to/assess their partner's argument and express their real opinions on the subject. (C) After this step, the whole class could be reconvened, and the instructor could ask students to manifest their true opinion about the image of the president by, for example, moving to a designated side of the classroom corresponding to their point of view (with one side of the classroom for the "pro" students and the other for the "con" students). In a distance learning context, like-minded students could be placed in large breakout discussion rooms. The students thus newly grouped might be asked to draw up a "master" list of the arguments supporting their assessment and then to reflect upon how their initial opinion might have been modified by the preceding discussion activities. (D) A final debate could be organized or (E) students could be asked to write an op-ed piece summarizing their thoughts. This writing activity could be followed by a reflection on the stylistic elements distinguishing such editorial texts

with a view to underscoring what types of rhetorical strategies can make opinion pieces more compelling.

3) Another way to ask students to consider how this photograph might affect the president's image would be to ask them to put themselves in the shoes of Macron's public relations director. What factors would inform this individual's reaction to the picture?[19] This perspective-adopting activity would naturally lead to a consideration of the role of the president because the reception of the image—positive or negative—would in large part be determined by whether we are considering Macron in terms of his domestic or international stature. Does international opinion impose different expectations than domestic opinion? Why? How would a similar photograph of an American president at a football, baseball, or basketball game be perceived (intercultural comparison)?[20] Can students think of or find images of American presidents in a similar posture?

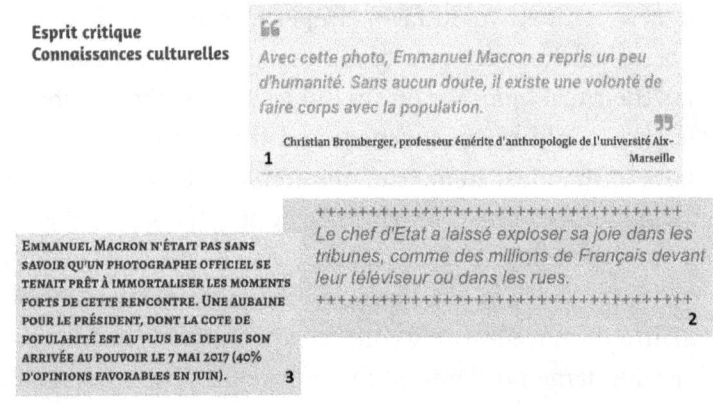

Figure 7.11 [21]

4) Another approach would be to ask students to read through a selection of reactions posted on francophone websites (in the form of articles, blog posts, videos, etc.), asking them to decode the terms of judgment and formulate opinions in light of these arguments. In addition to presenting students with interesting vocabulary and

grammatical constructions, this activity activates higher-order thinking and deepens cultural knowledge because students have to understand, interpret, and evaluate the thoughts of others and comprehend the context of the perspectives. For example, in the first quote shown in figure 7.11, we learn that Macron is perceived as distant or maybe even elitist. We could draw attention to this criticism by asking students to reformulate in French the judgment "a repris un peu d'humanité" in more straightforward terms. In their opinion, is it important that a leader seem like the rest of us? Why? The quotation in box 3 makes reference to low popularity ratings. Students could be asked to research online articles published around the date indicated (May 2017) to discover the political issues motivating criticism of Macron or they could simply propose conjectures as to why his ratings might be low.

Figure 7.12 World Cup Final: France versus Croatia, 2018. © Samir Sagolj.[22]

5) One could also sequence this activity in a way that would begin with a whole-class discussion in which students express whether they think the image conveys a positive or negative image of the president. Then, operating under the assumption that most students will perceive the gesture in a positive light, encourage them to reappraise the situation by introducing other photos

taken at the same event (figures 7.12–13). Students could then be asked to consider a newspaper article qualifying Macron's behavior as "sans retenu" (figure 7.14) and analyze why such an unbridled display of enthusiasm might be harmful to the president's image. To extend this analysis, students could examine a meme with the commentary "Quelle honte" that accompanied a blog post criticizing Macron's behavior (figure 7.15). Before seeing the meme in its editorial context, students could be asked to surmise why the blogger (and meme-maker) would condemn Macron's exuberance as shameful and undignified. Once the headline is introduced, the use of the word "hystérique" could be interrogated (*Que pensez-vous de l'emploi d'un mot comme "hystérique" pour qualifier le comportement du président ?*).

Figure 7.13 © BestImage; image reproduced with permission from Best Image.

Coupe du monde 2018 : une finale "sans retenue" pour Emmanuel Macron
LINFO.RE – créé le 16.07.2018

En quoi un chef d'État qualifié de "sans retenu" pourrait-il nuire à son image publique ?

Vocabulaire utile
- Se lâcher
- Se retenir
- Se maîtriser
- Respecter les codes du protocole
- Oublier les conventions
- Se comporter en président sérieux
- Être surexcité / hystérique

Emmanuel Macron nous fait honte devant Poutine en étant hystérique en finale de coupe du monde

Partager sur Facebook Twitter Google + Il a fallu que Moi Soleil se fasse encore plus remarquer, à croire qu'il était sous poudre de perlimpinpin l'hystérique, les Bleus n'allaient pas lui voler la vedette, franchement, c'était inimaginable, du coup to...

Figures 7.14 and 15 Screen capture[23]

If students haven't mentioned it themselves, attention could be drawn to Vladimir Putin's presence (right corner). In this framing of the scenario, Putin's gaze complicates Macron's gesture in a way not in evidence in the photograph that went viral (figure 7.1), wherein the other people in the box, seen from behind, are not the prominent elements in the photograph. The question of the role of a head of state would impose itself in the context of this consideration (*Quel est le rôle du président de la Ve République ? En quoi consiste institutionnellement son pouvoir ? Quels comportements "spontanés" sont admissibles pour un chef d'état français ? En quoi le président de la République incarne-t-il les valeurs de la nation ?*), which in turn could lead to many cultural discoveries (like the origin, goals, structure, and history of the Fifth Republic) and intercultural comparisons: *Comment le rôle du président est-il conçu aux États-Unis ? Quelle est sa fonction ? Quels sont ses pouvoirs ? Quelles valeurs incarne-t-il ? Quels comportements "spontanés" de la part du président américain pourraient avantager ou nuire à l'image du pays ?* Circling back around, the critique of Macron's enthusiasm as shameful could be interpreted in light of the political bias of the blogger: Does this posting seem to be coming from the political left or right? Are there clues that imply the blogger's political orientation? How might the political orientation of the blogger influence their opinion?[24] Do the blogger's political leanings affect students' reception of their critique?[25]

Cross-Cultural Comparisons: Sports, Culture, and Politics

Figure 7.16 © BestImage; image reproduced with permission from Best Image.

This last series of questions pertaining to the perception of a head of state by the public opens out onto another fructuous terrain for intercultural inquiry and self-reflection (in Byram's sense of encouraging students to be aware of their own historical situatedness and cultural biases, for each nation valorizes sports and its leader's relationship to sports in a very different way).[26] Interrogating the historical, cultural, and ideological underpinnings of observable differences could yield some illuminating insights and lead to a deepened comprehension of both the target and home cultures. For example, images abound of an often-shirtless Vladimir Putin engaged in all kinds of sports typically associated with virility (figures 7.17–19), allowing for comparisons with Macron's very different management of his athletic image. A comparison of the two presidents assuming boxing stances speaks volumes as to the difference in the image they seek

Figure 7.17 www.kremlin.ru27

Figure 7.18 www.kremlin.ru28

Figure 7.19 www.kremlin.ru29

to project.³⁰ Whereas Putin's instrumentalization of his physical prowess and fitness level is engineered to communicate the image of a sort of "surhomme,"³¹ in publicity shots of Macron promoting Paris as host for the 2024 Olympics, there is none of the chest-baring bravado we see in the Putin photographs. Macron plays tennis in his suit and tries his hand at playing para-tennis.³² Although Macron is in fact an avid tennis player, the images of him in tennis contexts that we find on the internet do not feature him as an individual engaging in sport but rather as a head of state participating in sports as they purport to French national goals and collective practices. His interest in seeming like "one of the people" (*jouer la proximité*) is at diametric odds with the rugged individualism and machismo connoted by the Putin shots. What does this difference indicate concerning the values of the two cultures and the idea of leadership? After a serious examination of these questions, students could be "tested" by commenting on a meme making fun of the two presidents in precisely the sports context just considered (figure 7.20).

Figure 7.20 ³³

After students have analyzed and discussed various images of the French and Russian presidents, making comparisons and drawing conclusions, they could turn their attention to comparisons with America. What assumptions do students bring to the table and how do these preconceptions affect their ability to understand and analyze the behavior of leaders from other countries and the role of sports in society? Let's consider, for example, the way in which sports are glorified in the United States as an embodiment of American values. Images abound of American presidents involved in sports: Abe Lincoln chopping wood, the macho Teddy Roosevelt involved in a wide range of sporting activities, the iconic pictures of JFK tossing a football, Gerald Ford as a football star, and Obama playing basketball, football, and golf (figures 7.21–24).[34] Students can be asked to consider what images of American presidents engaged in sports are meant to communicate and what this sports association implies about American values. A speech given by Barack Obama at the Healthy Kids and Safe Sports Concussion Summit in 2014 offers a useful synthesis of how Americans think of sports as reflecting national character: "Sports is fundamental to who we are as Americans and our culture. We're competitive. We're driven. And sports teach us about teamwork and hard work and what it takes to succeed not just on the field but in life." [35] Students could be shown the first part of this assertion ("Sports is fundamental to who we are as Americans and our culture") and asked to respond to questions pertaining to how they understand it (*Êtes-vous d'accord avec cette assertion ? Expliquez votre position. À votre avis, comment cette opinion se justifie-t-elle ? Quelles valeurs américaines le sport incarne-t-il ? Pourriez-vous imaginer un chef d'état français faisant cette identification ?*). Students would probably not have enough exposure to French culture to respond to the last question proposed—*Pourriez-vous imaginer un chef d'état français faisant cette identification ?*—but its inclusion is meant to prepare the way for the reflection to follow. Students could then be shown a longer section of Obama's speech and asked to identify and discuss the values articulated (figure 7.25). The exercise of translating the text into French would be conducive to deeper thinking about the terms in question, especially in the instances where the translation is not straightforward. For example, what does the inappropriateness of the direct translation of "hard work" as *"le travail acharné"* suggest? Is this notion understood differently in the two cultures? Is it valued in the same way?[36]

Figure 7.21 The Railsplitter by J. L. G. Ferris, 1909.[37]
Figure 7.22 "Terrible Teddy" waits for "the unknown" / Keppler, 1904.[38]

In order to begin to make comparisons with the role of sports in French society (and the implications thereof), students can be asked to research images of the last four[41] French and American presidents that feature them in sports contexts and bring their findings into class to be compared and discussed (figure 7.26). Ideally, students can print out the images they find, and the instructor can tape them onto the walls so that the class members can circulate to observe and discuss the images before a whole-class discussion.[42] What kinds of conclusions can we draw by comparing the images? Are the French as invested in sports as Americans? Do they value the same things in sports? How can we tell? Whereas most modern presidents (and indeed most US presidents throughout history) have been strongly and favorably associated with their athleticism,[43] French presidents are not similarly packaged. The images of French presidents that students will find predominantly

Figure 7.23 Gerald Ford on the football field at University of Michigan, 1933.[39]

Figure 7.24 Obama plays basketball with personal aide Reggie Love, 2009.[40]

Voici un extrait plus long du discours dans lequel Obama traite de l'importance du sport dans la conscience collective américaine.
- Quelles sont les valeurs évoquées ?
- Comment traduiriez-vous ce texte ? Y a-t-il des mots pour lesquels il est plus difficile de trouver une bonne traduction en français ?

> "Sports is fundamental to who we are as Americans and our culture. We're <u>competitive</u>. We're <u>driven</u>. And sports teach us about <u>teamwork</u> and <u>hard work</u> and what it takes to succeed not just on the field but in life."
>
> ~ Barack Obama

Figure 7.25

feature them in their official function attending sporting events and lauding the successful exploits of French athletes and teams. What does this difference in orientation suggest? Why don't French presidents integrate their personal engagement with sports as part of the public image they project?[44] What comparisons can we make with respect to ideas of individualism, national feeling, competition, and solidarity? Does the French president's role as official spectator place an emphasis on collective national spectatorship (figure 7.27)?[45]

Comparaisons interculturelles

Recherches — Faites des recherches sur Internet pour trouver des images des derniers quatre présidents de la République dans des contextes sportifs. (*Mitterrand - Chirac – Sarkozy – Hollande*)

Faites les mêmes recherches pour les derniers quatre présidents américains.

Conclusions — Quelles comparaisons pouvons-nous faire sur la manière dont le sport est instrumentalisé par les hommes politiques dans les deux pays ?

Figure 7.26

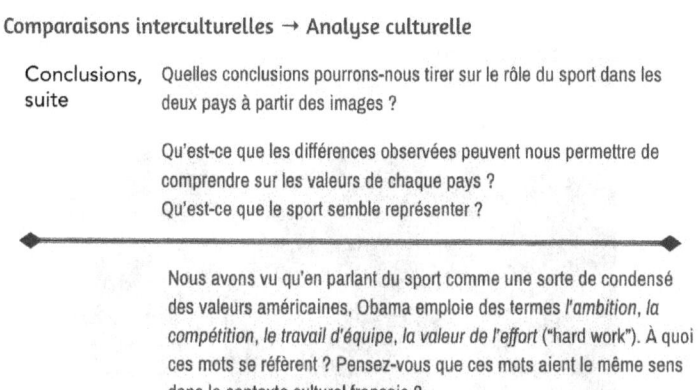

Figure 7.27

Soccer: The Universal Sport

The place of soccer in French (and European, American, and worldwide) culture is another path opening out onto myriad cultural reflections and comparisons. Why is soccer considered the universal sport? Why is its popularity growing in the United States? The increasing popularity and media attention devoted to the FIFA Women's World Cup also provides much material for reflection and allows for the integration of topics concerning gender, sexuality, and parity.[46] Students could be asked to look at posters and other images marketing the event to analyze how the female championship is marketed.[47] How are the players represented? Do these representations defy gender stereotypes? Can they be considered feminist? How does the marketing of the American team compare? One could even integrate into a lesson plan the internet memes generated around Megan Rapinoe, a media star of the US team who has been very vocal about an array of social issues (Rebucci 2019; Dorangeon 2019; Geais 2019). Why would she be pictured in a face-off with Donald Trump?[48]

Figure 7.28 Screen capture of photomontage posted to Twitter by ElElegante101 (@skolanach).[49]

If students were to research some of the issues Rapinoe fights for, it could be interesting to discover whether these issues are of similar importance in France. One could also discuss why Rapinoe's gesture, like Macron's, captured the public imagination and inspired memes. What kinds of observations could a comparison of her gesture and Macron's yield? More concretely, we could ask students (individually or in groups) to choose and research one of the players from the French women's soccer team.[50] The exercise could be rendered more analytical by asking students to focus on the players' countries of origin so as to discuss questions of citizenship, diversity, and perceptions of belonging, as Kristen Nugent and Theresa Catalano propose in a lesson plan based on soccer (2015, 21–22). Students could research the history of women's soccer,[51] or, to practice audio comprehension, students could listen to an interview with Emmanuel Macron concerning the French women's team (Remia 2019). The French and the

American presidents' support of the women's teams could be researched and compared.

One could ask students to assess the idea of soccer as an instrument of social change. For example, since France's last triumph at the World Cup in 1998, the mantra of *Black-Blanc-Beur* has circulated as a way to celebrate cultural diversity in France. How have the slogan and the hopes it expresses held up over time?[52] France's colonial history could also be considered through the lens of soccer (Diome 2005). One could look at how soccer engages with political issues, such as pay equity (evoked above) or social injustice. The comparison of Megan Rapinoe's "taking a knee" and the French team's refusal to sing the French national anthem (*siffler "La Marseillaise"*) could offer a rich cross-cultural context for reflection. The possibilities for cultural exposure, intercultural comparisons, and critical reflection are endless.

PART II: WHAT'S IN A MEME? ANALYZING THE DISCURSIVE FUNCTION OF MEMES AS UNITS OF COMMUNICATION

In the preceding section, we focused on how a single photograph of the president of the French Republic could be used as a point of departure for the exploration of a variety of social, cultural, and political topics, notably the role and function of sports in society, the expectations attendant to representations associated with a head of state, and how a sitting president might use sports to reflect their role. In the next two sections, I would like to look at how the Macron image captured the public's attention and inspired countless internet memes in order to consider ways to translate this cultural phenomenon into productive classroom material. The transformation of Macron's image into a viral internet meme offers a rich opportunity to engage students in the analysis of the discursive specificities of an internet meme. How does this hybrid mode of online communication function, and what are its implications?

Let's begin with a definition of an internet meme. The term "meme" was proposed in 1976 by Richard Dawkins in his book *The Selfish Gene* to describe, by way of a genetic analogy, the manner in which cultural ideas and habits (such as religion or customs) replicate, circulate, and evolve over generations. The term was later co-opted to describe the internet phenomenon of images being annotated or recontextualized and circulated through social media channels in order to convey messages. A meme is described as "viral" when it captures the attention of a critical mass of people and is replicated to a heightened degree. Some well-known viral internet memes are the "Gangnam Style" video or the distracted boyfriend meme.[53] Students are very familiar with this cultural form, and many probably use memes on a regular basis to express ideas, but they may not have spent a lot of time reflecting on the nature and implications of this textual form. What makes this mode of communication so successful, so "viral"? Are internet memes an "impactful" means by which to communicate information? Do messages that are transmitted through this medium stick? Are memes a legitimate form of communication? Are there dangers implicit in this hybrid form? Below is a possible sequence for engaging students with these questions.

1. A first step could be to show students how the image of Macron's celebratory gesture was extracted from its context, converted into a .png file with a green backdrop, and associated with the hashtag #PoseTonMacron in order to invite internet users to recontextualize it ("*le détourner*") as a meme (figure 7.29).[54] Students could be asked to guess the meaning of the hashtag #PoseTonMacron, with prompts to lead them to deduce that the verb "poser" refers to the image's placement in different contexts (figure 7.30). To follow up, they could be asked what other sorts of gestures come to mind and if they can think of other contexts in which to reposition the image.

Figures 7.29[55] and 30

2. To focus on grammar and vocabulary, the instructor could exploit some of the more playful versions of the meme and ask students to translate the various situations into words.[56] Memes could be selected and grouped according to theme in order to target specific lexical fields.

For example, many of the transpositions feature Macron in ludic sports situations; memes of this type could be used to work on sports vocabulary and the grammar associated with it through an open-ended communicative activity asking students to describe what they see, a vocabulary matching exercise, or a cloze activity targeting grammar points like *jouer à* and *faire de* + name of sport (figures 7.31–33).

Figures 7.31[57] and 32[58]

Parties du corps
Faire des développés avec des haltères est une excellent manière de renforcer les muscles des **épaules** et du haut du **dos**.

Jouer à un sport / Faire du sport
Il fait **de la** musculation.
Il joue **au** basket.
Il fait **de la** boxe.

 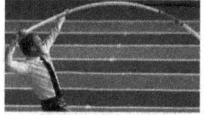
Verbes au présent / L'emploi de l'infinitif
Il **saute** en l'air pour marquer un panier.

Il **tient** une perche pour **faire** du saut à la perche.

Figure 7.33

3. In order to facilitate reflection on the mechanics of memes, we can ask students to work with well-known memes from their own culture before addressing the Macron meme specifically. The class could be divided into groups of three or four with a different meme attributed to each group. Some examples of well-known memes are "This is fine,"[59] "One does not simply,"[60] and the distracted boyfriend.[61] Students could be asked to describe the representations and explain the phenomenon or type of situation addressed by each meme. Following are some other suggested activities that vary in difficulty and complexity so as to be exploitable in a variety of pedagogical contexts.

4. "This is fine" (figure 7.34) is the simplest of the memes. Students can imitate its most popular variation—replacing the dog with a political figure—to share opinions on social and political issues that interest them.[62] Or, more simply, the meme could be used to initiate a discussion wherein students talk about their own experiences

with difficult situations and how they tend to cope while learning new idiomatic vocabulary.⁶³

Figure 7.34 "This is fine." ©KC Green, reprinted with artist's permission.

5. The "One does not simply" meme, which plays on Boromir's exasperated protestation that "One does not simply walk into Mordor" in the film *The Lord of the Rings*, allows students to talk about a popular movie franchise but also brings up questions of translation, for the tone and nuance of the expression "One does not simply . . ." is not easily translated into French.⁶⁴ Asking students to try to come up with an adequate translation will call their attention to how rarely translation offers an exact match and could also be used to draw their attention to certain grammar points such as the adverbial group "si facilement" and the use of the geographical preposition "en" with Mordor. The work with translation could also lead to a discussion of the cultural specificity of humor. Are there French versions of this meme? What does an American meme's presence, absence, or adaptation in the landscape of French meme-making imply or reveal? Students can go to the website MemeCenter, an aggregator of French memes, and consider and decipher the French variants of the meme.⁶⁵ More simply, students could collaboratively or individually add their own captions

to the meme using a meme generator site like imgflip or makeameme.⁶⁶

Figure 7.35 Meme produced by Heidi Holst-Knudsen.⁶⁷

6. The distracted boyfriend meme is one of the most well-known and viral of all memes. After discussing one of its iconic iterations—Socialism / The Youth / Capitalism (figure 7.36)—students could modify the meme with texts of their own making. This meme also lends itself to discussions about gender stereotypes and sexism, having provoked much criticism because of the gender norms and power structure it implies (Levenson 2018).

Figure 7.36 Twitter post by @OmarEssamLhc; reprinted with author's permission.⁶⁸

7. After students have been warmed up by their discussion of specific memes, they could be asked to extend their reflection by engaging with a series of more fine-tuned questions. This exercise should probably be done as homework, either as a written assignment or as a discussion board posting, to allow students to think deeply about the questions and come to class primed for participation in higher-order critical activities. The following is a list of possible questions:

   1. *Qu'est-ce qu'un mème ? Comment les mèmes sont-ils transmis ?*
   2. *Quels sont les attributs stylistiques des mèmes ?*
   3. *Quels types de messages transmet-on généralement avec des mèmes ?*
   4. *Quelles sortes de réactions visent-ils ?*
   5. *Qui se sert de ce format pour communiquer ses idées ?*
   6. *Le mème internet, est-ce un mode efficace de transmission des idées ?*
   7. *Y a-t-il des raisons de se méfier des mèmes ?*

8. This reflection exercise could be followed by a preliminary brainstorming activity that would allow the class to pool ideas and see how everyone's ideas about memes correspond. An online polling platform such as Poll Everywhere or the polling function on the Zoom platform would allow the instructor to post a question such as "*Quels mots vous viennent à l'esprit quand vous pensez à un mème internet ?*" Students could respond by proposing terms with their smart phones, tablets, or computers. Their responses would be immediately aggregated and projected onto a large screen: as students write, their words pop up in real time for everyone to see.[69] Poll Everywhere allows the instructor to select how the words

are displayed: for example, as a word cloud or ranked in order of frequency. With student ideas immediately accessible, the instructor can use their words as prompts to ask for explanations, challenge assumptions, or make connections. The words will also serve as segues to the discussion of the reflection questions assigned for homework. For example, qualifying words like "drôle," "caricature," "viral," or "intertextuel" purport directly to questions of style, transmission, communicative function, and judgments as to whether memes are a serious mode of communication (figure 7.37). A desirable product of this first brainstorming activity would be a list of defining features of an internet meme, thereby formulating a collaborative response to reflection question 2 (*Quels sont les attributs stylistiques des mèmes ?*).[70]

Discussion d'ensemble

Êtes-vous d'accord avec toutes ces qualifications ?
Y a-t-il das mots ou des descriptions qui vous étonnent / intéressent … ?

Figure 7.37

9. Activities following this exercise could be devised to get students to test their hypotheses in the light of practical examples. For example, in order to address question 4 (*Qui se sert de ce format pour communiquer ses idées ?*), the instructor could lead students through a consideration of internet memes of different types, such as "reaction" memes,[71] memes used for marketing purposes,[72] or political memes. An interesting case study could be the infamous "The Wall Is Coming" meme that Donald Trump posted to his Twitter account, in which he uses a reference to popular culture (the television series *Game of Thrones*) to communicate his intention to build a wall between Mexico and the United States (figure 7.38). Consideration of this meme would encourage critical reflection that integrates the students' previous reflections on the role and comportment of a head of state. A selection of *détournements* of the Macon meme for political commentary could nourish a consideration of questions 3, 5, and 6 (figure 7.39).

Figure 7.38 Screen capture of a tweet posted by Donald Trump, January 5, 2019.[73]

Comparez la fonction de communication de ces deux mèmes.

Pensez-vous que les mèmes soient un moyen de communication efficace ? Justifiez votre réponse.

Figure 7.39[74]

PART III. #POSETONMACRON AS VECTOR ONTO FRENCH CULTURE

One of the aims of these reflection exercises is to underscore how culturally embedded memes are. Images attract attention and "stick" as a function of how they capture the preoccupations of a given moment in a given society. Their reception and subsequent proliferation depend on how well they tap into and express cultural assumptions, attitudes, and referents. If these elements are poorly communicated or not recognized, a meme will not "take." Trump's "The Wall Is Coming" meme loses a measure of its sinister overtone if the intertextual reference to *Game of Thrones* and the wordplay on the show's famous expression "Winter is coming" are not recognized. The use of popular culture by the president of the United States to communicate his position on immigration is a charged and extremely culturally specific gesture that allows for much critical reflection about ideology, political values, attitudes toward violence, popular culture, appropriate presidential registers, and so on. Many of the memes inspired by Emmanuel Macron's World Cup exultation offer similarly productive windows into French culture. In this final section, I will focus on a selection of the Macron memes that serve as entry points into the treatment of a variety of topics in French culture. The examples that follow offer ideas for exposing students to contemporary political issues, French history, French art, and aspects of daily life in France.

Politics

Figure 7.40 Screen capture of a tweet posted to Twitter by @_miss_ives_.[75]

The meme of a drowning Macron (figure 7.40) could serve as a good introduction to lessons on French political issues because the simplicity of the image allows for its use in more elementary classrooms. Students could begin, as usual, by finding the words and syntax to describe the image and then interpret its message. After students have expressed that the image is a metaphor for a failed political agenda or diminishing approval ratings, they could be asked to research Macron's political platform and which of his programs have come under attack. They could come to class ready to share what they have learned via a short exposé or through other, more collaborative exercises.

Another follow-up activity after students have researched Macron's political program as homework would be to have them interpret a group of memes making reference to some of his contested initiatives or polemical statements. An assortment of such memes could be presented, and students, in groups, could try to explicate as many as possible in light of their research. Or, alternatively, students could be assigned the memes and asked to research the references evoked by them and interpret their critique. Figures 7.41 to 7.47 offer some examples, and figure 7.48 proposes the assignment.

Figure 7.41 Meme posted by @airwone17.[76]

Figure 7.42 Meme posted to Twitter by @Zilou7.[77]

Figure 7.43 Twitter post by @RoseDeBerne.[78]

Figure 7.44 Twitter post by @teddyruptif.[79]

Figure 7.45 Instagram post by bertrand_gicquiaux.[80]

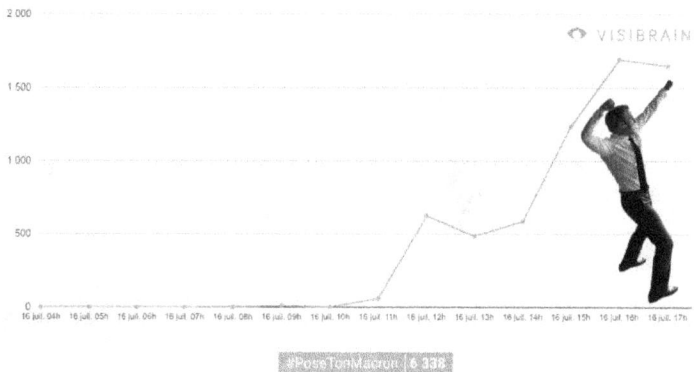

Figure 7.46 Meme posted to Twitter by @visibrain.[81]

Figure 7.47 Instagram post by @cedfernand.[82]

Faites des recherches sur le mème qui vous a été attribué pour comprendre l'allusion polituque et venez en cours prêt·e à partager ce que vous avez appris avec la classe.

Pensez-vous que les mèmes soient un moyen de communication efficace ?

Figure 7.48

Art History

Art history is another cultural angle to which internet memes of Macron offer access. The superposition of Macron's image onto iconic works of art serves as a perfect prompt for making connections between foreign language study and other disciplines (Kern 2008). Consider, for example, André Gunthert's meme in which he integrates Macron into Jacques-Louis David's 1785 painting *The Oath of the Horatii* (figure 7.49), Kt Kt's substitution of Macron in Bonaparte's place in Jacques-Louis David's *Bonaparte Crossing the Great Saint-Bernard Pass* (1800–1805) (figure 7.50), and Antoine Colombani's reinterpretation of Eugène Delacroix's *Liberty Leading the People* (1830) (figure 7.51).

Besides exploring with students these nineteenth-century painters and the political contexts in which they were working, one could also ask students to interpret the memes' political critique in the light of contemporary politics. Why, for example, does the revolutionary context impose itself as a reference? In the case of the comparison to Napoleon, students could be asked what characteristics they associate with Napoleon and which ones might be considered as negative in a modern-day president and why. As a follow-up activity, they could be shown an assortment of caricatures of Macron activating different aspects of the Napoleon trope and asked to collaboratively decode the cartoons.[86]

Figure 7.49 Twitter post by @gunthert.[83]

Figure 7.50 "Macroleone" by Kt Kt.[84]

Figure 7.51 Twitter post by @gugus_colmbn.⁸⁵

Cultural Practices

Other variations on the Macron meme point to cultural practices. To cite two examples, the positioning of Macron cheering the school lunch menu (figure 7.52) allows for a discussion of the French gastronomic tradition and its importance even at the level of school lunches. Students could be asked if they know what *cordon bleu* is and if they would expect such a dish to be served in their cafeteria. Why not? Do they find it surprising that this type of dish is a normal offering in French schools? How might they explain this? Macron positioned astride a fighter jet in the context of a Bastille Day celebration (figure 7.53) could be used to discuss the French holiday, the history to which it refers, and the nature of the institutional commemoration of it (*la grandeur française?*) and how the ceremonies reflect the French nation's sense of itself (with comparisons to how the Fourth of July is officially celebrated in the United States). To what does "l'erreur" refer?

Figure 7.52 Meme posted to Twitter by @Raffassine.[87]

Figure 7.53 Twitter post by @Antoine_ESL.[88]

CONCLUSION

The activities presented in this chapter were formulated with a view toward consistently anchoring language acquisition activities within rich cultural contexts that not only allow for exposure to elements of French culture but also push students to think critically about important social and political issues through intercultural comparison. The hope is that by consistently reflecting back on their own culture while learning about the target culture, they will sharpen their analytical skills, enrich their perspectives, and become comfortable questioning cultural norms that they might otherwise take for granted. An associated goal is that through their analysis of internet memes, students will become more attuned to how this very pervasive form of communication functions and therefore adopt a more critical stance in their reception of this and other forms of rapidly disseminated media. The internet memes reviewed in this chapter are meant to offer a fun, multifaceted, and productive point of engagement to inspire reflection on both French and American culture.

NOTES

1. Michael Byram, *Teaching and Assessing Intercultural Communicative Competence* (Clevedon, UK: Multilingual Matters: 1997).
2. Richard Kern, "Reconciling the Language-Literature Split through Literacy," *ADFL Bulletin* 33, no. 3 (Spring 2002): 20–24.
3. Kate Paesani, Heather Willis Allen, and Beatrice Dupuy, *A Multiliteracies Framework for Collegiate Foreign Language Teaching* (Upper Saddle River, NJ: Pearson, 2016).
4. As of this writing, Donald Trump, Putin, and Bernie Sanders are among the most popular internet memes on sites like Twitter and Reddit (Leclerc 2018).
5. Paesani, Willis Allen, and Dupuy, *A Multiliteracies Framework*.
6. I always use a political cartoon featuring the French head of state as a first-day-of-class communicative exercise precisely because it offers an easy point of entry for students to make observations and express opinions. In addition, there is an abundance of this type of material on the web to choose from, with many such images associating the American and French presidents.

7. Padlet, https://padlet.com.
8. Photo: OECD/Andrew Wheeler; "OECD Forum 2018—Arrival of Emmanuel Macron—President of France," by Organisation for Economic Co-operation and Development, licensed under CC BY-NC 2.0, https://www.flickr.com/photos/32771300@N02/42402983352.
9. The photograph of Brigitte Macron is licensed under the Creative Commons Attribution 2.0 Generic license (https://creativecommons.org/licenses/by/2.0/): Brigitte Macron, July 6, 2017, cropped from https://commons.wikimedia.org/wiki/File:Visita_de_Trabajo_a_Francia_(35633555171).jpg.
10. Lorin W. Anderson and David R. Krathwohl, eds., *A Taxonomy for Learning, Teaching, and Assessing: A Revision of Bloom's Taxonomy of Educational Objectives* (New York: Longman, 2001).
11. William Grabe and Robert B. Kaplan, *Theory and Practice of Writing: An Applied Linguistic Perspective* (New York: Longman, 1996).
12. "Knowledge telling" discussion questions:
    1. *Aimez-vous regarder les matchs de sport ? Pourquoi ou pourquoi pas? Est-ce que tous les gens dans votre entourage (famille, amis) ont la même attitude que vous ?*
    2. *Si vous aimez assister aux matchs de sport...*
    3. *Préférez-vous aller voir des matchs en live ou regarder des matchs à la télévision (à la maison ? dans un bar ?) Au stade, quels sièges préférez-vous ? Préférez-vous être avec la grande foule ou rester à l'abri dans une tribune privée ? Comment vous habillez-vous quand vous allez à des matches de sport ? Pourquoi ?*
13. Higher-order critical thinking discussion (or short essay) questions:
    1. *Qu'est-ce que la manière dont une personne s'habille pour assister à un match de sport pourrait nous dire sur sa position ou sa fonction sociale ?*
    2. *Et sa place dans le stade ? Voyez-vous des injustices inscrites dans la question de l'accessibilité des sièges ?*
14. Mike Weed, "The Pub as a Virtual Football Fandom Venue: An Alternative to 'Being there'?" *Soccer and Society* 8, no. 2–3 (2007): 399–414.
15. Boris Helleu, "Voir ou vivre ? Qu'est-ce qu'être un spectateur d'un match de foot ?" *France Foot*, February 16, 2017.
16. Florent Guénard and Igor Martinache, "Dossier : L'empire du foot." La vie des idées (Collège de France website, 2010).
17. See Sasin 2018.
18. See Lesaffre and Galibert 2018 for an image of the front pages of several international newspapers featuring the photograph:

19. *Vous êtes la directrice des communications de Macron. Quelle est votre réaction à cette image et à sa large diffusion sur internet ? Pensez-vous que cela donne une image positive ou négative de la présidence ?*
20. *Quel type d'image un leader national doit-il cultiver et projeter ? Pourquoi ? Quelles valeurs le chef d'état est-il censé incarner ? En France, aux États-Unis ? Évoquez des exemples dans les deux contextes.*
21. Quotations 1 and 3: Fachaux 2018; quotation 2: "Mondial" 2018.
22. Photo reprinted with permission from Reuters.
23. Nanouche 2018. To access the meme made by the blogger, see http://lagauchematuer.fr/wp-content/uploads/2018/07/poutine-macron2.jpg.
24. The opinion piece was published on an extreme-right website called La Gauche m'a tuer. For a report on the political orientation and reliability of this website, see Andraca 2018.
25. *Cette critique semble-t-elle venir de la gauche ou de la droite ? Y a-t-il des indices à discerner quant à l'orientation politique du blogueur / de la blogueuse ? Comment son orientation politique pourrait-elle influencer sa prise de position ? Comment la position politique de l'auteur pourrait-elle influer sur votre réception de sa critique ?*
26. Byram 1997.
27. "Vladimir Putin in Tuva 2007," licensed under the Creative Commons Attribution 4.0 License, https://commons.wikimedia.org/wiki/File:Vladimir_Putin_in_Tuva_2007-49.jpg.
28. This file comes from the website of the President of the Russian Federation and is licensed under the Creative Commons Attribution 4.0 License, http://en.kremlin.ru/events/president/news/51153/photos/43024.
29. "Putin Sochi Ice Hockey 4 Jan 2014," licensed under the Creative Commons Attribution 4.0 License, https://commons.wikimedia.org/wiki/File:Putin_Sochi_ice_hockey_4_jan_2014_-_03.jpg.
30. See, for example, the juxtaposition of photos of Putin and Macron boxing: http://www.a-droite-fierement.fr/wp-content/uploads/2017/07/poutine-macron-en-boxeurs.jpg.
31. Astrid Landon, "Macron en Top Gun : pourquoi la communication de Macron n'est plus si drôle" (Challenges website, 2017).
32. Th.B. 2017; image available at https://www.leparisien.fr/resizer/H8J3VItOlF-Dzf5Us6HGA8oGU6SE=/932x582/arc-anglerfish-eu-central-1-prod-leparisien.s3.amazonaws.com/public/WC5FK5ZLTQMBUJEM2JTl3CHEJI.jpg.
33. Image posted on the website La Chronique Facile (du Mercredi) ("Pose ton Macron" 2018), author of the meme unknown, https://lachroniquefacile.fr/2018/07/18/pose-ton-macron-comment-se-moquer-dune-photo/. To

extend the activity to include a consideration of American presidents in this context, see variations on the Putin riding a bear meme featuring Trump astride a lion and Obama on a bike.

34. For these images and more, see the photo gallery of American presidents in sporting contexts associated with Kiger 2019. For an image of JFK playing football, see https://www.thesportscol.com/2019/06/the-kennedy-clan-and-sports/.
35. Obama 2014.
36. Possible translation: *Le sport est fondamental pour notre identité en tant qu'Américains et notre culture. Nous sommes* compétitifs. *Nous sommes ambitieux. Et le sport nous enseigne la valeur du* travail d'équipe *et de* l'effort *et ce qu'il faut pour réussir non seulement sur le terrain, mais dans la vie.*
37. Public domain, available at http://www.everythinglincoln.com/articles/autobio.html.
38. Public domain, available on the website of Library of Congress, https://www.loc.gov/pictures/item/2011645537/.
39. Public Domain, courtesy Gerald R. Ford Library, available at http://www.ford.utexas.edu/images/avproj/pop-ups/H0035-03.html.
40. Public domain, the Official White House photostream, https://www.flickr.com/photos/obamawhitehouse/3993800443/.
41. Obviously, choosing how far back to ask students to go would depend on the aims of the instructor. I chose as far back as four previous presidents in order to include François Mitterrand as an example of an especially intellectual, not particularly sporty president.
42. Or, in an online class setting, students could post images found to a common Google Slides document and review the images collaboratively in small groups (breakout rooms) before convening for a whole-class discussion.
43. For an overview of American presidents and the sports associated with them, see Kiger 2019.
44. See Billard 2017 for an interesting examination of this topic.
45. *De quelle manière les présidents français sont-ils associés au sport et pourquoi ? Comment le sport est-il perçu en France ? Quels sont les sports les plus pratiqués et les plus populaires en France ?*
46. See, for example, Polverini 2019; and "Inégalités salariales" 2019.
47. Official publicity poster for the 2019 Women's World Cup, https://imgur.com/r/soccer/zToOTCl.
48. Reproduced with permission from ElElegante101 (@skolanach); meme posted to Twitter, June 28, 2019, https://twitter.com/skolanach/status/1144722538129326080.

49. Reprinted with the creator's permission.
50. For descriptions of the twenty-three players on the French women's team, see Trilat 2019.
51. See, for example, the dossier dedicated to the evolution of women's participation in the sport published by Mediapart (Correia 2019).
52. See, for example, Leprince 2018; and Billard and Noisette 2018.
53. Detailed explanations of most memes can be found on the website Know Your Meme: https://knowyourmeme.com/memes/gangnam-style; https://knowyourmeme.com/search?q=distracted+boyfriend.
54. "La célébration de Macron" 2018. I am very grateful to Ronan Daniel, editor in chief of the website Topito, for sharing the origin of the hashtag, which he and collaborators at Topito created to inspire people to play with the image. To stimulate interest in the hashtag, Daniel and his collaborators created some of the first memes and associated them with #PoseTonMacron. They then shared the best versions in a blog post titled "Top 20 des meilleurs détournements photoshop de Macron pendant la finale."
55. Twitter post reproduced with permission from Ronan Daniel.
56. For an inventory of many of the memes created based on the Macron image, see Twitter #PoseTonMacron: https://twitter.com/hashtag/PoseTonMacron?src=hashtag_click and "Pose ton Macron" 2018.
57. I am grateful for the permission to refer to these memes granted to me by their creators: Ronan Daniels for the first three in clockwise order (rugby, pole vault, weightlifting); Anthony Hammard for the meme of Macron on horseback; @_Green_Shadow for the volleyball meme; Pierrot Dactile for the basketball meme. All of these memes appear on Twitter under the hashtag #PoseTonMacron: https://twitter.com/search?q=%23PoseTonMacron&src=typed_query.
58. I am grateful for the permission to include the boxing meme from its creator @Meeea (Twitter).
59. Image on the website Know Your Meme, https://knowyourmeme.com/memes/this-is-fine. For an explanation of the meme's enduring success, see Bartley 2020. See also Orsini 2016.
60. Image on the website Know Your Meme, https://knowyourmeme.com/memes/one-does-not-simply-walk-into-mordor.
61. Image on the website Know Your Meme, https://knowyourmeme.com/memes/distracted-boyfriend. For a discussion of the meme's origins and success, see Barrett 2017.
62. A famous example is the superimposition of Trump; a meme template of this version appears on the meme-generator website imgflip, https://imgflip.com/memetemplate/141027278/trump---this-is-fine.

63. *Y a-t-il une situation dans votre vie que vous hésitez à affronter ? Avez-vous tendance à fuir les problèmes ou à y faire face ? Faites-vous l'autruche quand vous ne savez pas comment régler un problème ? Voilez-vous la face ou affrontez-vous les situations difficiles ou conflictuelles ?*
64. A good translation, but not the only one, would be "*On n'entre pas si facilement en Mordor.*" The adverbial group and the geographic preposition could be interesting topics to discuss. For the now generic "One does not simply" meme, the translation "*Il ne s'agit pas de simplement*" could be an alternative.
65. http://www.memecenter.fr/meme/boromir/.
66. https://imgflip.com/memegenerator; https://makeameme.org/.
67. Meme created on imgflip on August 11, 2020, image link, https://imgflip.com/i/4b4122
68. For the image as cited in Barrett 2017, see https://pbs.twimg.com/media/DHl1OdZXYAQymnU?format=jpg&name=medium.
69. Poll Everywhere, https://www.polleverywhere.com/.
70. Example of a possible list:

    Caractéristiques d'un mème internet: communique une idée concise, syntaxe simple / minimale, ton : humoristique et / ou idéologique, référence intertextuelle, juxtaposition atypique, rapidement proliféré sur Internet, éphémère (. . . ?)
71. See, for example, the eye rolling Robert Downey Jr. meme (https://knowyourmeme.com/memes/eye-rolling-robert-downey-jr) or the Grumpy Cat meme (https://knowyourmeme.com/memes/grumpy-cat).
72. The company Go Study Australia uses a series of memes to communicate items of cultural interest to potential clients: https://www.gostudy.fr/blog/les-francais-en-australie-en-memes/.
73. At the time of writing this chapter and prior to this account's suspension, available at https://twitter.com/realDonaldTrump/status/1081735898679701505/photo/1. For a discussion of the meme, see Leclerc-Mougne 2019.
74. Thank you to Teddyswood (@Teddyruptif) for permission to reference his *La La Land* meme, posted to his Twitter account on July 16, 2018 (https://pbs.twimg.com/media/DiOkIC5WsAEz3Mr?format=jpg&name=medium). Thank you to Patrizio Miranda for allowing me to use the second image, which he first posted to his Facebook page in 2018 (https://scontent-bos3-1.xx.fbcdn.net/v/t1.15752-9/48417608_809280819420175_4578400112077701120_n.png?_nc_cat=103&_nc_sid=b96e70&_nc_ohc=aGuaOeIQKQcAX9LAJLY&_nc_ht=s-content-bos3-1.xx&oh=3e87e172e3ba683ba300ad5d50030e90&oe=5F38C7B6).

75. Posted to Twitter, July 17, 2018, https://twitter.com/hashtag/posetonmacron?lang=gl; image available at https://pbs.twimg.com/media/DiUmvebWAAE6uz_?format=jpg&name=large.
76. Meme cited in the article "Pose ton Macron : Comment se moquer d'une photo": https://lachroniquefacile.fr/wp-content/uploads/2018/07/DiNxol-GXcAAM5AK.jpg.
77. Reproduced with the permission of creator. Meme posted to Twitter, February 19, 2020, https://twitter.com/Zilou7/status/1233865373705031683/photo/1.
78. Meme posted to the #PoseTonMacron hashtag to Twitter, https://twitter.com/search?q=%23PoseTonMacron&src=typed_query; image available at https://pbs.twimg.com/media/DiOFzohWkAEoZBE?format=jpg&name=900x900.
79. Meme posted to Twitter, July 16, 2018, https://twitter.com/Teddyruptif/status/1018809051994615808. Reprinted with permission from author.
80. Posted to Instagram by bertrand_gicquiaux, https://www.instagram.com/p/BlXwAsVDX1N/?igshid=1726f79u0qfxj. Accessed July 5, 2020.
81. Meme posted to Twitter, July 16, 2018, https://twitter.com/hashtag/posetonmacron?lang=fr; image available at https://pbs.twimg.com/media/DiPTbj5XoAE57FZ?format=png&name=medium.
82. Posted to Instagram by cedfernand, https://www.instagram.com/p/BlXlxO-SHADC/?igshid=po2y7tjj8fo3. Accessed July 5, 2020. Reproduced with permission from author.
83. Thank you to André Gunthert for permitting me to reprint his Twitter post of July 16, 2018, https://twitter.com/hashtag/posetonmacron?lang=fr; image available at https://pbs.twimg.com/media/DiQB4a6WkAAt6rj?format=jpg&name=900x900.
84. Thank you to Kt Kt for giving me the right to reprint his meme, posted to his Facebook page in July 2018; image available at https://www.leparisien.fr/resizer/BB7345rlP2b8kKEcTSO5U3SY4lw=/1095x1280/arc-anglerfish-eu-central-1-prod-leparisien.s3.amazonaws.com/public/J4SJES5EESW2G26ISI5B-VW4TYI.jpg.
85. Posted to the #PoseTonMacron hashtag to Twitter, July 16, 2018, https://twitter.com/hashtag/PoseTonMacron; image available at https://pbs.twimg.com/media/DiQlyJYXcAECM97?format=jpg&name=900x900.
86. Here are some image addresses linking to a few examples: https://lh5.googleusercontent.com/Gjhsw_1KSxysNEoW-_hokZqWY64042g8vnTkc-BimSxqZktCArtu_SGno-rgL5Xe789cE2eiEuEW6IaLDttU-tiT-szLwIvPgzSIuCbP; and https://lh3.googleusercontent.com/Sour9HVP7zyF5nKWbuCizpwho-53roiZUyjWLCQwuMMd9lM_HDyY8fcNyK8vmwzrXoxv_DMVxtBNHh-2MEiA7RGR-935WeTV9DXpghjG27.

87. Posted to Twitter, July 16, 2018, https://twitter.com/Raffassine/status/1018879547004121089.
88. Posted to Twitter, July 16, 2018, https://twitter.com/hashtag/posetonmacron?lang=fr. Reproduced with permission from Antoine Eisele.

REFERENCES

"Mondial : Macron explose de joie sur le but français." 2018. *Sport24 Info* (blog), https://www.sport24info.ma/football/mondial-macron-explose-de-joie-sur-le-but-francais/. Accessed July 5, 2020.

Anderson, Lorin W., and David R. Krathwohl, eds. 2001. *A Taxonomy for Learning, Teaching, and Assessing: A Revision of Bloom's Taxonomy of Educational Objectives*. New York: Longman.

Andraca, Robin. 2018. "Le site «La gauche m'a tuer» est-il fiable ?" *Libération*, June 18. https://www.liberation.fr/checknews/2018/06/18/le-site-la-gauche-m-a-tuer-est-il-fiable_1659333.

Barrett, Brian. 2017. "The 'Distracted Boyfriend' Meme's Photographer Explains All." *Wired*, August 28. https://www.wired.com/story/distracted-boyfriend-meme-photographer-interview/?mbid=social_fb. French translation of the article in *Vanity Fair*: https://www.vanityfair.fr/savoir-vivre/story/le-photographe-derriere-le-meme-du-distracted-boyfriend-explique-les-raisons-de-son-succes/3472.

Bartley, Terry. 2020. "This Is Fine: The Meme's Meaning & Why It's More Relevant in 2020 Than Ever Before." *Screen Rant*, May 27. https://screenrant.com/this-is-fine-meme-meaning-relevance-2020/.

Billard, Sébastien. 2017. "Les présidents et le sport : qui imagine De Gaulle en short ?" *Le Nouvel Obervateur*, July 16. https://www.nouvelobs.com/politique/20170705.OBS1666/les-presidents-et-le-sport-qui-imagine-de-gaulle-en-short.html.

Billard, Sébastien, and Thierry Noisette. 2018. "Coupe du Monde 1998 : 'Blacks, blancs, beurs : pourvu que ça dure...' *Le Nouvel Observateur*, June 26. https://www.nouvelobs.com/sport/coupe-du-monde-2018/20180612.OBS8054/coupe-du-monde-1998-blacks-blancs-beurs-pourvu-que-ca-dure.html.

Britton, David. 2020. "The Best *Distracted Boyfriend* Memes." *The Dot*, April 3. https://www.dailydot.com/unclick/distracted-boyfriend-memes/.

Byram, Michael. 1997. *Teaching and Assessing Intercultural Communicative Competence*. Clevedon, UK: Multilingual Matters.

———. 2012. "Language Awareness and (Critical) Cultural Awareness—Relationships, Comparisons and Contrasts." *Language Awareness* 21, no. 1–2: 5–13.

Correia, Mickaël. 2019. "La longue marche féministe du football." Series of 5 articles. Mediapart, June–July. https://www.mediapart.fr/journal/dossier/international/notre-serie-la-longue-marche-feministe-du-football.

"Coupe du monde 2018 : une finale 'sans retenue' pour Emmanuel Macron." 2018. *L'Info.re*, July 16. https://www.linfo.re/sports/football/coupe-du-monde-2018-une-finale-sans-retenue-pour-emmanuel-macron.

Dawkins, Richard. 2006 [1976]. *The Selfish Gene*. New York: Oxford University Press.

Diome, Fatou. 2005. *Le ventre de l'Atlantique*. Paris: Livre de poche.

Dorangeon, Théo. 2019. "Alex Morgan et Megan Rapinoe, deux femmes en mission." *Le Parisien*, July 7. http://www.leparisien.fr/sports/football/coupe-du-monde/etats-unis-pays-bas-alex-morgan-et-megan-rapinoe-deux-femmes-en-mission-07-07-2019-8111337.php.

"En images : Les mille talents de 'Super Poutine.'" 2018. *Le Nouvel Observateur*, August 20. http://www.nouvelobs.com/galeries-photos/photo/20120509.OBS5199/en-images-les-mille-talents-de-super-poutine.html.

Fachaux, Laurie. 2018. "Coupe du Monde : Macron, une communication 2 étoiles." TV5, July 16. https://information.tv5monde.com/info/coupe-du-monde-macron-une-communication-2-etoiles-250041.

François. 2018. "Top 20 des meilleurs détournements photoshop de Macron pendant la finale." *Topito*, July 16. http://www.topito.com/top-meilleur-detournement-photoshop-macron.

Geais, Pierrick. 2019. "Megan Rapinoe, star du foot et nouvelle icône anti-Trump." *Vanity Fair*, July 5. https://www.vanityfair.fr/pouvoir/politique/story/megan-rapinoe-star-du-foot-et-nouvelle-icone-anti-trump/6604.

Grabe, William, and Robert B. Kaplan. 1996. *Theory and Practice of Writing: An Applied Linguistic Perspective*. New York: Longman.

Guénard, Florent, and Igor Martinache. 2010. "Dossier : L'empire du foot." La vie des idées (Collège de France website). https://laviedesidees.fr/L-empire-du-foot,1113.html.

Helleu, Boris. 2017. "Voir ou vivre ? Qu'est-ce qu'être un spectateur d'un match de foot ?" *France Foot*, February 16. https://www.francefootball.fr/news/Voir-ou-vivre-qu-est-ce-qu-etre-un-spectateur-d-un-match-de-foot/778610.

"Inégalités salariales, l'autre match du foot féminin." 2019. RTBF website, June 7. https://www.rtbf.be/sport/dossier/coupe-du-monde-feminine/detail_inegalites-salariales-l-autre-match-du-foot-feminin?id=10241094.

Kaplan, Robert B., and William Grabe. 2002. "A Modern History of Written Discourse Analysis." *Journal of Second Language Writing* 11, no. 3: 191–223.

Kern, Richard. 2002. "Reconciling the Language-Literature Split through Literacy." *ADFL Bulletin* 33, no. 3 (Spring): 20–24.

———. 2008. "Making Connections through Texts in Language Teaching." *Language Teaching* 41, no. 3: 367–387.

Kiger, Patrick J. 2019. "Oval Office Athletes: Presidents and the Sports They Played." History Channel website, January 29. https://www.history.com/news/us-presidents-athletes.

"La célébration de Macron pendant la finale du Mondial objet de nombreux détournements." 2018. RT France website, July 16. https://francais.rt.com/france/52510-celebration-macron-pendant-finale-mondial-objet-nombreux-d%C3%A9tournements-photos?fbclid=IwAR0I1ZvEnx6m49RsOjmdCTwGFqxUF5a59LFFM8ry7EFQ9I0wVddbui-f5Dc.

Landon, Astrid. 2017. "Macron en Top Gun : pourquoi la communication de Macron n'est plus si drôle." Challenges website, July 21. https://www.challenges.fr/politique/macron-en-top-gun-pourquoi-la-communication-de-macron-n-est-plus-si-drole_488845.

Leclerc, Ambre. 2018. "Des chercheurs ont analysé les mèmes les plus populaires d'internet." *TuxBoard* (October). https://www.tuxboard.com/des-chercheurs-ont-analyse-les-memes-les-plus-populaires-dinternet/.

Leclerc-Mougne, Antoine. 2019. "Le mème internet : nouvelle arme politique." *Antidote*, February 5. https://magazineantidote.com/societe/meme-internet-arme-politique/.

Leprince, Chloé. 2018. "'Black-blanc-beur' : petite histoire d'un slogan ambigu." France Culture website, July 13. https://www.franceculture.fr/sociologie/slogan-pejoratif-ou-cri-de-ralliement-dune-france-en-liesse-histoire-du-black-blanc-beur.

Lesaffre, Clément, and William Galibert. 2018. "Emmanuel Macron exulte pendant la finale de la Coupe du monde : les dessous d'une photo déjà culte." *Europe 1*, July 16. https://www.europe1.fr/Coupe-du-Monde/emmanuel-macron-exulte-pendant-la-finale-de-la-coupe-du-monde-les-dessous-dune-photo-deja-culte-3711803.

Levenson, Claire. 2018. "En Suède le mème du 'Distracted Boyfriend' jugé sexiste par l'observatoire de la pub," *Slate*, September 26. http://www.slate.fr/story/167720/suede-meme-distracted-boyfriend-juge-sexiste.

"Mondial : Macron explose de joie sur le but français." 2018. *Sport24 Info* (blog), https://www.sport24info.ma/football/mondial-macron-explose-de-joie-sur-le-but-francais/.

Nanouche. 2018. "Emmanuel Macron nous fait honte devant Poutine en étant hystérique en finale de Coupe du Monde." La Gauche m'a tuer website, July 16. http://lagauchematuer.fr/2018/07/16/emmanuel-macron-nous-fait-honte-devant-poutine-en-etant-hysterique-en-finale-de-coupe-du-monde/. Accessed July 5, 2020.

Nikolsky, Alexei. 2018. Photograph of Emmanuel Macron at World Cup Final in the Luzhniki Stadium in Moscow, Russia, on July 15, 2018. Sputnik, Kremlin Pool Photo via Associated Press.

Nugent, Kristen, and Theresa Catalano. 2015. "Critical Cultural Awareness in the Foreign Language Classroom." *NECTFL Review* 75 (January): 15–30.

Obama, Barack. 2014. "Remarks by the President at the Healthy Kids and Safe Sports Concussion Summit." Press release from the Office of the Press Secretary. The White House, Office of the President, May 29. https://obamawhitehouse.archives.gov/realitycheck/the-press-office/2014/05/29/remarks-president-healthy-kids-and-safe-sports-concussion-summit.

Orsini, Alexis. 2016. "De « this is fine » à « this is not fine », l'histoire d'un « meme » qui a du chien." *Le Monde*, August 4. https://www.lemonde.fr/pixels/article/2016/08/04/de-this-is-fine-a-this-is-not-fine-l-histoire-d-un-meme-qui-a-du-chien_4978393_4408996.html.

Paesani, Kate, Heather Willis Allen, and Beatrice Dupuy. 2016. *A Multiliteracies Framework for Collegiate Foreign Language Teaching*. Upper Saddle River, NJ: Pearson.

Polverini, Léa. 2019. "La visibilité des lesbiennes lors de la Coupe du Monde a un impact bien au-delà du terrain." *Slate*, July 6. http://www.slate.fr/story/179412/visibilite-lesbiennes-coupe-monde-foot-impact-jeunes.

"Pose ton Macron : comment se moquer d'une photo." 2018. *La Chronique facile (du mercredi)*. https://lachroniquefacile.fr/2018/07/18/pose-ton-macron-comment-se-moquer-dune-photo/.

Rebucci, Julien. 2019. "Megan Rapinoe, superstar du foot et poil à gratter de Donald Trump." *Les Inrockuptibles*, July 2. https://bit.ly/3B66epk.

Remia, Cedric. 2019. "Coupe du monde féminine de football 2019 : 'Les choses ne seront plus jamais pareilles' . . . Emmanuel Macron très confiant pour l'avenir du football féminin." *Téléloisirs* website, July 8. https://www.programme-tv.net/news/evenement/coupe-du-monde-feminine-de-football-2019/236076-coupe-du-monde-feminine-de-football-2019-les-choses-ne-seront-plus-jamais-pareilles-emmanuel-macron-tres-confiant-pour-lavenir-du-football-feminin-video/.

Sasin, Marie. 2018. "France-Croatie : la joie de Macron au coup de sifflet final." RTL, July 15. hhttps://bit.ly/34tdpMn.

Th.B. 2017. "Paris 2024 : Macron tombe la veste et s'essaye au fauteuil-tennis et à la boxe." *Le Parisien*, June 24. http://www.leparisien.fr/sports/JO/paris-2024/video-paris-2024-macron-tombe-la-veste-et-s-essaye-au-fauteuil-tennis-et-a-la-boxe-24-06-2017-7084311.php.

Trilat, Gaétan. 2019. "Coupe du monde feminine : qui sont les 23 joueuses de l'équipe de France ?" *Sud-Ouest*, June 7. https://www.sudouest.fr/2019/05/21/coupe-du-monde-feminine-qui-sont-les-23-joueuses-de-l-equipe-de-france-6106671-766.php.

Weed, Mike. 2007. "The Pub as a Virtual Football Fandom Venue: An Alternative to 'Being there'?" *Soccer and Society* 8, no. 2–3: 399–414.

CHAPTER EIGHT

CULTURE WITH PICTURES

blogs BD *for Multiple Literacies in the French Language Classroom*

Aurélie Chevant-Aksoy, Santa Monica College

Research has shown that comics provide alternatives to traditional texts, present lexical diversity, and introduce learners to the semiotics of other cultures in the language classroom.[1] In 2012, Christophe Evans and Françoise Gaudet reported that, in France, about 16 million adults read comic books, 92 percent for leisure and 78 percent for cultural, critical, and aesthetic interpretation.[2] With more than 3 million in existence, *blogs BD*, or blog entries using comics (*bandes dessinées*, or *BD*), are in part responsible for that popularity.[3] Because of their interactive format and their succinct and socioculturally relevant content, *blogs BD* provide a wealth of cultural references and information that can be used creatively in the language classroom. This chapter demonstrates why and how to use *blogs BD* at different levels of the French curriculum within the multiliteracies framework as described by the New London Group,

Rick Kern, and Kate Paesani, Heather Willis Allen, and Beatrice Dupuy.[4] *Blogs BD* offer educators the means to make cross-cultural comparisons; alert students to the social, cultural, historical contexts of communication; and immerse them in French-speaking online communities. The first part of this chapter explains terms that refer to this literary genre and how *bandes dessinées* are a key cultural element of French society. The chapter then discusses the benefits and drawbacks of working with *blogs BD* in the French language classroom. It also provides readers with a non-exhaustive list of *blogs BD* to use in their classes. Finally, the chapter concludes by presenting three instructional sequences on how to use *blogs BD* within the multiliteracies frameworks for elementary, intermediate, and advanced French classes.

CULTURAL IMPORTANCE OF *BANDES DESSINÉES* IN FRANCE

Instructors cannot overlook *bandes dessinées* when looking for different media resources to teach culture in the French language classroom. They have been part of the French cultural patrimony for a long time. Ann Miller identifies Alain Saint-Ogan's *Zig et Puce* as the first Franco-Belgian comic series to replace text beneath the frames with speech balloons in 1925.[5] In the 1930s, the first golden age of *bandes dessinées* happened in France partly due to the massive import of American comic strips to France.[6] A second golden age of *bandes dessinées* occurred in the 1940s and 1950s with the emergence of two main Belgian schools: l'école de Bruxelles (with *bandes dessinées* such as Hergé's *Tintin* and Edgar P. Jacobs's *Blake et Mortimer*) and l'école de Charleroi (with *bandes dessinées* such as Morris's *Lucky Luke* and Peyo's *Les Schtroumpfs*).[7] Such *bandes dessinées* can be referred to as *BD patrimoniales* (patrimonial comics or classics). They are comic series that feature daring adventures with elements of fantasy, action, mysteries, political thrillers, and science fiction, as well as a lot of humor.

The *bande dessinée* has since undergone an evolution in formats and socio-cultural themes in response to cultural and political trends. As a result, several subgenres have emerged in France: adult *bandes dessinées* in the 1960s, feminist *bandes dessinées* in the 1970s, more *BD* albums in the 1980s, and Japanese mangas in the 1990s. Additionally, the first *BD* salon appeared in 1972 in Toulouse, followed by one in Angoulême in 1974.[8] The Festival international de la bande dessinée (FIBD)[9] in Angoulême celebrated its forty-seventh birthday in January 2020 and is today one of the biggest, most revered comic conventions in the world. In 2019, the festival's artistic director, Stéphane Beaujean, explained that, in France, "the market has risen from 700 books per year in the 1990s to 5,000 this year."[10] By 2017, there were about 8.4 million of *bandes dessinées*, mangas, and comics buyers in France. This represents 15.5 percent of the whole population.[11] *BD*, mangas, and comics attract buyers that are usually younger (around forty years old) than book buyers (around forty-two to forty-three years old), and *bandes dessinées* usually attract a younger readership (ten- to seventeen-year-olds) and especially more women in the eighteen- to twenty-five-year-old demographic.[12] Because of their historical background, their diverse socio-cultural subject genres (coming-of-age stories, detective stories, historical testimonials, etc.), and the contemporary appeal to a wide French readership, it is obvious that *bandes dessinées*, known now as the "ninth art," are an important pedagogical resource to use to teach culture in the French language classroom.

BANDES DESSINÉES, COMICS, GRAPHIC NOVELS, AND *BLOGS BD*

When talking about *bandes dessinées*, it is possible to encounter many other different terms: comics, graphic novels, and *blogs BD*. What do all these terms mean? First, it is important to note key differences between *bandes dessinées* and what Americans commonly designate as "comics." On its website, the Cultural Services of the French Embassy in the United States explains these differences:

> In the U.S., "comic books" are thin periodicals of about 32 pages, mainly based on the adventures of superheroes, while the term "graphic novel" is given to illustrated hardcover books, and the audiences for these two categories do not always coincide. In France, however, both traditional *bandes dessinées* [series such as *Tintin* and *Astérix*] and *romans graphiques* are bound in hardcover, and are therefore all classified as "graphic novels" in the U.S.[13]

In fact, the traditional Franco-Belgian *bande dessinée* is usually about forty to fifty pages long and contains one- to two-page short stories (like in André Franquin's *Gaston Lagaffe*) or a complete story (like in Hergé's *Tintin* series). The plot and illustrations tend to be lighter in tone, and it usually offers fictional daily life events, detective stories, and international adventures. The format follows the *ligne claire* (clear line) traditional format with clear outlines and meticulous delineation of panels. On the contrary, graphic novels or *romans graphiques*, as the name indicates, tend to be full-fledged, novel-like narratives. They usually offer fictional and autobiographical stories, such as coming-of-age stories, travel diaries, and war testimonials. The format tends to be less traditional. For example, blurred delineations around panels, speech balloons, or captions are commonly used to reflect the complex narratives in *romans graphiques*.

In addition to those two categories, *blogs BD* in France also gather a large readership. *Blogs BD* began to popularize around 2004, and by 2008, more than 3 million were already in existence. Julien Baudry defines a *blog BD* as a platform used by authors to post mainly drawings and comics (and sometimes other media) instead of using simply written narrations. On a *blog BD*, you can find, for instance, the author's biography, text entries, webcomics, virtual sketchbooks, embedded videos/images/hypertexts, readers' commentaries, and links to other blogs.[14] *Blogs BD* tend to focus on daily life anecdotes and social and political satires or commentaries (LGBT+ and/or feminist questions, daily news, culinary interests, etc.). The success of a *blog BD* depends on how fast and often authors post information about their daily life (usually linked to contemporary pop culture references or interests) and comment on the news.[15] This chapter focuses on the use of *blogs BD* in the French language classroom because they not only provide contemporary and authentic content but also allow instructors to integrate more digital literacy in language instruction.

TEACHING WITH *BLOGS BD* IN THE FRENCH LANGUAGE CLASSROOM

Blogs BD are an incredible tool to use in the French language classroom primarily because of their authenticity and contemporaneity. As Sébastien Rouquette notes, *blogs BD* tend to have short and simple stories published quite regularly.[16] Due to such concise format and the use of visual language that is almost universally understood, students also tend to feel less intimidated by their content.[17] As *blogs BD* contain culturally authentic testimonials of contemporary issues, they enable students to examine cultural, social, and political references that resonate more with their daily life. It is important to note here that, whereas the production of Franco-Belgian comics tends to be dominated by male authors and a more masculine imaginary, *blogs BD* provide more diverse perspectives. Authors such as Pénélope Bagieu and Margaux Motin have paved the way for women's representation in the genre by offering an insight into the daily life of strong, single women. These authors comment on the business world, the beauty and fashion industry, and other socio-cultural issues.[18] Moreover, because *blogs BD* encompass a wide range of contemporary subjects, students can discover new vocabulary, especially puns, idiomatic expressions, and other transcriptions of native speech patterns. Finally, since students have access to *blogs BD* on the web, they can always continue surfing outside of class and find other sites (other interest groups or bloggers) mentioned on the blogs.[19] This can create more interaction with communities of francophone authors and readers.

However, it is important to note that *blogs BD* present some challenges as pedagogical materials. First, their content is not regulated, and they present little accountability for political correctness, or linguistic accuracy.[20] Vulgarity and grammar mistakes abound in *blogs BD*, making them sometimes tricky to use in the classroom. Additionally, *blogs BD* use colloquial grammar and vocabulary, sometimes making them hard to understand for beginner students with low levels of exposure to spoken French. As such, it can become time consuming for instructors to seek out the right blog entry to match a specific grammar, vocabulary, or socio-cultural point. That said, any instructor's first forays into this genre should begin with web browser searches of key terms such as "blogs BD France" or "nouveaux blogs BD." Hopefully, this will lead instructors to websites such as Bédé.fr (https://www.bede.fr) and SensCritique (https://www.senscritique.com) that list trending and active *blogs BD*. Famous newspaper websites such as *Le Monde* (https://www.lemonde.fr) and *Libération* (https://www.liberation.fr) also host interesting *blogs BD*. To help, below is a non-exhaustive list of *blogs BD* to use in the French language classroom at a college level. Note that it will be difficult to predict if this list will stand the test of time, as authors continue on paper format or other media such as Instagram, Facebook, or Tumblr.

Blogs on Daily Life Anecdotes

Boulet: http://www.bouletcorp.com

Level: beginner to advanced / Legibility: some difficulties / Drawings: some vulgarity

Boulet writes about daily life adventures and anecdotes such as going to the supermarket, being lazy, taking the subway in Paris during rush hour, or going back to his childhood home. His blog entries tend to be a bit long but can be used easily if broken down.

Soledad: http://www.blogdesoledadbravi.com

<u>Level:</u> beginner to advanced / <u>Legibility:</u> some difficulties / <u>Drawings:</u> childlike art style

Although this blog has not been updated since 2016, its topics are atemporal and its illustrations still appear in *Elle* magazine. Entries are illustrated lists of cultural facts providing answers for questions like such as "Que faites-vous pendant les vacances scolaires?" (What do you do with your school break?), or "Vous faites quoi dans le train?" (What do you do when you ride the train?).

Zo Illustrations: https://www.zoillustrations.com

<u>Level:</u> beginner to advanced / <u>Legibility:</u> French-English / <u>Drawings:</u> infographics, comics

Zo writes about daily challenges, the environment, real life vs. imagined life, and travels. Her blog entries are quite short.

Bigger than life: http://martinsinger.over-blog.net

<u>Level:</u> beginner to advanced / <u>Legibility:</u> easy / <u>Drawings:</u> illustrations and comics

Martin Singer does a lot of short illustrations that include or exclude text and speech bubbles. Some drawings are more abstract but there is a lot of potential for creative tasks at all levels.

Le blog de Zelba: http://zelba.over-blog.com

<u>Level:</u> intermediate to advanced / <u>Legibility:</u> some difficulties / <u>Drawings:</u> some vulgarity

Zelba is a German illustrator who has lived in France for more than fifteen years. She writes about her family life with teenagers and a husband. She portrays an alter ego called "Mademoiselle Choucroute" (Miss Sauerkraut) who gives culture and language lessons in German and French.

Blogs on the News and Social and Political issues

Plantu: https://www.lemonde.fr/blog/plantu/

Level: beginner to advanced / Legibility: some difficulties / Drawings: childlike art style

This blog can be found on the website of the newspaper *Le Monde*. His blog entries tend to be short (press cartoon), and they focus on French politics and famous political figures as well as burning social and political issues.

Chappatte: https://www.chappatte.com

Level: intermediate to advanced / Legibility: some difficulties / Drawings: press cartoons

Chappatte is a Swiss cartoonist who publishes cartoons in famous newspapers (*New York Times, Le Temps, Le Canard enchaîné*). His blog entries tend to be short (press cartoon), in French or in English, and they focus on pressing social and political international issues.

Tartrais: http://tartrais.net and https://tartrais.com

Level: intermediate to advanced / Legibility: easy / Drawings: press cartoons, single drawings

Blog entries contain one illustration with limited speech bubbles and focus on general social and political issues. The drawings are easy to identify, but the message tends to be a little obscure.

Urtikan.net: https://www.urtikan.net

<u>Level:</u> intermediate to advanced / <u>Legibility:</u> some difficulties / <u>Drawings:</u> some vulgarity

This website is for an independent satirical journal. It contains satirical press cartoons from bloggers and artists that target social and political issues and international news.

Blogs on Specific Socio-cultural Topics

Elise Gravel: http://elisegravel.com

<u>Level:</u> beginner to intermediate / <u>Legibility:</u> easy / <u>Drawings:</u> childlike art style

Elise Gravel illustrates in a poster format. She addresses a younger audience but usefully describes daily life topics such as types of families, environmental tips, or school bullying.

Une année au lycée:
https://www.lemonde.fr/blog/uneanneeaulycee/

<u>Level:</u> beginner to advanced / <u>Legibility:</u> some difficulties / <u>Drawings:</u> cartoonish

This blog by Fabrice Erre recounts a high school teacher's daily life and covers topics such as the educational system, cultural generational gaps, and the use of technology. Entries tend to be short.

À boire et à manger: https://long.blog.lemonde.fr/blog/long/

<u>Level:</u> intermediate to advanced / <u>Legibility:</u> some difficulties / <u>Drawings:</u> childlike art style

This blog by Guillaume Long can also be found on the website of the newspaper *Le Monde*. The blog entries are quite long, but they contain interesting recipes and other culinary facts.

Assignée garçon: https://assigneegarcon.tumblr.com

<u>Level:</u> intermediate to advanced / <u>Legibility:</u> easy / <u>Drawings:</u> childlike art style

The blog is updated regularly and includes short entries with interesting social comments on daily life as a transgender person (e.g., transitioning and the use of gender-fluid pronouns).

The aforementioned blogs are useful for in-class and homework activities, for linguistic and cultural analysis. For a more artistic approach to the use of *blogs BD*, teachers can look into websites such as Storybird (https://storybird.com), Pixton (https://www.pixton.com), Make Beliefs (https://www.makebeliefscomix.com), or Write Comics (http://writecomics.com). Such websites could be great tools to create comics for final projects.

TEACHING CULTURE WITH BLOGS BD WITHIN A MULTILITERACIES FRAMEWORK

As we just discussed, *blogs BD* are a great addition to language classes because their format seems less intimidating for students, and they contain culturally authentic testimonials of contemporary issues that resonate with students' daily lives. *Blogs BD* are, in fact, a great tool to teach culture in a more authentic way and can be fully integrated in weekly activities with other grammar and vocabulary exercises. In modern language instruction, teaching culture in the language classroom has been a source of numerous challenges and dilemmas. When teaching a language, traditionally, the topic of "culture" has often been an isolated component, separated from teaching grammar, vocabulary, and also literary texts. Although there are many approaches to teach culture in the language classroom, this chapter chooses to look into the multiliteracies framework to better integrate culture in the curriculum. Kern's work has been central to the development of a curriculum centered on multiliteracies, a term first introduced by the New

London Group in "A Pedagogy of Multiliteracies: Designing Social Future."[21] Within this framework, Kern defined literacy as:

> the use of socially-, historically-, and culturally-situated practices of creating and interpreting meaning through texts. It entails at least a tacit awareness of the relationships between textual conventions and their contexts of use and, ideally, the ability to reflect critically on those relationships. . . . It draws on a wide range of cognitive abilities, on knowledge of written and spoken language, on knowledge of genres, and on cultural knowledge.[22]

For Kern, multiliteracies instruction is an efficient way to "reconcile the teaching of 'communication'" (referring to the early levels of language teaching) with the "teaching of 'textual' analysis" (referring to the advanced levels).[23] *Blogs BD* work particularly well within a multiliteracies framework because they contain different genres, linguistic registers, and formats (written, visual). *Blogs BD* provide students with stimulating complex content to make connections between language and culture, from beginning to advanced levels of the language program. To understand how to use the multiliteracies framework in the classroom, we adopted Paesani, Allen, and Dupuy's use of the New London Group's four "pedagogical acts" (situated practice, overt instruction, critical framing, and transformed practice) to create instructional activities. Paesani, Allen, and Dupuy explained that, when planning classroom activities, the four "pedagogical acts" can overlap and are neither hierarchical nor sequential. Situated practice activities guide learners to tap spontaneously into their prior knowledge to interact with authentic texts. It is often referred to as experiencing the known and the new. Interestingly situated practice activities could include wiki/blog writing, information gap activity, digital voice recording, and paired oral interview.[24] In overt instruction activities, learners, with active instructor intervention, focus on language forms and conventions and develop the knowledge needed to understand how texts are constructed. Activities such as text mapping, revising/editing, and analyzing word/syntax relationships can be used here. [25] With critical framing activities, learners connect meanings to their social contexts and purposes and engage in constructive criticism of what they learn. Such activities prompt learners to make cross-cultural comparisons and to raise questions about their own cultures in relation to other cultures. Teachers can ask students to do presentations, reflective journaling, and comparison reading/analysis activities.[26] Finally, in transformed practice activities, "learners apply the understandings, knowledge, and skills gained through textual interaction and use them to produce language in new and creative ways."[27] Students can redesign through story retelling, panels or debates, and stylistic/genre reformulation of a text.

Additionally, when thinking of the multiliteracies framework in the globalized world of the twenty-first century, we agree with Chantelle Warner and Dupuy that instructors should also study and use information and communication media. Instructors should consider embedding in their curriculum "not only the types of visual media ... e.g., film, images, and posters, but ... any new literacy practices enabled through digital communications media."[28] In that respect, *blogs BD* are a great medium since students analyze written texts with images, gifs, and sometimes videos and other forms of animation. Because *blogs BD* are found online, on artists' own blogs, on famous newspaper websites, and on other social media, students also learn how to navigate different technological sources and their cultural and linguistic codes. The following instructional sequences provide various ways to integrate *blogs BD* to teach culture at different levels of the French curriculum using the four pedagogical acts.

Instructional Sequence at the Elementary Level

This sequence is appropriate for a second semester, elementary French class to talk about childhood/adolescence memories in comparison with contemporary habits and life and to practice the use of *imparfait* and *présent*. As situated practice, the instructor brainstorms with students on their late childhood: where they used to live; who used to be their friends and role models; what they used to like doing, eating, watching, listening to, and so on. The students use this activity to practice the *imparfait* and gather vocabulary that will be useful in the next phase of the sequence. This also leads to some critical framing and cross-cultural comparison of kids and adolescent cultural trends in the 1980s to 1990s: through the use of print and video advertisements, students compare the time periods and trends in France and the United States (and other countries). The instructor then provides a paper copy of a shortened version of the blog entry "Tempus Fugit"[29] by the French cartoonist Boulet (Appendix 8.1 on Fulcrum) and, as transformed practice, asks the students to work in groups to narrate what is going on in the images. Students narrate mostly in the third-person singular and use the *imparfait* and *présent*. Students usually grasp that the images in the bubbles represent the past, in comparison with the rest of the drawings that indicate present actions. They sometimes have a hard time understanding the second image on the top right corner—which can be interpreted as doing laundry. Groups then team up and compare their narrations before writing them on the board. As an overt instruction activity, students reflect on the use and construction of the *imparfait* and the *présent*. Additional grammar exercises can be added at this stage.

To finish the sequence, the instructor can return to a critical framing activity on childhood/adolescence objects by showing the last part of Boulet's blog entry (Appendix 8.2 on Fulcrum). The class can brainstorm together on several ideas that echo the first critical framing activity. In these activities, the instructor can pose the following questions: What kind of objects and places come to mind when you think of your childhood/adolescence? What do Boulet's objects tell us about his upbringing, where he grew up in France (and maybe his social class)? What do Boulet's objects tell us about French culture and French people's values? Finally, as a transformed practice and follow-up activity, students can write a short composition at home comparing their life during their late childhood/early adolescence to the present. In this activity, students may provide pictures or illustrations representing key objects or places symbolizing their past or the link between their past and present.

Instructional Sequence at the Intermediate Level

The following sequence is appropriate for a second semester, intermediate French language class. Press cartoons from *blogs BD* are utilized in a unit on the environment, which happens roughly in the middle of the semester (Week 6 or 7). It is important here to practice specific vocabulary and verify the prior knowledge of students on such an intricate topic. Therefore, instructors should start the class with the activity "Trouvez quelqu'un qui" (Appendix 8.3 on Fulcrum), used for situated practice. Students ask peers different questions about their connection to the protection of the environment and then discuss the answers as a whole class. The instructor uses this activity as critical framing to introduce important French-speaking organizations such as La Fondation pour la nature et l'homme in France, Équiterre in Canada, and TERRA Festival in Guadeloupe, as well as international and francophone environmental activists (such as Greta Thunberg, Nicolas Hulot, Yannick Jadot, Marion Cotillard, and Mélanie Laurent). After that, the instructor forms groups of about three to four students and gives each a press cartoon (Appendix 8.4 on Fulcrum). Each group reflects upon the characters, their actions and the written text, and the environmental problem represented. The instructor should circulate to help groups identify the characters (not everyone might know who Galileo is or recognize Greta Thunberg in the first drawing) and to explain vocabulary and the author's message (such as "climatosceptiques" or the symbolism of an American rich oilman in drawing number 4). After twenty minutes, each group presents its cartoon, and the class discusses the social, cultural, and political implications of each. To conclude this sequence, the instructor points out the form used in drawing number 4: "Il faut sortir de là, Pinocchio!" Students will hopefully recognize the use of "il faut + infinitive" to express necessity (this serves as the first part of a review of the subjunctive). As a final transformed practice in class, students are asked to write solutions to the problems studied in the cartoons using the "il faut / il est nécessaire / il est important que + infinitive" format. As a follow-up activity, once a week during the second half of the semester (Weeks 8 to 15), two pairs of students can present a press cartoon that they found online (Appendix 8.5 on Fulcrum) as a way to talk about more cultural contemporary issues in the language classroom.

Instructional Sequence at the Advanced Level

This sequence is appropriate for an advanced composition class. By the end of the second unit of this class, students learn the format and content of *un portrait* and they write a creative physical and psychological description of an important person in their life. Instructors should start this unit with situated practice: brainstorming gender stereotypes, especially ones concerning parents. Students are then provided with two illustrations from Soledad Bravi's *blog BD* (Appendix 8.6 on Fulcrum) to critique. Together and on the board, the class should list the information on being a father and a mother found in Bravi's illustrations. The instructor can then emphasize some cultural differences between Bravi's ideas and the students' families, origins, and cultural experiences linked to the family. This coincides with overt instruction, as students will gather vocabulary to describe a person's physical and moral characteristics. Here students work especially on adjectives and idiomatic expressions, such as "papa poule," "le papa à ses fifilles," and "G.O." (*gentil organisateur* au Club Med; exercises not included in this chapter).

After this vocabulary work, the class should look at a *blog BD* entry "Au magasin" by Guy Delisle. Before looking at the blog entry, the instructor should tell the students to pay attention to the father figure in the cartoons and ask them to describe their impressions of his physical appearance and personality traits. The instructor repeats this activity for the first four drawings of the *blog BD* (Appendix 8.7 on Fulcrum), and students develop a description of the father. By the end of the session, students use these notes to complete homework at home. Via their school's online learning management system, students find slides on VoiceThread[30] containing each drawing shown in Appendix 8.7 on Fulcrum (shortened version of Delisle's blog entry). On VoiceThread, students record themselves as if they were narrating the story from the point of view of the father. They are encouraged to use the past tenses and to creatively describe emotions and feelings.

CONCLUSION

Teaching culture in the language classroom is not always an easy task. Finding authentic ways to teach culture, without oversimplifying it, providing a monolithic representation of francophone culture(s), or even isolating it from grammar and vocabulary instruction can be challenging. Using a multiliteracies framework helps introduce texts (in various formats) at any level of the curriculum and provides students with authentic discourse, cues for meaningful communication, and knowledge of underlying linguistic codes in relation to different socio-cultural contexts and situations. However, as Warner and Dupuy mentioned, one of the challenges to adapting the multiliteracies framework to current programs is that "many of the currently available methods textbooks do not have a multiliteracies orientation"[31] and that "the thematic content of textbooks often continues to be introduced in a 'culturally neutral' way, often through short, author-created texts with no clear audience or intent in mind and devoid of ambiguous meaning."[32] In this chapter, instructors are provided one solution to start bridging that gap. By including activities using *blogs BD* in their curriculum, instructors can encourage students to explore the linguistic and cultural diversity of the French-speaking world, through various online and technological media, inside and outside of class. Even though the format and availability of *blogs BD* online (on blogs, Facebook, Instagram, Pinterest, etc.) are constantly evolving and changing, the methodology demonstrated here serves as a guide to map out new authentic activities. It is imperative that instructors work together and share more databases and links of activities and sequences such as those discussed in this chapter to continue building a more innovative and relevant curriculum for our students.

NOTES

1. Jacqui Clydesdale, "A Bridge to Another World: Using Comics in the Second Language Classroom" (Calgary: University of Calgary, 2017), http://citeseerx.ist.psu.edu/viewdoc/download?doi=10.1.1.568.6729&rep=rep1&type=pdf.
2. Christophe Evans and Françoise Gaudet, "La lecture de bandes dessinées," *Culture Études* 2, no. 2 (March 2012):1–8.
3. Alexis D'Hautcourt, "Un nouvel outil pour l'apprentissage de la lecture du français : les blogs BD," *Journal of Inquiry and Research* 87 (March 2008): 229–238.
4. New London Group, "A Pedagogy of Multiliteracies: Designing Social Future," *Harvard Educational Review* 66, no. 1 (Spring 1996): 60–92; Richard Kern, *Literacy and Language Teaching* (Oxford: Oxford University Press, 2000); and Kate Paesani, Heather Willis Allen, and Beatrice Dupuy, *A Multiliteracies Framework for Collegiate Foreign Language Teaching* (Upper Saddle River, NJ: Pearson, 2016).

5. Ann Miller, *Reading* bande dessinée: *Critical Approaches to French Language Comic Strip* (Bristol, UK: Intellect Books, 2007), 17.
6. Miller, 17.
7. Miller, 20–21.
8. Miller, 28–29.
9. For more information, check out the FIBD official website: https://www.bdangouleme.com/.
10. Seb Emina, "In France, Comic Books Are Serious Business," *New York Times*, January 29, 2019,https://www.nytimes.com/2019/01/29/books/france-comic-books-angouleme.html.
11. Antoine Oury, "France : qui sont les lecteurs de BD, mangas et comics ?" ActuaLitté, October 17, 2017, https://www.actualitte.com/article/monde-edition/france-qui-sont-les-lecteurs-de-bd-mangas-et-comics/85374.
12. Oury.
13. Cultural Services, French Embassy in the United States, "Why Do French Comics Sell Abroad?," n.d.,http://frenchculture.org/books-and-ideas/4093-why-do-french-comics-sell-abroad.
14. Julien Baudry, "Partie 3 : les blogs bd, une spécificité française ?" Neuvième art 2.0, May 2012, http://neuviemeart.citebd.org/spip.php?article395.
15. Baudry.
16. Sébastien Rouquette, "Les Blogs BD, entre blog et bande dessinée," *Hermès* 54 (2009): 119.
17. D'Hautcourt, "Un nouvel outil," 234.
18. Thierry Groensteen, "Femme (1) : représentation de la femme. Dictionnaire esthétique et thématique de la bande dessinée," Neuvième art 2.0, September 15, 2004, http://neuviemeart.citebd.org/spip.php?article677.
19. Rouquette, "Les Blogs BD," 121.
20. Rouquette, 120.
21. Chantelle Warner and Beatrice Dupuy, "Moving toward Multiliteracies in Foreign Language Teaching: Past and Present Perspectives . . . and Beyond," *Foreign Language Annals* 51, no. 1 (Spring 2018): 119.
22. Kern, *Literacy and Language Teaching*, 16.
23. Richard Kern, "Literacy as a New Organizing Principle for Foreign Language Education," in *Reading between the Lines: Perspectives on Foreign Language Literacy*, ed. Peter C. Patrikis (New Haven, CT: Yale University Press, 2003), 43.
24. Paesani, Willis Allen, and Dupuy, *Multiliteracies Framework*, 37.
25. Paesani, Willis Allen, and Dupuy, 38.
26. Paesani, Willis Allen, and Dupuy, 39.

27. Paesani, Willis Allen, and Dupuy, 39.
28. Warner and Dupuy, "Moving toward Multiliteracies," 123.
29. Boulet, "Tempus Fugit," Bouletcorp.com, August 8, 2006, http://www.bouletcorp.com/blog/2006/08/03/tempus-fugit/.
30. VoiceThread (https://voicethread.com) is a website that you can embed in Canvas. Instructors can upload a PowerPoint presentation and ask students to record their own narration onto each slide.
31. Warner and Dupuy, "Moving toward Multiliteracies," 121.
32. Warner and Dupuy, 122.

REFERENCES

Baudry, Julien. "Partie 3 : les blogs bd, une spécificité française ?" Neuvième art 2.0, May 2012. http://neuviemeart.citebd.org/spip.php?article395.

Boulet. "Tempus Fugit." Bouletcorp.com, August 8, 2006. http://www.bouletcorp.com/blog/2006/08/03/tempus-fugit/.

Bravi, Soledad. "Quel père êtes-vous ?" *Soledad*. Published in *Elle* magazine, July 29, 2016. http://www.blogdesoledadbravi.com/2016/07/29-juillet-elle-magazine.html.

———. "Quelle sorte de mère êtes-vous ?" *Soledad*, accessed August 9, 2019. https://www.facebook.com/cours.matelem/photos/avis-aux-mamansetvous-quelle-sorte-de-m%C3%A8re-%C3%AAtes-vous-illustration-soledad/10156152296586785/.

Cambon. "Climat : les jeunes en ont assez de l'irresponsabilité des adultes." Urtikan.net, February 22, 2019. https://www.urtikan.net/dessin-du-jour/climat-mobilisation-des-jeunes-a-paris/.

Chappatte. "Urgence climatique." Chappatte.com, October 11, 2018. https://www.chappatte.com/gctag/pollution/.

Clydesdale, Jacqui. "A Bridge to Another World: Using Comics in the Second Language Classroom." Calgary: University of Calgary, 2017. http://citeseerx.ist.psu.edu/viewdoc/download?doi=10.1.1.568.6729&rep=rep1&type=pdf

Cultural Services, French Embassy in the United States. "Why Do French Comics Sell Abroad?" n.d. http://frenchculture.org/books-and-ideas/4093-why-do-french-comics-sell-abroad.

Delisle, Guy. "Au magasin." guydelisle.com, accessed August 9, 2019. http://www.guydelisle.com/gdmp4-2/.

D'Hautcourt, Alexis. "Un nouvel outil pour l'apprentissage de la lecture du français : les blogs BD." *Journal of Inquiry and Research* 87 (March 2008): 229–238.

Elsner, Daniela, Sissy Helff, and Britta Viebrock. "Films, Graphic Novels & Visuals: Developing Multiliteracies in Foreign Language Education—An Interdisciplinary Approach." In *Films, Graphic Novels & Visuals: Developing Multiliteracies in Foreign Language Education—An Interdisciplinary Approach*, edited by Daniela Elsner, Sissy Helff, and Britta Viebrock, 7–13. Zürich: LIT Verlag, 2013.

Emina, Seb. "In France, Comic Books Are Serious Business." *New York Times*, January 29, 2019. https://www.nytimes.com/2019/01/29/books/france-comic-books-angouleme.html.

Evans, Christophe and Françoise Gaudet. "La lecture de bandes dessinées." *Culture Études* 2, no. 2 (March 2012):1–8.

Gindensperger, Sophie. "Les Blogs BD bougent encore." *Libération*, October 10, 2015.https://next.liberation.fr/culture/2015/10/10/les-blogs-bd-bougent-encore_1399927.

Groensteen, Thierry. "Femme (1) : représentation de la femme. Dictionnaire esthétique et thématique de la bande dessinée." Neuvième art 2.0, September 15, 2004. http://neuviemeart.citebd.org/spip.php?article677.

Kern, Richard. *Literacy and Language Teaching*. Oxford: Oxford University Press, 2000.

———. "Literacy as a New Organizing Principle for Foreign Language Education." In *Reading between the Lines: Perspectives on Foreign Language Literacy*, edited by Peter C. Patrikis, 40–59. New Haven, CT: Yale University Press, 2003.

Miller, Ann. *Reading* bande dessinée: *Critical Approaches to French Language Comic Strip*. Bristol, UK: Intellect Books, 2007.

Mutio. "Plastique : une pollution qui vire au désastre écologique." Urtikan.net, June 14, 2019. https://www.urtikan.net/dessin-du-jour/plastique-une-pollution-qui-vire-au-desastre-ecologique/.

New London Group. "A Pedagogy of Multiliteracies: Designing Social Future." *Harvard Educational Review* 66, no. 1 (Spring 1996): 60–92.

Oury, Antoine. "France : qui sont les lecteurs de BD, mangas et comics ?" ActuaLitté, October 17, 2017. https://www.actualitte.com/article/monde-edition/france-qui-sont-les-lecteurs-de-bd-mangas-et-comics/85374.

Paesani, Kate, Heather Willis Allen, and Beatrice Dupuy. *A Multiliteracies Framework for Collegiate Foreign Language Teaching*. Upper Saddle River, NJ: Pearson, 2016.

Plantu. "Canicule." *Blog de Plantu* (blog), August 27, 2016. https://www.lemonde.fr/blog/plantu/2016/08/27/canicule/.

Rouquette, Sébastien. "Les Blogs BD, entre blog et bande dessinée." *Hermès* 54 (2009): 119–124.

Warner, Chantelle, and Beatrice Dupuy. "Moving toward Multiliteracies in Foreign Language Teaching: Past and Present Perspectives... and Beyond." *Foreign Language Annals* 51, no. 1 (Spring 2018): 116–128.

PART IV

DIGITAL TECHNOLOGIES

CHAPTER NINE

ENGAGING STUDENTS INSIDE AND OUTSIDE OF THE CLASSROOM WITH YOUTUBE

Audra Merfeld-Langston, Missouri University of Science & Technology

Music, commercials, *courts métrages*, vlogs, news reports, documentaries, and more are among the rich authentic French-language materials available on YouTube. With a quick search, we can access content from across the francophone world. It has never been easier to find authentic videos for our courses. Instructors need only navigate to YouTube and enter basic search terms for their desired topic: "*publicités belges*," "*fêtes québecoises*," or "*musique au Sénégal*." One can find intellectual or mundane content and everything in between. Integrating such materials effectively into our courses, however, can be challenging. Barriers to moving beyond the entertainment value YouTube content provides for language learners[1] include the constantly evolving nature of language instruction,[2] rapidly changing technological developments and capabilities,[3] and the unfamiliarity of many language teachers with computer-assisted language learning (CALL),[4] including challenges creating effective listening activities for authentic materials.[5] As Janel Pettes Guikema and Mandy Menke explain, teachers gravitate toward teaching as they were taught, and even though they may be considered to be "digital natives" (Prensky's name for those born since 1980 who have presumably been immersed in technology), they may lack confidence in using technology to teach.[6] Nevertheless, studies have found that students expect instructors to use technology in their teaching[7] and that consequently, as language instructors, we need to adapt the delivery of our course content and methodology,[8] especially to foster digital literacy. Indeed, as Christoph Hafner, Alice Chik, and Rodney Jones indicate, "what it means to learn a language . . . has shifted," along with what it means to be literate in online content, including knowing how to decipher the multimodal ensembles we find there.[9] Significantly, using technology in language learning also figures as one of the key recommendations in the 2017 report by the American Academy of Arts & Sciences' Commission on Language Learning.[10]

YouTube's versatility lends itself well to integration in French courses at multiple levels and for diverse age groups, with minimal (if any) training required for teachers on how to use the technology, though they may still need guidance on how to design appropriate accompanying activities.[11] Many students are not only familiar with the format of YouTube, but they are regular users of it: "YouTube, on mobile alone, reaches more [18- to 34-year-olds in the United States] than any TV network," with the majority of views (70 percent) coming from mobile devices. Collectively, the audience of over one billion YouTube users watch one billion hours of videos a day.[12] Many K–12 students are also fluent in navigating YouTube's landscape, though perhaps more in terms of finding the latest episodes of their favorite gaming YouTubers. As language teachers, we can tap into students' interest in YouTube to foster interest in and interactions with French. Since it is mobile and can be viewed on many types of devices, both inside and outside the classroom, students can watch "assignments" multiple times and can choose to further engage with other content-related suggestions, thereby adding a level of autonomy to their experience. Moreover, online and blended courses are becoming increasingly popular, and YouTube videos are easy to embed in course content.[13]

Since many students already watch YouTube, adding language learning tasks within this environment has the potential to minimize any fear factor they may have about learning another language. Tentative findings indicate that compared with similar content on blogs, YouTube videos "promoted greater recall of the target words' grammatical functions and greater recognition and recall of their meanings."[14] The multilingual caption options available for many of these videos further aid in making the foreign familiar. And as Maribel Montero Perez, Piet Desmet, and Elke Peters note, captions—an "easily implementable" tool in classroom contexts—can "enhance attention and vocabulary learning through video."[15]

In addition to the authentic language in context that French-language YouTube videos provide (some aimed at language learners but most targeted toward native speakers), they are rich in their cultural diversity. YouTubers hail from around the francophone world. They are young and old, of diverse political leanings, and specialists (or amateurs) in many genres. Joseph Terantino suggests using YouTube in foreign language teaching for providing content and information, to "experience portions of other cultures including artifacts, history, and politics without physically traveling to the target country,"[16] for student-created videos, and for collaboration. Scott Taylor notes that venues like YouTube (and Netflix and Hulu) can "breathe life into language study, . . . connect students with the target culture, and . . . exercise a number of modalities for achieving the individualized goals of differentiated learning."[17] Indeed, the surrounding multimodal content of text, images, buttons, icons, and so on[18] create a type of cultural immersion unavailable in traditional printed materials. The user is in control of the experience. If students like the video they watch for class, they can continue their immersive experience by clicking on some of the suggestions on YouTube's side panel. They can learn more about the video in a text section under the video, where they can also add a thumbs-up or thumbs-down or add a comment to express their opinions and participate in a global online community. They can read through others' comments below the video, which are rich in terms of language and culture, often in multiple languages; as Phil Benson has shown, these spaces are prime areas where language learning can occur.[19]

YouTube connects us to a global community and contains content from across the francophone world. Users have access to speech samples that include many accents, registers, and speech patterns. Previously, as Claire Kramsch notes, "the real living monolingual NS in all his/her phonological, stylistic, ethnic, and social diversity was never the goal of instruction. The goal was always a standard variety of a more or less educated urban metropolitan speaker."[20] Textbooks reflect this approach. Kramsch continues:

> The gap between this target and the real, multilingual NS reality of today's world is growing larger because of the global mobility, the Internet, social networks, and the global influence of English and Anglo-American pragmatics. It doesn't mean we should stop teaching the standard, but we should stop pretending this is how all native speakers speak in all walks of life and in all circumstances.[21]

Hafner, Chik, and Jones similarly note the disconnect between "school-based language" that focuses on standardized forms and language used in online spaces, as does Robert Godwin-Jones.[22] Using well-structured YouTube activities in French courses can counteract this gap, and exposing students to the great diversity in speaking styles, vocabulary, attitudes, presentation styles, regional variances, and much more is a way instructors can contribute toward making "our students into multilingual individuals, sensitive to linguistic, cultural, and above all, semiotic diversity, and willing to grapple with differences in social, cultural, political, and religious worldviews."[23]

Finally, YouTube videos offer countless possibilities for integrating the American Council on the Teaching of Foreign Languages' (ACTFL) 5 Cs (Communication, Cultures, Connections, Comparisons, and Communities) into French courses at all levels and for all ages while also following the guidelines outlined in the Partnership for 21st Century Skills (P21) "21st Century Skills Map," such as integrating technology into instruction to enhance learning; seeking opportunities for learners to use language beyond the classroom; and personalizing real-world tasks[24] via interpersonal, interpretive, and presentational modes of communication.[25] YouTube further ties in particularly well with P21's maps for information literacy, media literacy, and technology literacy.

SAMPLE ACTIVITIES

Familiarity with YouTube is not in itself enough to ensure language learning. As Robert Blake indicates, instructors must thoughtfully construct tasks around the videos to ensure students' comprehension. This includes creating pre-listening activities to adequately frame the linguistic and cultural content, without which the second language (L2) learner can be overwhelmed by material created with a first language (L1) audience in mind.[26] Taylor similarly mentions the necessity of adequately structuring and sequencing lessons.[27] In the second part of this chapter, then, I will focus on practical strategies for incorporating YouTube in French-language courses via three types of activities that instructors can adapt for different ages or ability levels: video blogs (vlogs), integration of videos with other media, and playlists. Instructions and questions for students that accompany these activities could be in either English or French, depending on the goals for the course. Accordingly, I have used both in my examples.

ACTIVITY 1: VLOGS

Vlogs contain countless possibilities for the development of digital literacy, collaboration, multilingual peer learning, and intercultural exchanges, though this area remains relatively "unexplored in the context of French language learning."[28] In a vlog, a narrator shares their thoughts on topics with the viewers, much like a blog, but in video form. Vlogs are characterized by their focus on everyday experiences. Because of their informal nature, vlogs include ample examples of slang. The clips' brevity (generally five to fifteen minutes) means that students can watch them multiple times to maximize their comprehension, in terms of both language and culture. For pedagogical purposes, the best vlogs contain interesting and relatable topics that allow for cross-cultural comparisons and have the potential to generate student interest and engagement. As with other types of authentic discourse, when choosing which vlogs to use, instructors must consider learning objectives and design related activities accordingly. As Guikema notes in her discussion of podcasts for language learning, the level of difficulty of the discourse as well as students' familiarity with the subject should both be taken into consideration.[29] Each vlogger below hosts a channel on YouTube that includes videos and playlists with approachable content for classroom use. I have aimed in my selection to include a variety of perspectives, genres, accents, and cultures rather than to highlight only the best-known francophone vloggers whose subscribers number in the millions. A Google search for "Vlog in French" will produce numerous lists of the latter.

1. **Amini Cishugi** is a freelance blogger and novelist from the Democratic Republic of the Congo. With his vlogs,

he aims to "present beautiful places he visits and share information about Africa." He takes his audience to marketplaces ("A l'intérieur d'un marché africain d'épicerie") and schools ("A day in a Burundian public school"), to a zoo, and to various neighborhoods he encounters in his travels. In each episode, he narrates what he sees and offers details about local customs or history, much of which will be new to North American students. For example, in one episode, he explains, "L'Art de négocier un taxi vélo en Afrique, surtout au Burundi." Along with the richness of the scenery and the cultural insights the videos offer, viewers might appreciate their informal, authentic (non-contrived) format and the narrator's sincerity in sharing his experiences.

2. **Audrey D.** This primary school *vloggeuse* from Quebec touches on a variety of topics in her videos, which she summarizes as focusing on Quebec/France; educational and advice videos; videos "*sans tabous*"; vlogs; and her discoveries, thoughts, and opinions.[30] While she sometimes addresses controversial topics, she does so with the aim of teaching and learning something.[31] Audrey D. explores particularities of Québecois accents and vocabulary, which can be useful for introducing students to linguistic variety. Additionally, students and instructors may enjoy using some of her cooking videos—such as "Je cuisine une poutine maison"[32]—for hands-on activities. Finally, Audrey D. frequently invites her viewers to interact with her and to contribute ideas and questions.

3. **Ma vie aux États-Unis.** As the title implies, in this vlog series, the host, Yoann, shares with viewers some of his experiences living in the United States. Yoann, who hails from the North of France, studied and taught French in

the U.S. for four years.[33] His observations about Americans from the perspective of an outsider can encourage students to consider how "normal" differs from one culture to another. For example, in "Dire bonjour aux Américains: Les Hugs!" Yoann first explains how French people greet and take leave of one another and then details different types of American hugs, modeling them with a friend. In "Shopping in the United States," he visits Walmart; he is struck by the large size of milk jugs, tubs of butter and ice cream, the color of eggs, the amount of GMO meat products, and the abundant amount of plastic (bags, bread bags). Yoann's videos touch on sports, language, holidays, and more.

4. **Scilabus.** Viviane Lalande began her science vlog, Scilabus, in 2013; it sprang from her blog of the same name. An engineer by training, Lalande earned a PhD in biomechanics. Her videos feature the science of the every day, presented in a manner accessible to the general public. She explores themes such as "Pourquoi l'ourlet des t-shirts est-il indispensable ?" "Pourquoi y a t-il autant d'air dans les sacs de chips ?" and "Analyser les cris des joueurs permet de prédire le gagnant." While portions of each video include straight narration, she also goes on location to interview experts. She includes data and graphs, clips from other sources (e.g., from a tennis match), and some historical background. Additionally, the vlogger conducts simple experiments to test hypotheses. Overall, these videos feature an approachable mix of history, science, and curiosity and would be appropriate for any age/ability level.

What Can You Do with a Vlog?

The above examples represent a tiny sampling of French-language vloggers on YouTube. Vlog genres include comedy, language learning, gaming, beauty, DIY projects, politics, and much more. Compiled lists of vlogs (such as those found at https://frenchtogether.com/french-youtubers/ and https://www.frenchplanations.com/french-youtubers/) can help instructors identify appropriate material for use with a particular class. Once instructors have selected a vlog, the next step is to design related tasks that correspond with the overall goals and learners' needs. Tasks could be related to specific language objectives, to comparing and contrasting cultures (from the visual to the ideological), to discussing/analyzing/critiquing the content, or to all of the above. Pre-viewing scaffolding may include providing students with vocabulary, asking them to listen for specific information, having them read the transcript, or asking opinion or knowledge-based questions about the topic. A series of questions about both audio and visual content can guide students' viewing and help them navigate meaning, while follow-up discussion questions can foster cultural comparisons and larger-scale discussions. When time is limited, English may be preferable for addressing cultural comparisons, whereas if the goal is a focus on language proficiency, French would be more appropriate. Examples of during- and after-viewing questions generalizable to most videos include:

- Where is the vlogger filming? How does this person's home/office/school/environment compare to yours?
- How is the vlogger dressed? How does this compare with how people dress where you live?
- What topics does the vlogger address? How do they approach these topics?
- Are their attitudes toward these topics surprising? Why or why not?

- What do you think about what the vlogger presented? Explain.
- What does the speaker's voice sound like? Can you detect a particular accent? Are they speaking clearly or mumbling? What do these qualities reveal about the intent and level of formality of the video?
- If you had the opportunity to ask the vlogger three questions, what would they be?
- What can you deduce about the region/country where this person lives based on what you see and hear in the video?
- Where is the vlog post situated on the fact-opinion continuum? How can you tell?
- As a supplement to the above activities, instructors can use vlogs as a starting point for related projects. For example:
- Research one of the topics presented in the vlog and present it to the class or compose an essay about it.
- Find another vlogger who posts the same genre of videos and compare their styles.
- Watch more of the vlogs for a particular individual and explain how they relate to one another. What do we learn about the vlogger? What common threads unite the videos?
- Create your own vlog to present to your class. (This could be centered on a particular theme or modeled after a vlogger discussed in class.)
- Read the viewer comments for the YouTube video. In general, what types of views do they express about the video? If you were going to comment on the vlog, what would you say? (Instructors could also have students model the informality of the comments.)
- Find a vlogger from a different francophone country who creates similar content as the vlog we studied. Compare

and contrast their presentation styles, accents, and general approach.

A main goal in using vlogs is to get students engaged with culture in meaningful, engaging ways.

Activity 2: Using YouTube as a Springboard for Integrating Multiple Sources

Pascale Perraudin and Shannon Porfilio note the challenges of incorporating ACTFL's second C, Culture, into French-language courses, notably at the elementary level,[34] and advise against the "postcard approach," a superficial use of authentic materials (found in textbooks) that remains largely "touristic" and stereotyped and fails to adequately engage students with the material (and potentially creates negative attitudes toward the culture). Kramsch echoes this notion and asserts that "[t]he commodification of language and of language teaching materials in the new global economy has become a source of great concern to language educators."[35] While watching a given YouTube video can be an informative or entertaining stand-alone activity, it has the potential to become a "digital postcard" without the instructor's adequate consideration of objectives and without proper contextualization of and scaffolding for the students' experience. However, YouTube can also act as a springboard for broader and deeper exploration of people, ideas, and themes and create a multimodal learning experience.

Scilabus and STEM, in French

For example, following working with the Scilabus videos mentioned above, learners can deepen their experience at Viviane Lalande's website (https://www.scilabus.com). Students could familiarize themselves with sections of the website and further engage with content on specific pages. One page, "Collaborations et presse," links to written, audio, and video interviews with Lalande. These documents provide further cultural context to the video(s) the students view (as well as even more authentic language). In the interviews and news articles, we can read/hear about how she came to Quebec from France, why she started her vlog, and why she values sharing science with the public. We can also find critical perspectives about her vlogs. One article states, "Ce qu'on apprécie particulièrement, ce sont ses expériences pour prouver ce qu'elle avance. Et lorsqu'elle se demande si on peut tous devenir olympien, ou ce que les vols en avion font au corps humain, elle va directement interviewer une athlète ou un pilote."[36] After reading this article and others, students could discuss: Do you agree with this assessment? What do the various reviews of Scilabus's vlogs have in common? What elements of the vlogs do the reviews focus on? In a follow-up project, students might write a review of one of Lalande's vlogs or role-play an interview with her.

Another article Scilabus links to, "Sur YouTube, la science infuse," draws readers' attention to "l'émergence de talentueux vulgaristeurs [de science]," including Scilabus.[37] Here, we find a list of other science vloggers whose videos students could use for comparison and contrast with Scilabus. Topics for discussion might be: Which science vlogger do you prefer and why? Which is easiest to understand in terms of language? In terms of scientific explanations? What kinds of science do they discuss? How do these science vlogs relate to science vlogs from your home country? Another activity related to this article could be to investigate the authors' statement, "Tous les youtubeurs ne sont pas à l'aise devant une caméra, et les rares youtubeuses sont particulièrement timides." Why are there fewer *youtubeuses*? Do students agree that they are more timid than *youtubeurs*? Why are there fewer women in certain STEM fields? This last topic has the potential to bring Scilabus's vlogs into a much broader discussion about gender roles, gender equality, and gender stereotyping.

Viviane Lalande also wrote blog entries for the children's website Kidi'science (https://kidiscience.cafe-sciences.org) and links to these entries from her Scilabus website. Students could read one or more of her Kidi'science guest entries (for instance, "On est allés voir Pluton !") and analyze differences between those entries and her regular blog entries on Scilabus. How does her vocabulary change? Her tone? What register does she use? How does one adapt language and content to one's audience? A project could involve students writing two brief science blog entries (in French) on the same topic—one destined for adults and one for children. Finally, to complete the loop that opened with the viewing of the video, the class could discuss whether they prefer Lalande's blog or her vlogs and why. What are the pros and cons of each? Which is more effective?

Stromae, Debbouze, Corneille: Music, Society, History, Diversity

Using Scilabus's YouTube videos in class combines language learning, cultural competence, digital literacy, and STEM. The next activity sequence combines music, social issues, history, and diversity using a blend of YouTube videos, press articles, and social media. This sequence, which can be spread out over several weeks, also emphasizes the reach of the francophone world and traces of France's colonial past. Instructors can choose the steps that best fit their needs or complete the entire sequence with their students; some parts may need to be adapted for younger audiences.

1. The sequence begins with Stromae (Paul Van Haver), whose popular music many students may have heard already. Students will read several articles about Stromae from the American press. This serves as a quick introduction to Stromae and to his reception in the United States. With the title "Meet Stromae, the Most Famous Pop Star

You've Never Heard of," Tim Lowery already makes a statement about both Stromae's popularity and the United States' knowledge (or lack thereof) about other cultures. The accompanying image from the cover of *Time Out* (New York) is of Stromae as half "male," half "female," which his fans will recognize from his video "Tous les mêmes," and can spark discussions about gender and representation. Ian Parker's article "Ridiculous" highlights Stromae's blending of cultures, including via his heritage as half Belgian, half Rwandan. Readers learn about Stromae's importance in Belgium and about the death of his father in the 1994 Rwandan genocide. These two articles are aimed at teen or adult readers; other articles may be appropriate for younger audiences.

2. Next, students view Stromae's video "Alors on danse" on YouTube, either in class or as homework. Instructors will find plenty of discussion topics here (boredom at work, money, love, famine, the third world) that they can explore with students if desired; for this sequence, the video is mostly a catalyst for the activities that follow.

3. Third, students complete online research to learn about actor and comedian Jamel Debbouze. Likely, fewer students will be familiar with him. Sample questions include: *Quelle est sa profession ? Où a-t-il grandi ? D'où vient sa famille ? Quelles langues parlent-ils ? Pourquoi est-il connu dans le monde francophone ? Quel accident lui est-il arrivé ? Quel effet cela a-t-il eu sur sa vie ?*[38] The answers to these questions will bring geography, ethnicity, immigration, and disability into the discussion.

4. The students return to YouTube to watch a video in which Debbouze coaches Stromae through the creation

of his hit song "Alors on danse." A search for "Stromae Debbouze Alors on danse" will bring up several versions of the video, which lasts approximately six minutes. The video's humor is evident even if students do not understand the entire dialogue. Comprehension questions can include time codes to assist students' in clarifying meaning: What does Stromae want Jamel to do (0:00–0:20)? How long does Stromae ask Jamel to stay (1:19–1:22)? Jamel suggests they need some lyrics to produce a specific emotion, followed by a refrain that makes you want to celebrate. What is this emotion (3:20–3:50)? Post-viewing discussion questions invite students to analyze the humor, compare and contrast, and consider broader cultural implications: *Quels sont les éléments comiques ? Qu'est-ce que Stromae et Debbouze ont en commun ? Pourquoi collaborent-ils, pensez-vous ? Que veut dire "la francophonie" ?*[39]

5. The sequence can end with the previous step, or it can continue with what follows here (which could also be its own sequence), centered on singer and author Corneille (Cornelius Nyungura), who, like Stromae, has roots in Rwanda.

   a. First, students work with the lyrics to Corneille's "Le Jour après la fin du monde" in class. This could focus on vocabulary, general comprehension, verb tenses, or another aspect of the song. (Lyrics are easily findable online via a search engine.)
   b. The students then imagine (aloud or on paper) what the video will be like, based on the lyrics.
   c. The class views the video together (https://youtu.be/Khz6ud6wFcw) and reacts. How does the video compare to what they had imagined it would be? Do the

lyrics go along with the visual aspect of the video? With the sound of the song?

d. The instructor introduces an image of the cover of Corneille's 2016 autobiography, *Là où le soleil disaparaît*, without revealing that the book recounts the events surrounding the murder of Corneille's family during the Rwandan genocide. Students respond to questions such as, What do you think the topic of his book is? How do you interpret the title?[40]

e. The instructor chooses one or more press articles about the book's publication for students to read. The instructor can also use YouTube video interviews with Corneille about his book. The reading/viewing should be accompanied by comprehension and discussion activities to engage the students.

f. The class discusses "Le Jour après la fin du monde" again, in light of the new information. Questions might include: Has your perspective about the video changed in any way? If so, how? Is your interpretation of the lyrics modified? If so, how? Why?

6. The sequence closes with a discussion (or projects) related to the Rwandan genocide, which students were first introduced to via Stromae. *Qu'est-ce que le génocide ? Que s'est-il passé au Rwanda ? Quels sont les effets du génocide rwandais aujourd'hui ? Quelle est l'importance d'étudier cette histoire ? Quel rôle jouent des gens célèbres en attirant notre attention sur cette tragédie ? Connaissez-vous d'autres sources d'information ou de représentations du génocide rwandais ? Comment représentent-elles ce qui s'est passé ?*[41]

The Scilabus and Stromae/Debbouze/Corneille sequences offer multiple avenues to pursue in extending the impact of, and learning associated with, one YouTube video.[42] With careful preparation and structuring, instructors can create meaningful and captivating experiences for language learners that extend in multimodal directions.

Activity 3: YouTube Playlists

YouTube playlists are collections of videos that users curate.[43] They can be grouped by any theme the user chooses and can be shared with others. Some instructors may already maintain playlists for their classes, though as Blake points out, this may place "a heavy burden on the instructor who needs to frame these materials linguistically and culturally in ways that will be meaningful for L2 learners."[44] In contrast, having students create their own playlists can personalize their experiences, instill autonomy, expose them to authentic language, introduce them to new ideas/music/regions/cultures, catalyze classroom discussions, foster sharing in the classroom, and allow for interactions with a wider (global) community.

To create a playlist, students will need to sign in to YouTube. If school restrictions or privacy-related concerns do not allow this, they could save the individual links for each video elsewhere. While the look of and use of a separate list of links may be clunkier, it will ultimately serve the purpose of gathering the material together.

For use in French courses, instructors will first need to create overarching objectives for the assignment. These could involve discovering new music, increasing debate skills in French, following and analyzing news coverage of a topic, or comparing manifestations of a particular concept or idea in different countries. The objectives can be adjusted to meet the overall goals and needs of the course. Students' playlists could be centered on a specific type of video (*publicités, clips de musique, vlogs, actualités,* or *bandes annonces*), a topic (*la santé, le sport, les femmes, la diversité, l'écologie*), or a subcategory of any of these. Alternatively, playlists could be a mixture of genres and topics, each connected by class assignments or the individual student's personal projects and preferences. Or the students could have multiple playlists, categorized according to theme. There are numerous text and video tutorials online about how to create a YouTube playlist, and as the specific steps to follow change as YouTube updates its site, the focus here will be instead on what to do with this type of activity.

A search on YouTube for "French playlist" will yield examples of existing playlists. Many YouTube channels also contain curated playlists. To find such channels, users enter a search term ("français," "diversité," "francophonie," "actualités") within YouTube's search box and use the filtering tool under the search box to limit results to channels or playlists. Additionally, the Ministère de la Culture's publication *350 chaînes YouTubes culturelles et scientifiques francophones* contains an annotated list of 350 YouTube channels with educational potential, categorized by subject.[45] While preexisting playlists can serve as examples for students to get started, the idea here is that students will be generating their own playlists, whether individually or in groups. An assignment of this type could be a unit within a larger lesson, or it could be an ongoing project throughout the course.

A sample music playlist assignment could be as follows: each week students add one French-language song to their playlist. On a class discussion board, they post a link to their playlist and song of the week, along with a three- to five-sentence explanation about why they chose that song. They will also comment on a classmate's post and once a week converse with a partner or in a group about their selections. If desired, instructors could require students to more formally present a song to the class, including an analysis of the lyrics and the visual images. This activity encourages student-centered personalization of language learning and interaction with French outside of class. A music playlist, in particular, is something the students might use even after the course is completed.

Another type of assignment could direct students to compile a playlist as a final project, accompanied by a written document or oral presentation in which they analyze and critique the content they selected. In this model, students could also be responsible for reviewing and expressing opinions about the videos found in classmates' playlists. Or the entire class could maintain a playlist, with one student per week responsible for presenting new content to add, along with their rationale for adding it. There are many possibilities for using playlists in French classes. Though the instructor provides goals and guidance, the students ultimately control the content of their playlists and choose which cultural elements to interact with.

Multiple viewings

In the above examples, the videos suggested are all relatively short. Thus, multiple viewings are possible, and perhaps preferable, in order to develop different skills and address different goals. First, the students could watch the video without sound, to focus on what they can discern about the situation from viewing the images. During a second viewing, students could focus on the sounds they hear, without subtitles. Many videos feature captions in English and French (adjustable in the settings for the video). As studies have shown, captions in the target language lead to improved listening comprehension.[46] Thus, a third viewing could involve hearing French and reading French subtitles, and a fourth viewing could involve hearing French and reading English subtitles. A final viewing without subtitles could complete the process. Any combination of these viewings could work, depending on the goals of the lesson. For example, goals could include a focus on linguistic matters: vocabulary acquisition, pronunciation practice (by repeating after the speaker), or comparing spoken French with English subtitles (Are they accurate? What expressions are lost in translation?). These are just a few examples of focus areas for multiple viewings.

CONCLUSION

YouTube, with its vast array of free content, is a rich source of authentic linguistic and cultural content. With planning, instructors can adapt its content to work with any course and thereby contribute to cultivating digital literacy, which Guikema and Williams note is currently lacking in foreign language learning and teaching[47]:

> Much more than a set of skills or competencies, digital literacies are conceptualized as a way of being an engaged, responsible reflective citizen in a 21st-century global community permeated by multimodal technologies. It is therefore critical that digital literacies be integrated throughout foreign/second language education, where multiple communities, identities, languages, and cultures converge.[48]

The activities presented above can encourage students to interact with French language and francophone cultures inside and outside the confines of courses and to "engage in nonhierarchical free play with new media and allow themselves to be creative, critical, and even audacious."[49] While students can use what they learn in the classroom to help them process and understand what they see/hear in French on YouTube, ideally, interacting with French-language and francophone-related content online will lead students to avoid considering French as merely a subject they study in school and instead as a part of everyday life in a global community—a community that they are able to understand and in which they can participate.

NOTES

1. Joseph M. Terantino, "YouTube for Foreign Languages: You Have to See This Video," *Language Learning & Technology* 15, no. 1 (2011): 11.

2. Pascale Perraudin and Shannon Porfilio, "Au-delà de la carte postale : culture et documents authentiques au niveau élémentaire," *French Review* 84, no. 3 (February 2011): 500–501.
3. Scott Taylor, "Integrating Performance Studies into the Foreign Language Curriculum via Digital Media: New Adventures in Multiliteracies," *French Review* 87, no. 1 (2013): 114.
4. Greg Kessler, "Technology and the Future of Language Teaching," *Foreign Language Annals* 51, no. 1 (2017): 206; Philip Hubbard, "CALL and the Future of Language Teacher Education," *CALICO Journal* 25, no. 2 (2008): 176; Janel Pettes Guikema and Mandy R. Menke, "Preparing Future Foreign Language Teachers: The Role of Digital Literacies," in *Digital Literacies in Foreign and Second Language Education*, ed. Janel Pettes Guikema and Lawrence Williams (San Marcos, TX: CALICO, 2014), 265–285; and Silvia Benini and Liam Murray, "Challenging Prensky's Characterization of Digital Natives and Digital Immigrants in a Real-World Classroom Setting," in Guikema and Williams, *Digital Literacies*, 69–85.
5. Robert Blake, "Technology and the Four Skills," *Language Learning & Technology* 20, no. 2 (2016): 133.
6. Guikema and Menke, "Preparing Future Foreign Language Teachers," 266–268
7. Kessler, "Technology," 2018; and Dolores Durán-Cerda, "Language Distance Learning for the Digital Generation," *Hispania* 93, no. 1 (2010): 109.
8. Terantino, "YouTube," 11; Durán-Cerda, "Language Distance Learning," 109–110; and Guikema and Menke, "Preparing Future Foreign Language Teachers."
9. Christoph A. Hafner, Alice Chik, and Rodney H. Jones, "Digital Literacies and Language Learning," *Language Learning & Technology* 19, no. 3 (2015): 1–2.
10. American Academy of Arts & Sciences, *America's Languages: Investing in Language Education for the 21st Century*, Commission on Language Learning (Cambridge, MA: American Academy of Arts & Sciences, 2017), ix, 11–13, https://www.amacad.org/sites/default/files/publication/downloads/Commission-on-Language-Learning_Americas-Languages.pdf. Using YouTube in French-language classrooms assumes access to technology, which, of course, remains problematic in some schools and for some learners and teachers. As the overall theme of this volume is on innovative ways of teaching culture and not on addressing social, economic, and technological challenges, this chapter will set aside the question of access to technology to focus instead on ways to use YouTube to introduce culture in French-language classes.
11. In contrast to Marc Prensky, Heather Lotherington and Natalia Ronda assert that "Authentic communication in the digital world is made not born. There

is no speaker native to the virtual world, and the concept of digital native (Prensky, 2001), which assigns innate expertise by birthright, is both dated and ageist. Digital competencies are socially learned, not innately developed." Heather Lotherington and Natalia Ronda, "2B or Not 2B? From Pencil to Multimodal Programming: New Frontiers in Communicative Competencies," in Guikema and Williams, *Digital Literacies*, 23. See also Marc Prensky, "Digital Natives, Digital Immigrants," *On the Horizon* 9, no. 5 (2001): 21.

12. YouTube, "YouTube for Press," accessed June 21, 2019, https://www.youtube.com/intl/en-GB/yt/about/press/.
13. Chareen Snelson, "YouTube across the Disciplines: A Review of the Literature," *MERLOT Journal of Online Learning and Teaching* 7, no. 1 (2011): 160.
14. Henriette L. Arndt and Robert Woore, "Vocabulary Learning from Watching YouTube Videos and Reading Blog Posts," *Language Learning & Technology* 22, no. 3 (2018): 135, https://www.lltjournal.org/item/3084.
15. Maribel Montero Perez, Piet Desmet, and Elke Peters, "Enhancing Vocabulary Learning through Captioned Video: An Eye-Tracking Study," *Modern Language Journal* 99, no. 2 (2015): 324.
16. Terantino, "YouTube," 11 and 14.
17. Taylor, "Integrating Performance Studies," 116.
18. Phil Benson, *The Discourse of YouTube: Multimodal Text in a Global Context* (New York: Routledge, 2017), 2.
19. Phil Benson, "Commenting to Learn: Evidence of Language and Intercultural Learning in Comments on YouTube Videos," *Language Learning & Technology* 19, no. 3 (2015): 88–105.
20. Claire Kramsch, "Teaching Foreign Languages in an Era of Globalization: Introduction," *Modern Language Journal* 98, no. 1 (2014): 305.
21. Kramsch, 305.
22. Hafner, Chik, and Jones, "Digital Literacies," 3; and Robert Godwin-Jones, "Emerging Technologies: Integrating Intercultural Competence into Language Learning through Technology," *Language Learning & Technology* 17, no. 2 (2013): 1–11.
23. Kramsch, "Teaching Foreign Languages," 305.
24. American Council on the Teaching of Foreign Languages (ACTFL) and Partnership for 21st Century Skills (P21), "21stt Century Skills Map," March 2011, 4, https://www.actfl.org/sites/default/files/resources/21st%20Century%20Skills%20Map-World%20Languages.pdf
25. ACTFL and P21, 5.
26. Blake, "Technology," 133.
27. Taylor, "Integrating Performance Studies," 116.

28. Christelle Combe and Tatiana Codreanu, "Vlogging: A New Channel for Language Learning and Intercultural Exchanges," in *CALL Communities and Culture—Short Papers from EUROCALL 2016*, ed. Salomi Papadima-Sophocleous, Linda Bradley, and Sylvie Thouësny (Voillans, France: Research-publishing.net, 2016), 120, 123.
29. Janel Pettes Guikema, "Discourse Analysis of Podcasts in French: Implications for Foreign Language Listening Development," in *Electronic Discourse in Language Learning and Language Teaching*, ed. Lee B. Abraham and Lawrence Williams (Amsterdam and Philadelphia: John Benjamins Publishing Company, 2009), 181.
30. Audrey D., "Audrey D., Youtubeuse québecoise: About," YouTube, accessed July 15, 2019, https://www.youtube.com/user/DododFun/about.
31. Audrey D., "Présentation de ma chaîne," YouTube, October 4, 2017, https://youtu.be/eoDIdNuOHcl.
32. Audrey D., "Je cuisine une poutine maison (recette poutine québécoise)," YouTube, June 8, 2019, https://www.youtube.com/watch?v=HQlCkJhjLiQ.
33. Pauline P., "Ma Vie aux Etats-Unis-Récit d'expatrié," SC Magazine, May 01, 2017, https://www.sprachcaffe.com/francais/sprachcaffe-magazine-article/ma-vie-aux-etats-unis-recit-dexpatrie-2017-05-01.htm
34. Perraudin and Porfilio, "Au-delà de la carte postale," 487.
35. Perraudin and Porfilio, 302.
36. Liv Audigane, "Six youtubeurs pour vous réconcilier avec les sciences," *Les Echos Start*, February 10, 2017, https://start.lesechos.fr/actus/cultures-medias/six-youtubeurs-pour-vous-reconcilier-avec-les-sciences-7322.php.
37. Erwan Cario and Camille Gévaudan, "Sur YouTube, la science infuse," *Libération*, September 7, 2016, https://www.liberation.fr/futurs/2016/09/07/sur-youtube-la-science-infuse_1488980/.
38. Translation: What is his profession? Where did he grow up? Where is his family from? What languages do they speak? Why is he well known in the francophone world? What accident befell him? What was its effect on his life?
39. Translation: What are the comic elements? What do Stromae and Debbouze have in common? Why do you think they are collaborating? What does "la francophonie" mean?
40. Optional: The instructor then provides students with samples of fans' comments about the book, using screenshots or transcribed text from Corneille's Facebook page. The class could discuss fans' reactions and/or analyze language use in terms of vocabulary or grammar. Instructors can find posts related to Corneille's autobiography by navigating to his Facebook page,

clicking on "posts" in the navigation menu, and then entering the book's title in the search engine ("Search for posts on this Page").

41. What is genocide? What happened in Rwanda? What are the effects of the Rwandan genocide today? What is the importance of studying this history? What role do celebrities play in drawing our attention to this tragedy? Do you know of other sources of information or representations of the Rwandan genocide? How do they represent what happened?

42. Further ideas for such types of "beyond the video" activities are plentiful in Jayne Abrate et al., *Martinique : culture, histoire et environnement en contexte pour la classe de français* (Marion, IL: American Association of Teachers of French, 2019). The entire volume is focused on using YouTube videos about Martinique in French-language classrooms.

43. For further ideas for using playlists, see Audra Merfeld-Langston, "Mobilizing French: Using YouTube Playlists to Personalize Language Learning," *American Association of Teachers of French National Bulletin* 43, no. 3 (2018): 17.

44. Blake, "Technology," 133.

45. Mathilde Hutin, *350 chaînes YouTubes culturelles et scientifiques francophones*, Langue française et langues de France, Ministère de la Culture, November 9, 2018, https://www.culture.gouv.fr/Sites-thematiques/Langue-francaise-et-langues-de-France/Ressources/Ressources-pedagogiques-et-sensibilisation2/350-ressources-culturelles-et-scientifiques-francophones-en-video.

46. Isabel Borrás and Robert C. Lafayette, "Effects of Multimedia Courseware Subtitling on the Speaking Performance of College Students of French," *Modern Language Journal* 78, no. 1 (1994): 61–75; and Perez, Desmet, and Peters, "Enhancing Vocabulary Learning."

47. Janel Pettes Guikema and Lawrence Williams, "Digital Literacies from Multiple Perspectives," in Guikema and Williams, *Digital Literacies*, 1.

48. Guikema and Williams, 3.

49. Lotherington and Ronda, "2B or Not 2B?," 23.

REFERENCES

Abrate, Jayne, Catherine Daniélou, Anne Jensen, and Audra Merfeld-Langston. *Martinique : culture, histoire et environnement en contexte pour la classe de français*. Marion, IL: American Association of Teachers of French, 2019.

American Academy of Arts & Sciences. *America's Languages: Investing in Language Education for the 21stt Century*. Commission on Language Learning. Cambridge, MA: American Academy of Arts & Sciences, 2017. https://www.

amacad.org/sites/default/files/publication/downloads/Commission-on-Language-Learning_Americas-Languages.pdf.

American Council on the Teaching of Foreign Languages (ACTFL). *World-Readiness Standards for Learning Languages*. Accessed June 6, 2019. https://www.actfl.org/sites/default/files/publications/standards/World-Readiness-StandardsforLearningLanguages.pdf.

American Council on the Teaching of Foreign Languages (ACTFL) and Partnership for 21st Century Skills (P21). "21st Century Skills Map." March 2011. https://www.actfl.org/sites/default/files/pdfs/21stCenturySkillsMap/p21_worldlanguagesmap.pdf.

Amini Cishugi. YouTube. https://www.youtube.com/channel/UCrEbDdjhkfKd66Yx_rvxTOw.

———. "A Day in a Burundian Public School—VLOG #26." YouTube, April 8, 2020. https://youtu.be/Dowt1FeceLU.

———. "L'art de négocier un taxi vélo en Afrique, surtout au Burundi—VLOG #36." YouTube, June 17, 2020. https://youtu.be/2Nsv6hjonfI.

———. "A l'intérieur d'un marché africain d'épicerie—VLOG #3." YouTube, June 20, 2020. https://youtu.be/28Qd6ka4rz4.

Arndt, Henriette L., and Robert Woore. "Vocabulary Learning from Watching YouTube Videos and Reading Blog Posts." *Language Learning & Technology* 22, no. 3 (2018): 124–142. https://www.lltjournal.org/item/3084.

Audigane, Liv. "Six youtubeurs pour vous réconcilier avec les sciences." *Les Echos Start*, February 10, 2017. https://start.lesechos.fr/actus/cultures-medias/six-youtubeurs-pour-vous-reconcilier-avec-les-sciences-7322.php.

Audrey D. "Audrey D., Youtubeuse québecoise : About." YouTube text, accessed July 15, 2019. https://www.youtube.com/user/DododFun/about.

———. "Je cuisine une poutine maison (recette poutine québécoise)." YouTube, June 8, 2019. https://www.youtube.com/watch?v=HQlCkJhjLiQ.

———. "Présentation de ma chaîne." YouTube, October 4, 2017. https://youtu.be/eoDIdNuOHcl.

Benini, Silvia, and Liam Murray. "Challenging Prensky's Characterization of Digital Natives and Digital Immigrants in a Real-World Classroom Setting." In *Digital Literacies in Foreign and Second Language Education*, edited by Janel Pettes Guikema and Lawrence Williams, 69–85. San Marcos, TX: CALICO, 2014.

Benson, Phil. "Commenting to Learn: Evidence of Language and Intercultural Learning in Comments on YouTube Videos." *Language Learning & Technology* 19, no. 3 (2015): 88–105.

Benson, Phil. Commenting to Learn: Evidence of Language and Intercultural Learning in Comments on YouTube Videos." *Language Learning & Technology* 19, no. 3 (2015): 88–105.

———. *The Discourse of YouTube: Multimodal Text in a Global Context*. New York: Routledge, 2017.

Blake, Robert. "Technology and the Four Skills." *Language Learning & Technology* 20, no. 2 (2016): 129–142.

Borrás, Isabel, and Robert C. Lafayette. "Effects of Multimedia Courseware Subtitling on the Speaking Performance of College Students of French." *Modern Language Journal* 78, no. 1 (1994): 61–75.

Cario, Erwan, and Camille Gévaudan. "Sur YouTube, la science infuse." *Libération*, September 7, 2016. https://www.liberation.fr/futurs/2016/09/07/sur-youtube-la-science-infuse_1488980/.

Combe, Christelle, and Tatiana Codreanu. "Vlogging: A New Channel for Language Learning and Intercultural Exchanges." In *CALL Communities and Culture—Short Papers from EUROCALL 2016*, edited by Salomi Papadima-Sophocleous, Linda Bradley, and Sylvie Thouësny, 119–124. Voillans, France: Research-publishing.net, 2016. https://doi.org/10.14705/rpnet.2016.eurocall2016.548.

Corneille. *Là où le soleil disparaît*. Paris: Xo éditions, 2016.

Corneille. "Le Jour après la fin du Monde." YouTube, July 22, 2011. https://youtu.be/Khz6ud6wFcw.

DGLFLF (Délégation Générale à la Langue Française et aux Langues de France), Ministère de la Culture. "Avant-propos." In *350 chaînes YouTubes culturelles et scientifiques*, by Mathilde Hutin, 203. Langue française et langues de France. Ministère de la Culture, November 9, 2018, 2–3. http://www.culture.gouv.fr/Thematiques/Langue-francaise-et-langues-de-France/Ressources/Ressources-pedagogiques-et-sensibilisation/350-ressources-culturelles-et-scientifiques-francophones-en-video.

Durán-Cerda, Dolores. "Language Distance Learning for the Digital Generation." *Hispania* 93, no. 1 (2010): 108–112.

Godwin-Jones, Robert. "Emerging Technologies: Integrating Intercultural Competence into Language Learning through Technology." *Language Learning & Technology* 17, no. 2 (2013): 1–11.

Guikema, Janel Pettes. "Discourse Analysis of Podcasts in French: Implications for Foreign Language Listening Development." In *Electronic Discourse in Language Learning and Language Teaching*, edited by Lee B. Abraham and Lawrence Williams, 169–189. Amsterdam and Philadelphia: John Benjamins Publishing Company, 2009.

Guikema, Janel Pettes, and Mandy R. Menke. "Preparing Future Foreign Language Teachers: The Role of Digital Literacies." In *Digital Literacies in Foreign and Second Language Education*, edited by Janel Pettes Guikema and Lawrence Williams, 265–285. San Marcos, TX: CALICO, 2014.

Guikema, Janel Pettes, and Lawrence Williams. "Digital Literacies from Multiple Perspectives." In *Digital Literacies in Foreign and Second Language Education*, edited by Janel Pettes Guikema and Lawrence Williams, 1–7. San Marcos, TX: CALICO, 2014.

Hafner, Christoph A., Alice Chik, and Rodney H. Jones. "Digital Literacies and Language Learning." *Language Learning & Technology* 19, no. 3 (2015): 1–7.

Houy, Benjamin. "41 Popular French Youtubers That Will Help You Better Understand Spoken French." *French Together*, accessed June 20, 2019. https://frenchtogether.com/french-youtubers/.

Hubbard, Philip. "CALL and the Future of Language Teacher Education." *CALICO Journal* 25, no. 2 (2008): 175–188.

Hutin, Mathilde. *350 chaînes YouTubes culturelles et scientifiques francophones*. Langue française et langues de France. Ministère de la Culture, November 9, 2018. http://www.culture.gouv.fr/Thematiques/Langue-francaise-et-langues-de-France/Ressources/Ressources-pedagogiques-et-sensibilisation/350-ressources-culturelles-et-scientifiques-francophones-en-video.

Kessler, Greg. "Technology and the Future of Language Teaching." *Foreign Language Annals* 51, no. 1 (2017): 205–218.

Kramsch, Claire. "Teaching Foreign Languages in an Era of Globalization: Introduction." *Modern Language Journal* 98, no. 1 (2014): 296–311.

Lalande, Viviane. "On est allés voir Pluton !" Kidi'Science, July 15, 2015. https://kidiscience.cafe-sciences.org/articles/on-est-alles-voir-pluton/.

Lotherington, Heather, and Natalia Ronda. "2B or Not 2B? From Pencil to Multimodal Programming: New Frontiers in Communicative Competencies." In *Digital Literacies in Foreign and Second Language Education*, edited by Janel Pettes Guikema and Lawrence Williams, 9–28. San Marcos, TX: CALICO, 2014.

Lowery, Tim. "Meet Stromae, the Most Famous Pop Star You've Never Heard of." *Time Out* (New York), April 28, 2014. https://www.timeout.com/newyork/music/meet-stromae-the-most-famous-pop-star-youve-never-heard-of.

Ma Vie aux États-Unis. YouTube. https://www.youtube.com/c/MavieauxEtatsUnis/featured.

———. "Dire bonjour aux Américains : Les Hugs !" YouTube, December 7, 2015. https://youtu.be/5wPcaQ-5mr4.

———. "Shopping in the United States." YouTube, July 29, 2015. https://youtu.be/jywwFGQWLKw.

Merfeld-Langston, Audra. "Mobilizing French: Using YouTube Playlists to Personalize Language Learning." *American Association of Teachers of French National Bulletin* 43, no. 3 (2018): 17.

P., Pauline."Ma Vie aux Etats-Unis-Récit d'expatrié." *SC Magazine*, May 01, 2017. https://www.sprachcaffe.com/francais/sprachcaffe-magazine-article/ma-vie-aux-etats-unis-recit-dexpatrie-2017-05-01.htm.

Parker, Ian. "Ridiculous." *New Yorker*, June 30, 2014. https://www.newyorker.com/magazine/2014/07/07/ridiculous-2.

Perez, Maribel Montero, Piet Desmet, and Elke Peters. "Enhancing Vocabulary Learning through Captioned Video: An Eye-Tracking Study." *Modern Language Journal* 99, no. 2 (2015): 308–328.

Perraudin, Pascale, and Shannon Porfilio, "Au-delà de la carte postale : culture et documents authentiques au niveau élémentaire," *French Review* 84, no. 3 (February 2011): 486–502.

Prensky, Marc. "Digital Natives, Digital Immigrants." *On the Horizon* 9, no. 5 (2001). https://www.marcprensky.com/writing/Prensky%20-%20Digital%20Natives,%20Digital%20Immigrants%20-%20Part1.pdf.

Scilabus. YouTube. https://www.youtube.com/user/scilabus.

———. "Ce que les cris des joueurs communiquent à l'adversaire." YouTube, June 5, 2019. https://youtu.be/TATMgXt2jvE.

———. "Pourquoi l'ourlet des t-shirts est-il indispensable ?" YouTube, June 19, 2019. https://youtu.be/FJ3Jb4SUvf8.

———. "Pourquoi y a t-il autant d'air dans les sacs de chips ?" YouTube, May 1, 2019. https://youtu.be/1k8BuOLoixA.

Snelson, Chareen. "YouTube across the Disciplines: A Review of the Literature." *MERLOT Journal of Online Learning and Teaching* 7, no. 1 (2011): 159–169.

Son, Jeong-Bae. "Learning about Computer-Assisted Language Learning: Online Tools and Professional Development." In *Computer-Assisted Language Learning: Learners, Teachers and Tools*, edited by Jeong-Bae Son, 173–186. Newcastle upon Tyne, UK: Cambridge Scholars Publishing, 2014.

Stromae. "Stromae—Alors On Danse (Clip Officiel)." YouTube, April 28, 2010. https://youtu.be/VH0T4N43jK8.

Taylor, Scott. "Integrating Performance Studies into the Foreign Language Curriculum via Digital Media: New Adventures in Multiliteracies." *French Review* 87, no. 1 (2013): 113–124.

Terantino, Joseph M. "YouTube for Foreign Languages: You Have to See This Video." *Language Learning & Technology* 15, no. 1 (2011): 10–16.

YouTube. "YouTube for Press." Accessed June 21, 2019. https://www.youtube.com/intl/en-GB/yt/about/press/.

CHAPTER TEN

CHARTING THE COURSE

Online Maps as a Tool in the French Culture Classroom

Carrie O'Connor, Boston University

INTRODUCTION

Among the many digital and interactive learning tools available to language learners today, shared mapping applications present a multimodal source with numerous possible pedagogical benefits. Online maps that include user-created content, such as Google Maps, can be used in a range of language courses, from beginner to advanced content-based curricula. As freely adaptable, continually changing information sources, online maps enhance the learner's connection to the places in which different languages are spoken, providing a glimpse into both contemporary life as well as changes over time. In addition to connecting with cities and villages far from home or the classroom, students can also read and view the user-created text, photos, and videos; what's more, the tool allows users to interact with this content, so students can pose questions to and solicit feedback from locals or visitors alike, essentially creating borderless learning communities.

How can we, as facilitators of language learning, contextualize the use of shared maps so as to maximize their functionality both in and outside the classroom? How, then, can students use their own creativity and digital savvy in order to connect language to place, both in real and virtual spaces? Furthermore, how can instructors and students work together to enlarge and deepen the linguistic and cultural knowledge fields by integrating maps in various activities and projects?

This project aims to illuminate some of the possible uses of shared online mapping tools in language instruction. In order to do so, I will refer to the already robust and growing field of place-based education (and its more recent offshoot—virtual place-based education). Additionally, I will outline a specific application of Google My Maps from a final assessment for an Advanced French for Business course at an American university. Using American Council on the Teaching of Foreign Languages (ACTFL) language proficiency guidelines, I demonstrate how this project fulfills a multitude of learning outcomes across two of the four skills (namely, writing and speaking) as well as intercultural competency. Using this project as a successful model, I will then explore further innovative uses of the digital mapping tool in a variety of language-learning environments with the aim of contributing to and advancing a forum in which educators can find inspiration and share their own successes and challenges. Finally, it is necessary to recognize the possible challenges in using online platforms so that students, as well as their personal information, remain protected.

CONTEXT

Traditionally in language classrooms, students have engaged in a multitude of ways with or in the target language using role-playing, realia-based activities, and so on. As educators, our role has multiple facets, but ideally, we are learning facilitators and coaches, especially in a flipped, student-centered classroom. As students (and the world writ large) have become more and more immersed in (and arguably, dependent upon) digital technologies, so too has the classroom and the tools that it encompasses. Therefore, we as instructors have needed to adapt to integrate new digital and interactive tools in addition to those tried and true tools and methods in our teaching. The purpose of this project is to probe the current foreign language learning tools in order to inquire how they can be applied most effectively to achieve various learning outcomes, specifically in a content-based language course. In this type of learning environment, students not only engage with the language and content, but they develop multiple literacies that will eventually support them in their chosen profession (business, in this example). Interaction with online shared maps in the final assessment supports each of the four literacies commonly referred to under the umbrella of multiple literacies: visual, textual, digital, and technological.

MAPS AS AN INSTRUCTIONAL TOOL

Drawn maps depicting topography and political boundaries are ubiquitous inside the front and/or back covers of language textbooks. Sometimes, we may refer students to these colorful maps at the beginning of a course in order to illustrate the scope of a language's geographical reach. Perhaps a unit on history or culture later in the course will include a more detailed map of a region or country that is less well known to the general population. In lessons aimed at reinforcing grammatical structures such as the imperative verb form, we may turn to more localized maps of cities or neighborhoods so that students can give and follow cardinal directions. In these instances, images of places and how they are situated in the world are essential for students to connect to the content, whether it be linguistic or cultural. There are, of course, other ways that instructors have incorporated maps into their teaching over the years, as many blogs and online fora attest. Building upon these teaching strategies with new technologies is not only useful but many would argue necessary in a rapidly changing global environment in which students need a multitude of skills in order to be successful global citizens.

In order to capitalize on students' already strong familiarity with digital tools, we can use online shared maps, such as Google My Maps, in the physical or virtual classroom to enhance existing effective pedagogical methods and models. Shared online maps have the "potential to make student-centered learning a reality by promoting learner agency, autonomy and engagement in social networks that straddle multiple real and virtual communities independent of physical, geographic, institutional and organisational boundaries," as Catherine McLoughlin and Mark Lee observe.[1] The online maps connect individuals and groups through digital means to places and spaces that they might not otherwise encounter in reality. They can experience the geography, both physical and political, of places that are relevant to learning about the histories and cultures associated with the languages that they are studying. Additionally, students can connect with one another in the virtual spaces created by shared online maps, creating new, parallel communities to the one already established in the classroom. If doing so is deemed appropriate and useful, students also have the opportunity to engage with other users in public digital spaces associated with their own maps. Through this use of maps as an innovative teaching tool, students are able to experience greater control of their own learning and thus (hopefully) become more engaged and successful overall. This, in turn, supports a student-centered learning environment.

GOOGLE MY MAPS

Google offers a tool within its broad suite of applications called My Maps, a separate tool that can be accessed from within the Google Maps tool. I focus on this particular online mapping tool, instead of others,[2] to highlight its functionality in a variety of task-based lessons and projects, specifically in one student project that I will develop in a later section. Google Maps, in general, are definitely useful in place of the more traditional drawn maps referenced earlier. Students can easily navigate cities, see satellite images, and virtually "walk" the streets past businesses, parks, and residences from their computers or mobile devices. In order to create a personalized map with saved locations, annotations, and more features, one must have a Google ID (most commonly obtained through the use of the Gmail tool) and use of a web browser. Once a user is signed in, they can navigate to Your Places from the Google Maps menu, then click on the Maps tab in order to create a new map or access existing personal maps. Google provides instructions on how to access and use the function through its Support page.[3] Students are mostly familiar with the Google suite of applications and can quickly learn how to use My Maps effectively.

Of particular interest to language instructors is the ability to use Google tools in a variety of languages so that students can interact directly in the target language when using their personalized maps. This serves multiple functions: on assignments and projects, it is not necessary to instruct or guide using English in order to use the tool; students learn the relevant vocabulary and nomenclature through direct interaction with the maps rather than through teacher-centered presentation and explanation. Place names, directions, even distances are all presented in the target language (and unit of measure), which enables students to absorb potentially new content in an already comfortable interface, thus relieving some of the stress or resistance that some learners are bound to experience.

THE COURSE AND FINAL PROJECT

With the historical and more recent interactive uses of maps in mind, I now turn to a presentation of a successful example of a college-level final assessment using Google My Maps. In an Advanced French for Business course that I taught to students during the summer prior to their semester or year abroad in France,[4] I piloted a final project based on creating a *plan perso*, or personal map, of Paris using the Google My Maps tool. The students taking the course were mostly rising juniors who had completed at least six semesters of college-level French.[5] Therefore, their French skills were judged to be at roughly the equivalent of the Intermediate Mid sublevel, according to ACTFL. In addition, their major (or second major, if French was also their major) was in a business field, so this course was also content specific and the second course in a two-part sequence (they completed the first course during the previous spring semester). The syllabus outlined the course objectives and goals as follows:

> Students will develop their competence in the interpersonal, interpretive, and presentational modes of communication through activities that focus on grammar, vocabulary, and culture. Specifically, students will be able to:
>
> - understand the organization of commercial firms in France.
> - understand etiquette and social dynamics within a French company.
> - determine a product's compatibility with French markets and devise a French marketing campaign.
> - have a deeper understanding of French written and conversational business practices.
> - understand and analyze press documents.

Using authentic materials ranging from newspaper and magazine articles, print and video advertisements, publicly available corporate organizational documents (e.g., organizational structures, business strategies, marketing plans, etc.), students were able to learn specifics and from them compile general inferences about French business practices. Although this course was taught in a traditional classroom on an American university campus, these realia documents allowed students to immerse themselves in a specific professional and cultural milieu that was further enhanced by classroom language immersion. Because the course targeted students studying in France, the content was also largely focused on the Hexagon and, specifically, its capital, Paris.[6] Realia with associated place-focused grammar activities as well as cultural and historical readings paired naturally with using maps in class to enhance the content. In the "Learning Outcomes" section, I will elaborate on how other educators have successfully integrated place-based education (PBE) methods in other domains.

Beyond the daily assignments and class presentations/discussions, the Advanced French for Business course culminated in a final project designed to showcase the breadth and depth of skills and knowledge that students had acquired. This final project was to create, as stated above, a *plan perso* of Paris and consisted of two interrelated assessments aimed at evaluating students' linguistic aptitudes (in presentational speaking and writing) as well as their research and business analysis capabilities. The first part of the project asked students to identify and research five (or more) sites in Paris according to a theme that was personally interesting or relevant to them (ranging from lesser-known public parks to nightclubs).[7] They then situated these five sites on their Google My Maps of Paris and gave a short presentation of each location and how they wished to discover them while in France. The description included practical information, such as precise geographical location, historical background, and personal relevance, to name a few elements. Then, in a second part of the oral presentation and written report, students focused on just one of the chosen sites to give in-depth information. I required that students perform adequate primary and secondary research in order to discuss the history; public reception; past, present, and/or future marketing/publicity strategies; and overall evolution about that one site.

In order to guide students in this research portion of the project, I gave them the example of the first McDonald's restaurant in France. Given the fast food restaurant's rocky history with France and the French, there is ample historical and current information to develop a robust and detailed presentation of the business in this specific context. Drawing upon this example, one student, a self-proclaimed "foodie" who loved trying out different bakeries and restaurants (an activity that she also enjoyed around her university in Boston), chose, among her five sites, one bakery focused on gluten-free breads and pastries that had recently opened in the increasingly hip, lesser-known 11th district of Paris. During her research to identify this one site, she also learned of several other bakeries that she would add to her own enlarged *plan perso* to actually visit and try out while in Paris, beyond just the sites required for the class project. As a way to encourage maintaining the classroom community throughout the students' time in France, I suggested that they share their personal maps with their classmates and continue adding to them as they discover the city "in real life." In future iterations of this course or project, I would like to propose additional activities that students could engage with while on site as well as upon return to their home institution. This seems to be the place, in my experience and research, where interactive community-based projects end but where they have the potential to grow and continually enrich the students and course in general.

Creating a student-centered model for the final project, all the while insisting upon rigorous linguistic and research skills, allowed students to become personally invested in their work. This not only makes the required "work" more pleasurable and relatable but also ensures that students feel an important ownership of their knowledge. As McLoughlin and Lee insist, "In today's knowledge based society, characterised by rapid change, dynamic communication and knowledge advancement, core competencies needed are self-direction, problem solving, critical inquiry, creativity, teamwork and communication skills, which can be fostered through engagement with pedagogies that leverage digital tools, content and services."[8] In order to meet these "real-world" objectives, digital shareable mapping tools can be leveraged in many ways and are not limited to the scope of the final assessment detailed above.

LEARNING OBJECTIVES AND OUTCOMES

The learning objectives of the two-part final project, thus, focused on the students' writing and speaking skills, all within a content-based framework. Beyond the linguistic learning objectives (developed below), students would be able to enhance their geographical and cultural understanding of the city of Paris according to the specific locations that they selected and presented to the class. Additionally, they would continue to develop multiple literacies through firsthand interaction with digital and technological tools.

In accordance with ACTFL language proficiency guidelines, the My Maps final project assessed students' speaking competence on an Advanced Low to Advanced Mid level, placing emphasis on their abilities to link ideas together in paragraphs, present on topics of personal and public interest with relative ease, and use a wide general vocabulary as well as accurate specific vocabulary in a particular subject area. Overall, most students performed at the Advanced Mid level, with a few at the Advanced Low level due to some inclusion of false cognates or native language influence in the vocabulary or construction areas. Students were encouraged to interact with their peers following the oral presentations by asking for clarification, elaboration, or other pertinent information relative to the sites and/or research performed for the project. This activity gave students further opportunity to interact with individuals of a similar proficiency level in a relatively low-stakes environment. Again, the student-centered topic allowed each individual to take ownership of their work and to essentially become an "expert" vis-à-vis their peers. At the same time that the student shared recently acquired knowledge, they were enlarging that of their classmates and perhaps inspiring them to continue learning about the specific place. Students could begin to make connections between their chosen sites and engage in dialogue that would, hopefully, continue beyond the classroom walls to the very places discussed within them.

When I assessed students on their presentational writing proficiency, I directed them to write in their highest possible level based on their previous knowledge and the more in-depth study on advanced and problematic structures in the language that we had explored in class. They typically performed at the Intermediate High and sometimes Advanced Low levels. They were able to communicate adequately about information of public interest that demonstrated comprehension of topic-specific (business) vocabulary. However, some students wrote in a style very similar to their spoken French and often missed some of the more nuanced stylistic markers of higher proficiency levels. Their writing could be understood by most non-native speakers, but some meaning could be lost to native readers.

The students would ideally exit this Advanced French for Business course with high enough (Intermediate Mid to Advanced Mid) proficiency levels in all four language skills to communicate on a variety of personal and public interest topics, using appropriate vocabulary and structures. Furthermore, they would feel comfortable interacting with native speakers in a professional environment upon commencement of their internships in France. Ultimately, the course would give students the necessary tools and confidence to communicate effectively while they continued to progress and improve in a true immersive environment.

PLACE-BASED EDUCATION

Beyond the ACTFL language proficiency learning guidelines, this project using online, shareable maps was intended to enlarge students' cultural and historical knowledge of a specific place—Paris. Scholars have argued the merits of place-based education (PBE) for decades, often in an environmental or ecological framework.[9] One of the leading scholars and pioneers of PBE, David Sobel, defines the model as "the process of using the local community and environment as a starting point to teach concepts in language arts, mathematics, social studies, science and other subjects across the curriculum."[10] He argues further that "[e]mphasizing hands-on, real-world learning experiences, this approach to education increases academic achievement, helps students develop stronger ties to their community, enhances students' appreciation for the natural world, and creates a heightened commitment to serving as active, contributing citizens."[11] Often, as Sobel describes, PBE has traditionally meant taking students out into nature or the community adjacent to the school so that they are able to interact directly with the places around them and, ultimately, positively impact those places through their presence. And although Merrilyne Lundahl's argument for using PBE in a secondary school English class to connect students to their immediate environments through literature—"when people connect to place and make it personal, they become more committed to it"—it is, in my view, equally apt for the language and culture classroom.[12]

Using PBE as an educational model puts students directly in the place being studied in order to enhance the assignments, lessons, and learning outcomes. Again, Sobel argues that "[place-based] curriculum can mirror the expanding scope of the child's [or adult's] significant world, focusing first on the home and school, then the neighborhood, the community, the region, and beyond."[13] Following these descriptions and examples, it would seem that the PBE model is best suited for classes that aim to study and/or impact the places immediately surrounding the classroom.

Perhaps it is possible to envision PBE as an appropriate model for foreign language classes only in a study abroad framework, where students are physically located in the very places on which their courses focus. However, as teaching and learning have developed to include more digital communication tools and interactivity, so too have pedagogical models, including PBE.

In more recent years, our ways of understanding and implementing PBE have evolved to include the use of these new digital technologies. The *virtual* place-based educational model, as defined by Reneta Lansiquot and Sean MacDonald, is when a "virtual location is used to realize the concept of place where access to the geographic location is not possible. In such cases, the virtual becomes innovative and creative, making the place real and transcending the limitations of, or access to, the physical space."[14] For Lansiquot and MacDonald, VPBE became not only helpful but also at times necessary for their interdisciplinary classes at the New York City College of Technology (City Tech) in Brooklyn. Due to the highly urbanized surroundings of the campus as well as the financial limitations of the student body, educators were encouraged to look outside the traditional classroom in innovative ways to enhance their courses. When real places were inaccessible, they used "virtual worlds" in order to engage students in experiential activities, even while they did not change their "real-world" classroom location. Lansiquot and MacDonald's book, *Interdisciplinary Place-Based Learning in Urban Education*, is an excellent compilation of educators' attempts at pushing the boundaries of what place-based education is and can be when paired with other pedagogical models (such as interdisciplinarity and learning communities) as well as digital technologies. The examples undertaken at City Tech reflect this movement toward new possible adaptations of PBE and how it can be applied in varied circumstances and environments.

David Gruenewald, for one, also proposes a new framework placing PBE alongside critical pedagogy: a critical pedagogy of place. He stresses that one cannot dissociate place from the very real impacts that students (people) have upon it; in short, he claims, "Acknowledging that experience has a geographical context opens the way to admitting critical social and ecological concerns into one's understanding of place, and the role of places in education. This is the goal of a critical pedagogy of place."[15] Although this may at first blush seem self-evident, Gruenewald carefully examines the effects of using PBE in diverse ways and, more importantly, defines an overarching theoretical model that educators can point to when implementing innovative techniques in the classroom.

I have introduced here but a mere few examples of scholars adapting and creating new pedagogical models that best suit their individual class needs; as they ponder and evaluate the immediate effects of these innovations, other educators can benefit from new definitions and goals of these models. For my purposes, the virtual place-based nature of the Advanced French for Business *plan perso* project enhances students' cultural literacy by requiring them to imagine inhabiting a place (which would indeed become their future home, at least for a short time). Through this virtual geographical interactivity, students remove themselves, at least mentally, from the physical classroom space and are able to think about and explore a completely unknown place thousands of miles from their actual location.

FURTHER APPLICATIONS OF ONLINE MAPS IN LANGUAGE INSTRUCTION

The Google My Maps *plan perso* project that I conducted in my Advanced French for Business course is obviously just one use of digital interactive maps in a language class. Other language instructors, such as middle school French teacher Samantha Decker of the blog *The French Corner*,[16] have integrated maps longitudinally starting with absolute beginners. Decker uses Google Maps in a *chasse au trésor* (treasure hunt) activity wherein students are directed to specific addresses in francophone locations in order to answer questions related to the location (café, shop, bakery, etc.) in the Street View photographs. Google Lit Trips, a nonprofit organization, invites scholars and educators of a broad range of fields to design and submit their own examples of virtual trips that include locations of note on a variety of topics.[17] Existing examples on the higher education level include sites associated with James Joyce, Cormac McCarthy, and others. It is plain to see that the field is wide open to submissions in a multitude of genres, languages, and geographical locations.

In the French language, culture, and literature courses that I have taught over the years, I use maps in class to situate fictional literary or historical scenes such as the Maison Vauquer in Honoré de Balzac's *Le Père Goriot* or the bayous of Louisiana shown in the music video of Christophe Maé's song *Tombé sous le charme*. In the first case, students begin to visualize the street where the fictional house is described as being located, then the surrounding neighborhood and perhaps the characters' views of other parts of Paris. In the second example, students have a visual reference and song lyrics to draw from, but the map gives those images a relatable location that students can use to contextualize the message and references in the song. Maps, in these examples, are either starting points or additional aids that form a larger picture and enhance a student's understanding of content.

Since students are already so familiar with digital mapping applications, much can be done in the language classroom to exploit these skills. For example, they can form groups in class to navigate, explore, and share information. They can save specific locations, organize them using color-coded symbols, annotate with comments and narration, and then collaborate on the maps that they have created. More broadly, students can share and interact with others through the public forum provided in the Google Maps application. Using the Tour Builder function through Google Earth (in beta) (or Expeditions Pro), it is also possible to create a virtual voyage from place to place. With a (free) Google account, one can set the time spent at each location, the order in which a user "visits" each location, and add audio narration or text.

POSSIBLE SHORTCOMINGS

As noted in my introduction, many other shareable map applications are publicly available either for free or with fees. In my explorations of each of them, including Google My Maps, I did encounter some disadvantages.[18] Like any shared online platform, the use of online map tools presents challenges and possible threats to the user. First, and perhaps most important, there is no guarantee that a student's personal information is kept private or safe when using an online application or forum, especially one that is available at no or low cost. It is, therefore, imperative that students and instructors pay close attention to the ways that they share and interact on various platforms. One can access content uploaded by other users, but one has to remain vigilant about one's own interaction with this content as well as what personal information one chooses to share with the larger community. There are modes of using the tool wherein students can keep their information private or share it with only select groups of users, such as the instructor and classmates. However, it is necessary to carefully read and understand the terms of service of any such platform before agreeing to them.

Second, in terms of functionality, most digital mapping tools require a web browser and computer to create and edit personalized maps. This may not seem to be a significant detriment to the possible pedagogical advantages of using the tools, but in an era when students primarily use either tablets or cell phones to interact with digital content, this shortcoming proves problematic. It is possible to interact with Google My Maps and to create using all of the functionality that I've outlined, but only while using a computer and web browser. The My Maps are accessible for viewing on a mobile device, which is certainly helpful if and when one is physically in the geographical location of the map. However, it would be useful to have editing capabilities from all devices, not just computers. Moreover, some applications, such as Google Earth, need to be downloaded and used solely on a computer for both manipulation and consultation. In short, the available digital mapping applications are not yet perfected for optimal classroom use.

CONCLUSIONS

Taking into consideration the innumerable successful uses of maps, both physical and digital, in foreign language curricula over time, we can envision further beneficial pairings as additional technologies are developed and integrated. For example, the continued improvements in augmented and virtual reality (AR and VR, respectively) technologies as they relate to education announce exciting possibilities beyond traditional physical textbooks and classroom walls. As these tools have become more cost effective and accessible, educators have consequently begun to test their utility in diverse disciplines of study.[19] As McLoughlin and Lee conclude in their study on new media and social software, "there is a need to expand our vision of pedagogy so that learners become active participants and co-producers rather than passive consumers of content and learning processes are participatory and social."[20] Place-based education, and its later evolution to virtual PBE, has certainly expanded students' realms of learning, in both the surrounding real world and the (possibly) far-off virtual world. As this example of using online digital maps in an advanced French language and content course as well as other proven and potential ideas in diverse fields have shown, there is an infinite virtual world that is ready to be mapped and explored using our current technological tools and pedagogical models.

NOTES

1. Catherine McLoughlin and Mark J. W. Lee, "Mapping the Digital Terrain: New Media and Social Software as Catalysts for Pedagogical Change," in *Proceedings of the 25th ASCILITE Conference*, ed. Roger Atkinson and Clare McBeath (Melbourne: ASCILITE, 2008), 641.
2. Animaps, Scribble Maps, and various other Google tools (e.g., Earth, Lit Trips) provide some of the same features as Google My Maps, but for the scope of this project, I assess the functionality of just the latter tool. This is also not an endorsement of Google, and I am in no way compensated by the company.
3. "My Maps Help," https://support.google.com/mymaps/.
4. All but one (who would live in Reims) of the seven students in the class were to study and participate in internships in Paris.
5. Or the equivalent in high school.
6. In a typical French language class, I (among many of my peers) would focus not only on France but also on the many other French-speaking countries and regions throughout the world in order to highlight the vast diversity of cultures associated with the language.
7. If students had been informed of their future internship site, then this could be used as the basis for the final assessment. However, the design of the program did not allow for this option.
8. McLoughlin and Lee, "Mapping the Digital Terrain," 646.
9. See, for example, David A. Gruenewald, "The Best of Both Worlds: A Critical Pedagogy of Place," *Educational Researcher: A Publication of the American Educational Research Association* 32, no. 4 (2003): 3–12; and David Sobel, *Place-Based Education: Connecting Classrooms and Communities*, 2nd ed., Nature Literacy Series (Great Barrington, MA: Orion Society, 2013).
10. Sobel, *Place-Based Education*, 11.
11. Sobel, 11.
12. Merrilyne Lundahl, "Teaching Where We Are: Place-Based Language Arts," *English Journal* 100, no. 3 (January 2011): 45.
13. Sobel, cited in Gruenewald, "Best of Both Worlds," 8.
14. Reneta D. Lansiquot and Sean P. MacDonald, *Interdisciplinary Place-Based Learning in Urban Education: Exploring Virtual Worlds* (Cham, Switzerland: Palgrave Macmillan, 2018), 2.
15. Gruenewald, "Best of Both Worlds," 9.
16. Samantha Decker, *The French Corner* (blog), http://www.thefrenchcorner.net.
17. Google Lit Trips, https://www.googlelittrips.org.

18. My personal experiences with any of the online mapping tools is not necessarily indicative of the greater public's experiences and should not be taken as an endorsement or rejection of them.
19. See, on this topic, Sue Gregory and Denise Wood, eds., *Authentic Virtual World Education: Facilitating Cultural Engagement and Creativity* (Singapore: Springer Nature, 2018), for example.
20. McLoughlin and Lee, "Mapping the Digital Terrain," 649.

REFERENCES

ACTFL Proficiency Guidelines. 3rd ed. Alexandra, VA: American Council on the Teaching of Foreign Languages, 2012.

Gregory, Sue, and Denise Wood, eds. *Authentic Virtual World Education: Facilitating Cultural Engagement and Creativity*. Singapore: Springer Nature, 2018.

Gruenewald, David A. "The Best of Both Worlds: A Critical Pedagogy of Place." *Educational Researcher: A Publication of the American Educational Research Association* 32, no. 4 (2003): 3–12.

Lansiquot, Reneta D., and Sean P. MacDonald. *Interdisciplinary Place-Based Learning in Urban Education: Exploring Virtual Worlds*. Cham, Switzerland: Palgrave Macmillan, 2018.

Lundahl, Merrilyne. "Teaching Where We Are: Place-Based Language Arts." *English Journal* 100, no. 3 (January 2011): 44–48.

McLoughlin, Catherine, and Mark J. W. Lee. "Mapping the Digital Terrain: New Media and Social Software as Catalysts for Pedagogical Change." In *Proceedings of the 25th ASCILITE Conference*, edited by Roger Atkinson and Clare McBeath (Melbourne: ASCILITE, 2008). http://www.ascilite.org.au/conferences/melbourne08/procs/mcloughlin.html.

Sobel, David. *Place-Based Education: Connecting Classrooms and Communities*. 2nd ed. Nature Literacy Series. Great Barrington, MA: Orion Society, 2013.

CHAPTER ELEVEN

DEVELOPING INTERCULTURAL COMMUNICATIVE COMPETENCE VIA VIDEO-BASED SYNCHRONOUS COMMUNICATION AMONG L2 FRENCH LEARNERS

Virginie Cassidy, University of Denver, and Hongying Xu, University of Wisconsin-La Crosse

There has been some consensus reached about the importance of developing intercultural competence over the past decade. In 2005, the Association of American Colleges and Universities (AAC&U) launched a national advocacy and campus action initiative to provide guidance for liberal education, Liberal Education and America's Promise (LEAP), to cater to the demand for "more college-educated workers and more engaged and informed citizens."[1] Under the category Personal and Social Responsibility, intercultural knowledge and competence was listed as one of its essential learning outcomes.

In 2007, the Modern Language Association (MLA) released a report that emphasized the need to teach students how to "operate between languages"[2] to develop "translingual and transcultural competence."[3] This call to action echoed Michael Byram's advocacy for foreign language education to foster, in Byram's words, language learners with "an ability to interact with 'others,' to accept other perspectives and perceptions of the world, to mediate between different perspectives, to be conscious of their evaluations and differences."[4] Being an intercultural speaker entails being both linguistically and interculturally competent, able to interpret and evaluate the cultures of the target language and one's own. The MLA report also called for a restructuring of language programs in higher education by "replacing the two-tiered language-literature structure with a broader and more coherent curriculum in which language, culture, and literature are taught as a continuous whole."[5]

In foreign language education, the importance of Intercultural Communicative Competence (ICC) has also been highlighted. In 2015, the American Council on the Teaching of Foreign Languages (ACTFL) released a revised version of its 1996 *World-Readiness Standards for Learning Languages* as "a roadmap to guide learners to develop competence to communicate effectively and interact with cultural understanding."[6] Listed as one of the goals is learners' ability to "investigate, explain, and reflect on" the relationship between products, practices and perspectives of the target culture.[7] In 2017, a revised version of "Can-Do Statements" was released with a set of specific proficiency benchmarks, performance indicators, and examples to assess learners' intercultural communicative competence at different levels.[8]

With new guidelines on learning objectives and assessments, the question for educators is how to integrate culture within a course curriculum that focuses on language components and proficiency. Scholars and educators have pointed out the challenges or issues of actually integrating culture in the curriculum and making the development of ICC as one of the essential learning outcomes. Introducing culture has usually been postponed until learners have reached a higher proficiency level.[9] Additionally, in language courses, its role is often limited to being something extra, and, as such, culture is usually marginalized and "relegated to the background" because the priority has been given to the growth of language proficiency. Regarding content, the teaching of culture also faces the risk of oversimplification of the second language (L2) culture, thus reinforcing "homogeneous and essentialized perceptions of culture." The oversimplification of cultural content may partially be attributed to the fact that "the cultural information provided in most textbooks fails to provide instructors with adequate resources and strategies." One last issue mentioned by Marianne Bessy is that students solely rely on the instructor to know everything about the L2 culture. To resolve most of these issues, Bessy calls on all practitioners to adopt a student-centered approach to develop learners' autonomy in their cultural discoveries.[10]

Advocating for the inclusion of language and culture throughout the curriculum through a content-based instruction approach, Jason Martel and Nicole Pettitt suggested that textbooks can be used as a starting point but not as the sole resource of culture. As research shows that language educators prioritize culture products and practices over perspectives in planning their lessons, the authors propose to view the development of ICC as "the organizing feature of a curriculum."[11] An example is the class involved in the present study: a 300-level French course titled Sound, Speech and Proficiency, focusing on improving learners' pronunciation and speech. Adopting *Sons et sens : la prononciation du français en contexte*, the most recent textbook for French phonetics on the American market, helped introduce cultural elements into every class by contextualizing phonetic sound and transcriptions within thematic chapters bringing forth cultural elements; however, fostering intercultural competence remained a challenge.

One way to address this challenge is using technology to give students more exposure to L2 culture in different ways. Aleidine

Moeller and Kristen Nugent listed activities that can be used in language classrooms to build ICC among language learners by using examples from previous studies, including the "Cultura online blog exchange," "attitude exploration with OSEE tool[s]," "documenting transformation collectively," "proverbs," and "artifact exploration."[12] Most of the activities involve in-class interactions between language learners or between learners and artifacts. However, in recent years, the use of online tools in developing intercultural competence has increased.

COMPUTER-MEDIATED COMMUNICATION IN LANGUAGE EDUCATION

As articulated by Robert Blake, computer-mediated communication (CMC), asynchronous or synchronous, is best suited to carry out interactionist concepts relevant to second language acquisition (SLA).[13] Written synchronous CMC is particularly beneficial in lowering learners' affective filter and slowing down the pace of discussion.[14] Oral synchronous CMC enhanced both students' cultural awareness and motivation via meaningful authentic discussion with a partner.[15]

Socio-cultural researchers, such as Byram, Steven Thorne, and Robert O'Dowd, advocate for a CMC model that adds an intercultural competence outcome to the linguistic ones. Online Intercultural Exchange (OIE), also known as virtual exchange or telecollaboration, "refers to the engagement of groups of students in online intercultural interaction and collaboration with partners from other cultural contexts or geographical locations under the guidance of educators and/or expert facilitators."[16] Research has shown that telecollaboration provides "learners with a different type of knowledge from that which they usually find in textbooks"[17] and contributes to "the development of critical cultural awareness, as learners have opportunities in their online interaction to engage in intense periods of negotiation of meaning in which they can discuss cultural 'rich points' and elicit meanings of cultural behavior from 'real' informants in the target culture."[18] In a review of telecollaboration and language learning, Chun identifies two essential points: first, the development of ICC is a complex process that requires a relatively long period, and second, in-class discussions should follow online interactions.[19]

Broadening the research scope, Maria Avgousti analyzed findings from a total of fifty-four articles on ICC and online exchanges reporting data collected between 2004 and 2014. Her synthesis, like O'Dowd's, found that a focus on intercultural competence helped unveil multiple identities and eliminate stereotypes. However, Avgousti points out, "research on the application of synchronous Web 2.0 technologies on ICC development and its use in teaching is still quite limited."[20] One of her suggestions for future research was to "focus on the development of learners' ICC in informal contexts"[21] or "in the wild," "situated in arenas of social activity that are less controllable than classrooms or organized online intercultural exchanges might be."[22]

New technologies allow synchronous CMC to take place in a less controlled way. Commercialized video chatting tools such as TalkAbroad (2009) or Boomalang (2014) provide settings in which there can be an exchange of information with native speakers from different countries. Informational exchanges in these environments are not telecollaborative exchanges, which often pair students from different countries with common learning outcomes and tasks in play, nor are they completely in the wild even when they include native speakers who are not participating for educational gain. In this environment, native speakers receive training in ways to interact with language learners, are remunerated, and are chosen by the participants for fifteen- or thirty-minute sessions to discuss a topic previously entered by the instructor on the video conferencing platform. In our study, topics were closely related to what students were learning in class, but the prompts were broad and brief so that there was room for different contents and directions. In other words, in this setting, as in the wild, students are required to adjust to the interactive environment, to adapt and react to the content of the conversation, and to negotiate meaning.

BYRAM'S FRAMEWORK ON ICC

The present project adopted one of the video chatting platforms, Boomalang, and assigned it as an out-of-classroom task to help students develop their intercultural communicative competence (ICC). What exactly is ICC? As Janet Bennett points out, intercultural competence has been described variously as "a global-mindset," "global competence," and "intercultural effectiveness," among other descriptions.[23] Through research, a consensus has been reached among scholars that cultural competence entails "a set of cognitive, affective, and behavioral skills and characteristics that support effective and appropriate interaction in a variety of cultural contexts."[24]

In this project, the model proposed by Byram[25] was adopted to assess the presence and absence of intercultural competence before and after the use of the online video chatting platform. In his 1997 monograph, *Teaching and Assessing Intercultural Communicative Competence*, Byram suggested that intercultural communicative competence consists of a combination of linguistic competence, socio-linguistic competence, discourse competence, and intercultural competence, all of which enable a person to interact effectively with people from another culture in a foreign language. Byram defines intercultural competence through three areas: knowledge, attitudes, and skills. Speakers with ICC should have knowledge of the social groups and cultures of others as well as their own. They should also have knowledge of the processes of interaction at both individual and social levels, which, according to Byram, is fundamental. The second area includes curiosity toward other cultures that are perceived as different, with openness and with willingness "to suspend disbelief about other cultures and belief about one's own."[26] With the right attitude and sets of knowledge, a speaker should also possess two sets of skills: (1) skills in interpreting and relating and (2) skills in discovery and interaction. The former includes the skills of critically evaluating the products, practices, and perspectives of one's own culture and of other cultures. The latter refers to skills of acquiring "new knowledge of a culture and cultural practices" and the ability to "operate knowledge, attitudes and skills under the constraints of real-time communication and interaction."[27] All these factors contribute to the development of learners' critical cultural awareness, which is "an ability to evaluate critically and on the basis of explicit criteria perspectives, practices, and products in one's own and other cultures and countries."[28] Since the publication of Byram's monograph, his model has been widely used by teachers and researchers to assess intercultural competence among language learners.

As can be seen from the framework, some of the skills and abilities can hardly be developed through teaching cultural knowledge from textbooks in the classroom, not even through communicating with other L2 learners outside of the classroom. L2 learners should be given opportunities to communicate with native speakers from the L2 communities. Unfortunately, not every language can find a group of native speakers in the local community. The video-based synchronous chatting platforms make this possible.

APPLICATION TO THE CLASSROOM

FRE 301: Sound, Speech and Proficiency was developed to replace the more traditional French Phonetics course and adopted a task-based approach to the learning of the international phonetic alphabet. The curricular revision was motivated by the needs of the student body at a midwestern comprehensive institution. As described in the syllabus:

> This course first aims to improve students' pronunciation by providing an introduction to the principles of French phonetics and the study of stress, rhythm, and intonation. The course is designed to develop oral interactions through a pragmatic approach to language as students identify and practice different speech acts in their sociocultural contexts, applying interpersonal, interpretive, and presentational means of communication as defined by the ACTFL guidelines to achieve oral proficiency.

Therefore, in this course, learners study phonetics to help them better communicate in authentic situations, for instance while interacting with native speakers, a situation that can rarely take place on a campus lacking in diversity.

Inspired by the content-based instruction approach, the authors of *Sons et sens : la prononciation du français en contexte* elected to organize their book around cultural topics. For instance, chapter 5 explores the theme of marriage and the various formats it can take in France while introducing the concept of occlusive consonants and practicing their production. Relying on this double framework—task-based and content-based—as a design principle, the course is organized into three modules that ask students to reflect on each of the following essential questions:

- Module 1: How do language and culture influence one's identity?
- Module 2: Sport and leisure activities: What does "having fun" mean according to one's culture?
- Module 3: Performing Arts: How can the Arts call into question one's cultural perspectives?

Incorporating video chatting with francophone native speakers from a variety of countries allows the application of both frameworks. Students are able to have non-scripted, authentic conversations while they also explore a cultural topic by sharing their viewpoints, thus being potentially exposed to new perspectives.

This fifth- or sixth-semester course is one of the first three upper-level courses focusing on communication required of all French minors and majors. This study included eleven undergraduate students—ten female, one male, all white midwesterners. The class met for seventy-five minutes twice a week; the instructor and students were asked to have eight fifteen-minute sessions with a native speaker on Boomalang distributed over a twelve-week period. Only two students had studied abroad in France prior to taking the course. Thus, the interactions with video chatting partners represented a majority of the students' first experience, other than that with their language instructor, of meeting and negotiating meaning with a native speaker.

ACTIVITY DESCRIPTION

- Setting the context: Starting Week 3 of the semester, students began their video chatting experience via Boomalang. To promote a certain diversity in the representation of the cultures of the francophone world, interactions with at least three different partners from distinct francophone communities were required. The instructor provided topics written in French ahead of time through the learning management system (LMS) element and on the Boomalang dashboard[29], with a 500-word limit. For example, the conversation associated with the textbook chapter on education was "Explain the education system of your country. What are its strengths and weaknesses? What are its main challenges nowadays?"[30] It is important to note that the partners do not have access to these entries as the goal of the app is to provide the most authentic conversations. However, when booking a chat with a partner, students have the opportunity to type in anything they might want to discuss. As topics were framed with the cultural theme of a given chapter, students were to complete a set of three related activities: (1) an interpersonal communication activity; (2) a journaling, reflecting activity; and (3) a sharing group discussion, in-class activity. All three components were graded and assessed on a complete/incomplete scale.

- Reflecting on the experience: Within a week following a video chatting activity, participants were required to turn in their journal reflection through the LMS and prior to the day of our class discussion. Going through an individual reflection first allowed a scaffolding of the activity that would hopefully lead to richer and more in-depth class group discussion. To gather perspective data on the overall experience and to get students to provide an in-depth individual reflection, the journaling activity was completed in English and consistently included the same set of questions regardless of the theme explored in the video chatting.[31]

Sharing the experience with their peers: The in-class group (three to four members) discussions would generally serve as warm-up activity. A short prompt was provided for guidance to the groups who could interact in the language of their choice. Referring to the education theme again, the shared prompt was "(1) Report on your discussion with your conversation partner, (2) How can you compare and contrast the educational systems you discussed, (3) Write down at least three observations from your group conversation." Group conversations would take fifteen to twenty minutes of class time, depending on the level of engagement of students for a given topic.[32] To conclude the sharing activity, each group would then share its three main points with the whole class. The ten-minute activity would often last longer as other students contributed to the whole class discussion. This activity is a chance to make students aware that the native speaker's perspective was only one among many and that it would take more conversations with other members of the same culture, or even better, an extensive stay in this culture, to be able to develop a well-informed point of view on the subject.

WHAT WE FOUND IN OUR PROJECT

Growth Perceived by Students: Results from Pre- and Post-surveys

In order to assess the occurrence of changes and relying on Byram's framework, we designed a survey with a 5-point Likert scale to collect students' self-evaluations on their ICC before and after the conversation sessions. The survey's results are summarized in figure 1. They were grouped into three areas: attitudes, knowledge, and skills. Average scores on the post-conversation survey indicated an increase in attitudes, knowledge, and skills over scores shown on the pre-conversation survey. The biggest improvement was seen in "knowledge": the average score on the pre-conversation questionnaire was 3.42, around the *neither agree nor disagree* option, indicating that students did not think they had much knowledge about the francophone cultures or their own. However, on the post-exchange questionnaire, the points increased to 4.10, around the *agree* option, showing that students believed they had acquired some knowledge of both cultures. Similar patterns were found in the attitudes and skills sections. The average point score on the pre-conversation questionnaire, 4.27, showed that the participants already had open attitudes toward the target culture, but their attitudes became more positive afterward. On the post-conversation questionnaire, the score increased to 4.73, indicating an increase in their openness and willingness to change their attitudes. Points in the skills section were 3.51 on the pre-conversation questionnaire, denoting a lack of confidence. This score increased to 3.99 on the post-conversation questionnaire, demonstrating some improvement in their confidence in their skills. However, it must be pointed out that since this was a small group, it was not ideal to do any further statistical analysis, such as t-tests, to identify any significance. The results are descriptive in nature, but they do show some growth and are encouraging enough for further larger-scale projects along this line.

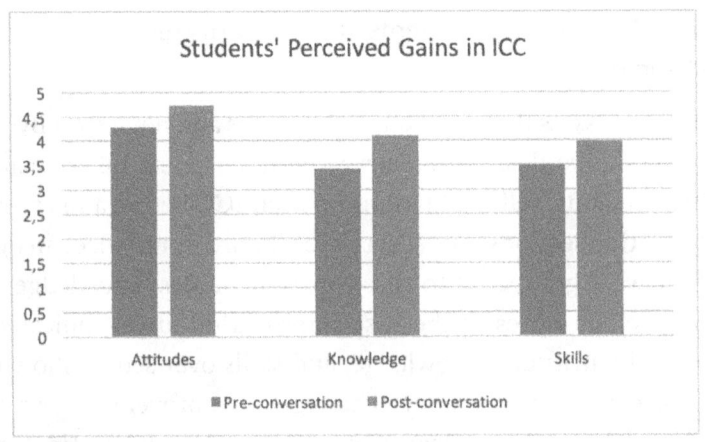

Figure 1. Average points for attitudes, knowledge, and skills before and after exchanges.

Growth Reflected in Students' Journal Entries

The journal entries were read by both writers independently, using Byram's framework as the coding scheme. Examples were cited to show students' growth in attitudes, knowledge, and skills. Therefore, we report our findings in the same order as follows. Attitudes

Attitudes, in Byram's model, is defined as "curiosity and openness, readiness to suspend disbelief about other cultures and belief about one's own."[33] Curiosity is the one factor that all participants exhibited from their first journal entries to their last. Instances of students looking forward to the next online conversation abound. However, a shift occurred in the reasons for such curiosity over the course of the semester. This shift was related to the attitude, or the readiness to suspend disbelief, about other cultures and their own.

At the beginning of the semester, students' curiosity and their willingness to pursue a discussion further arose from making connections and identifying a "sameness" in their partner:

> Considering what we talked about, our perspectives were quite similar. . . . I realized that we had tons to talk about, and I'm excited to talk about those things either with the same conversation partner or a new one. [Journal 1]

From the third journal entries on, a more frequent occurrence of the suspension of disbelief toward the other's cultures was noticeable, leading students to shift their perspectives toward their partner's culture as well as their own.

> I never expected where you get married to be so influenced by culture. However, that is kind of silly of me to have never considered that. Everything is affected by culture, and affects culture. [Journal 3]

> I think it is cool that comic books are not just categorized by one group of people liking them. It is also cool that you can find a lot of different types of comic books there. I wish that that was the case here, I think it is ridiculous people are categorized by who likes to read them. [Journal 6]

> We talked a bit about how our regions affect the foods we eat and we talked about how in Haiti they use a lot of spices . . . he described some of them and I just really want to try them now. [Journal 6]

The journal excerpts show that students started to realize their existing assumptions about others' cultures and that they were willing to suspend preexisting beliefs about either cultural practice or products in favor of exploring new perspectives. They also started to discuss with their conversational partners the reasons for cultural products or practices, which is one step further toward the understanding of perspectives, something ignored or lacking in culture teaching in language classes.

The students' changes over these online conversations conformed, to some extent, to the Developmental Model of Intercultural Sensitivity (DMIS) proposed by Bennett in 1993.[34] When L2 speakers experience cultural differences, their reactions vary at different stages of language learning. They start with their own culture as the center and the norm, against which others' cultures are viewed and evaluated. They either deny or minimalize the cultural differences or defend their own culture as being "superior." Later on, their reactions shift, and they start to experience their own culture in the context of others' cultures. They begin to accept cultural differences and show respect toward these differences. Finally, they start to adapt their views and behaviors by integrating different perspectives and constructs from other cultures. In other words, they learn to decentralize their own culture and relativize their perspectives.

In students' journals, we did not see much defense of students' own culture, but we did see examples of students minimizing cultural differences or highlighting sameness, which made them feel comfortable at the beginning of this project. Later on, we started to see examples of students recognizing cultural differences and reacting to them with openness and willingness to understand others' perspectives. This is an important step toward the next stage: to view and to behave appropriately while encountering others' cultures.

Knowledge

The first factor according to Byram's framework is "the knowledge of social groups, their products and perspectives in one's own and one's interlocutor's country, and of the general processes of societal and individual interactions."[35] From the first to the third journal entries, participants' interactions showed that the general process of societal and individual interaction was one of their main concerns. One student declared, "I know that Americans speak very 'vividly' so I tried not to get too excited or talk too fast." These comments on their interactions were often followed by thoughts from individual students on their social interaction with their peers. One participant focused particularly on interruptions with her partners: "When I interrupted, she expected me to keep talking so she stopped talking, but I did not want her to stop talking. I feel like that is an American way of signaling in a conversation that you are listening." By entry 3, this participant had concluded that the process of interrupting, and dealing with interruption, is a characteristic of a given culture.

One of the journal questions alerted students to the instances of nonverbal communication they might encounter.[36] While a few students tried to analyze the meanings of body languages (e.g., different noises made to show attention), most did not. However, students did realize that nonverbal communication was an inherent part of all interactions they had: "I originally thought that I wouldn't be able to understand someone's body language if they were trying to tell me something and I didn't hear/understand them, but most of the time, I actually understood."

From the third journal entry on, interactions with the speakers spurred students to further reflect on their own culture. They shared knowledge of their own culture as American citizens, including comments regarding celebrations and wedding ceremonies: "U.S. citizens like to be unique and over the top" and "I personally realized why everyone says America is so 'fun.' We take celebrations beyond and above [sic] what other cultures do."

A few students came to the conclusion that they might not, in fact, know everything about their own country: "We talked about the differences between a PACS [a civil partnership in France] and a marriage and she asked if there was something like that in the U.S. and I wasn't sure. I told her no or if there was, I didn't know of it." In only one instance was a student able to identify a cultural product's role (the comic book) in determining various social groups in both countries:

> Comic books are treated very differently within our two cultures. In France, everyone reads comic books; they are a normal thing for people of all ages and groups to enjoy. . . . Here in the U.S. people who read comic books are often classified as nerds. [Journal 6]

Regarding the knowledge of products, practices, and perspectives of their partners' cultures, students' entries indicate that they were often surprised at their lack of knowledge about their partners' countries. These admissions usually occurred after the third journal entry and included such epiphanies as "I realized I never got a full picture of what Comic Book culture was like in France before. I was only exposed to a tiny portion of it," and "I was surprised at [the fact that joining the military is not a widespread option to graduating French high schoolers]. I thought it was pretty common in Europe, and pretty much anywhere, to join the military." One student made it straightforward: "From today's conversation I gained a better understanding of the differences in education systems between our two countries [United States and France]."

Students also showed some reflection on the stereotypes they had about others or groups within their own culture. For example, one student said that she assumed that "they [French people] were very rude and judgmental." After having a conversation on travel, one student reported, "I was really surprised that she [conversational partner] had met so many Texan tourists because I have a perceived notion about Texans as people who aren't extremely cultured and would not want to go to France." During the conversation of wedding ceremonies, the conversational partner was surprised to learn that wedding ceremonies are sometimes outside in an open area. This triggered the realization from the student that "where you get married [is] so influenced by culture." Then the student generalized her realization: "Everything is affected by culture, and affects culture." We saw in this student the growth of knowledge of how people from different cultures function.

Skills

Byram proposed two sets of skills in his model. The first set, interpretation and relating, refers to the "ability to interpret a document or event from another culture, to explain it and relate it to documents or events from one's own."[37] The second, discovery and interaction, refers to the "ability to acquire new knowledge of a culture and cultural practices and the ability to use knowledge, attitudes and skills within the constraints of real-time communication and interaction."[38] In the first journal entry, most participants expressed their lack of confidence in their communicative skills. For example, one student wrote, "I was nervous and imagined it being dry and boring." Some students reported a lack of ability to interpret the conversation or to ask questions to acquire the knowledge to interpret it. For instance, one entry noted the use of more gestures and lip movement in the student's conversation partner but did not interpret it beyond saying, "I think this made the conversation fun."

Some students reported their difficulty asking questions: "At one point he asked me if I had anything to ask him and I wasn't expecting it and there were some awkward pauses . . ."; "Another challenge for me is to come up with questions to ask on the fly."

When students tried to ask questions to learn about the other culture, they could not make themselves understood even after they tried to rephrase it in another way. Other students reported that they forgot to ask questions, focusing only on explaining their own culture.

After three exchanges, participants began to show evidence of improvement in their skills to relate, interpret, discover, and interact. For example, a student who wanted to learn about the location of a wedding in France or in Europe asked a question that was misunderstood, so she rephrased her question and successfully redirected their conversation. Students also started to relate what they learned about francophone cultures to their own culture and to explain their differences. When discussing the locations of wedding ceremonies in France and those in the United States, a student noticed the difference in the wedding locations and related this difference to the role that religion plays in the weddings. Another student observed that an American wedding ceremony is more personal as attendance is usually reserved for family members and close friends. She then attributed this difference to the relationship between religion and weddings: "[I]n the U.S., the ceremony is private because of the religious aspect." They may not have reached the stage of adapting their perspectives during the communication, but at least they started to show some awareness of the relationship between perspectives and cultural practice.

After six exchanges, participants recorded more instances of their ability to relate, to comprehend, and to interact, which was indicated by their willingness to ask for clarifications when confusion arose. For example, when one student heard her partner talk about a famous person from French culture whom she did not know, she was able to indicate "that [she] didn't know who [her partner] was talking about." Students also began showing awareness of the necessary adjustments that had to be made. As one student put it, "it was refreshing to speak with a new partner and see how they interacted differently from the others." Another student noticed that whereas one native speaker was good at filling the "quiet moments," another was not. To adjust, she wrote down some topics for her next interaction to prevent such gaps. Therefore, students started to employ strategies to facilitate their interactions. One student, for instance, reported that she noticed she used her hands "a lot more" when "building off" her ideas. Students also found themselves explaining to their partners more about their culture and their own stories. This "reversed role" [leading the conversation], according to one student, made her feel more confident.

Although critical cultural awareness is not the focus of this study, we did notice some evidence suggesting its development. For example, after discussing the differences between weddings in France and those in the United States, one student started to *see* her own culture: "I don't really think about the U.S. having a 'culture' but we do when people from other countries look at us." She also made comments on learning about one's own culture in general: "When you live in the culture, it doesn't feel like a 'culture' but having to explain it to other people shows that there is in fact a culture in the U.S."

To sum up, students' journal entries did show that throughout these online exchanges, students experienced growth in the different aspects of ICC. They showed progress in their knowledge of, and in their attitudes toward the cultures of, the francophone world and in their skills in interpreting the knowledge and relating it to their own culture and experience as well as their skills to discover new knowledge and to interact with speakers from the francophone world.

Perceived Gains from Students' Experience of the Online Video-Based Conversations

We included questions in the guided questions for students' journal entries to collect feedback on their experience of using the online video-based exchanges. In general, participants gave positive feedback about their experiences. Students considered it "cool" to talk directly to native speakers from francophone communities and "to talk with someone with a genuine accent and hear their pronunciation and grammar," which helped them become "better French speakers" and better "understand French culture." The benefits they reported in their journal entries are summarized in the following aspects.

Increased confidence

Many students talked about how conversing with native speakers online improved their confidence and helped take them out of their comfort zone. In the words of one student, "One thing that's rewarding is gaining that confidence from them when they understand my French and both [my partners] said . . . that I spoke French well which was a confidence booster." In a later entry, she restated this with a more specific example: "Fanny said that I spoke fast and had a good accent and that I understood really well and that it was a really good conversation and that was really nice to hear. I think that sometimes I'm not as confident in my French abilities but it feels good to have a native speaker say that I actually sort of know what I'm doing." After talking to the same native speakers several times, one student commented, "Speaking more and more with Lucie, I find myself [moving] out of my comfort zone and trying harder than I have in the past."

Improved linguistic skills

Many students reported that their linguistic skills, including listening, pronunciation, and vocabulary, improved over time. Most of them expressed their nervousness in the first few journal entries using phrases such as "nerve-racking," "awkward silences," and "struggle." They had to listen very attentively to understand what their partners were saying. As their listening skills gradually improved, one student declared that "[i]t felt like a normal conversation I would have with a friend in English." When making mistakes, they enjoyed being corrected so they "could learn from [their] mistakes and continue to improve."

Improved communicative skills

Students also reported an improvement in communicative skills such as asking questions and the use of nonverbal tools, including voice, body language, and facial expressions. Most students noticed their lack of ability to ask questions during the first few exchanges and, therefore, worked consciously on that in later exchanges, sometimes with the help of their conversation partners. They remarked on their progress: "[I]t felt like the smoothest of the past conversations. We were both asking and answering questions." Another student noted, "I felt that this [later] conversation was one of my better ones. I asked Ionela a lot of questions, and we were able to keep the conversation going."

Interestingly, most students noticed the difference between their use of nonverbal communicative tools and that of their partners, and they continuously adjusted their use to facilitate communication. For example, a student incorporated more gestures while explaining her ideas and observed the following: "I noticed that when I am more comfortable with my conversation partner, I use more body language and I see the same [in] whoever I am speaking with."

It must be pointed out that not all students perceived the aforementioned benefits from the first online exchange nor did they all perceive these benefits after each exchange. However, the trend showed that the more they participated in online exchanges, the more the students perceived the benefits and their progress. One student who was at first a bit resistant to talking to a stranger online said, "It is so hard to understand a native speaker through a computer and headphones. I feel [that] if I was able to talk in person... it would be less challenging." However, after further online exchanges, she noted a change: "I really enjoyed this conversation. I liked being able to go wherever it took us, and I felt like the two of us could just keep it going." She also enjoyed talking to different native speakers online: "It was refreshing to speak with a new partner and see how they interacted differently from the others."

INSTRUCTIONAL TAKEAWAY

The study results and student feedback were so satisfying that it was decided to implement video chatting interactions with native speakers in all future FRE 301 courses. This ended up being the perfect experience to bring together the spontaneous conversation component for increasing students' proficiency level and the reflective cultural component for developing an awareness of other cultures and of their own. Speaking to millennials from across the globe (Haiti, Belgium, Switzerland, France) contributed to materializing *francophonie*, the fact that one language may be what brings together diverse cultures of the francophone world.

While students benefited from the variety of cultural perspectives and speaking accents, selecting many partners also meant that for each conversation, time would be spent on introductions and breaking the ice. As a result, it would take longer for students to feel at ease to discuss the task at hand while still having some time to freely discuss other topics. In this context, the fifteen-minute sessions were deemed too short. However, many students felt uncomfortable at the beginning of the experiment, wondering how they could speak for fifteen minutes, a feeling that faded over time. In the future, having longer sessions toward the end of the semester will be considered.

The modules' essential questions anchored the video chatting experiment to the course, as students were asked to provide a written answer through the Discussion section of the LMS, furthering the reflection by synthesizing several sets (conversation/reflecting/sharing). It would be beneficial for students to be able to share their experience with their peers, to expand on the sharing component. A panel for an audience of peers in other French courses or even in other disciplines (such as anthropology or sociology) would spread the interest for valuing other perspectives and learning about other cultures.

NOTES

1. "Liberal Education and America's Promise," AAC&U, accessed July 24, 2019, https://www.aacu.org/leap.
2. Mary Louise Pratt et al., "Transforming College and University Foreign Language Departments," *Modern Language Journal* 92, no. 2 (2008): 289.
3. Pratt et al.
4. Michael Byram, Adam Nichols, and David Stevens, introduction to *Developing Intercultural Competence in Practice*, ed. Michael Byram, Adam Nichols, and David Stevens (Clevedon, UK: Multilingual Matters, 2001), 5.
5. Modern Language Association Ad Hoc Committee on Foreign Languages, "Foreign Languages and Higher Education: New Structures for a Changed World," *Profession* (2007): 234–235.
6. World Readiness Standards for Learning Languages, ACTFL, accessed July 24, 2019, https://www.actfl.org/publications/all/world-readiness-standards-learning-languages.
7. "World Readiness Standards for Learning Languages Summary," ACTFL, accessed July 24, 2019, https://www.actfl.org/sites/default/files/publications/standards/World-ReadinessStandardsforLearningLanguages.pdf.
8. "Can-Do Statements," ACTFL and NCSSFL, accessed July 24, 2019, https://www.actfl.org/publications/guidelines-and-manuals/ncssfl-actfl-can-do-statements.
9. Sandy Cutshall, "More Than a Decade of Standards: Integrating 'Cultures' in Your Language Instruction," *Language Educator* 7, no. 3 (2012): 34.
10. Marianne Bessy, "Rethinking the Teaching of Culture at the Beginning Level: The Online Francophone Cultures Portfolio Project," *French Review* 93, no. 3 (2020): 67–68.
11. Jason Martel and Nicole Pettitt, "Mindsets and Tools for Developing Foreign Language Curriculum Featuring Thoughtful Culture-as-Content," *French Review* 90, no. 2 (2016): 171–174.

12. Aleidine J. Moeller and Kristen Nugent, "Building Intercultural Competence in the Language Classroom," in *Unlock the Gateway to Communication*, ed. Stephanie Dhonau (Eau Claire, WI: Crown Prints, 2014), 9–14.
13. Robert J. Blake, *Brave New Digital Classroom: Technology and Foreign Language Learning* (Washington, DC: Georgetown University Press, 2008), 70.
14. J. Scott Payne, "Making the Most of Synchronous and Asynchronous Discussion in Foreign Language Instruction," in *The Heinle Professional Series in Language Instruction*, vol. 1, *Teaching with Technology*, ed. Lara Lomicka and Jessamine Cooke-Plagwitz (Boston: Heinle, 2004), 79–93, quoted in Blake, *Brave New Digital Classroom*, 76–77.
15. Blake, *Brave New Digital Classroom*, 78.
16. Robert O'Dowd, "Online Intercultural Exchange and Language Education," in *Language, Education and Technology*, 3rd ed., ed. Steven L. Thorne and Stephen May (Cham, Switzerland: Springer International Publishing, 2017), 208.
17. Robert O'Dowd, "Telecollaboration and CALL," in *Contemporary Computer-Assisted Language Learning*, ed. Michael Thomas, Hayo Reinders, and Mark Warschauer (London: Bloomsbury Academic, 2014), 130.
18. O'Dowd, 131.
19. Dorothy M. Chun, "Language and Culture Learning in Higher Education via Telecollaboration," *Pedagogies: An International Journal* 10, no. 1 (2015): 11.
20. Maria Iosifina Avgousti, "Intercultural Communicative Competence and Online Exchanges: A Systematic Review," *Computer Assisted Language Learning* 31, no. 8 (2018): 832.
21. Avgousti, 845.
22. Steven L. Thorne, "The 'Intercultural Turn' and Language Learning in the Crucible of New Media," in *Telecollaboration 2.0: Language, Literacies and Intercultural Learning in the 21st Century*, ed. Sarah Guth and Francesca Helm (Bern: Peter Lang, 2010), 144.
23. Janet M. Bennett, "Cultivating Intercultural Competence: A Process Perspective," in *The Sage Handbook of Intercultural Competence*, ed. Darla K. Deardorff (Thousand Oaks, CA: SAGE Publications, 2009), 122.
24. Janet M. Bennett, "Transformative Training: Designing Programs for Culture Learning," in *Contemporary Leadership and Intercultural Competence: Exploring the Cross-Cultural Dynamics within Organizations*, ed. Michael A. Moodian (Thousand Oaks, CA: SAGE Publications, 2008), 98.
25. Michael Byram, *Teaching and Assessing Intercultural Communicative Competence* (Clevedon, UK: Multilingual Matters, 1997).
26. Byram, 50.

27. Byram, 6.
28. Byram, 53.
29. See Appendix 11.1 on Fulcrum for a screenshot of the dashboard.
30. See Appendix 11.3 on Fulcrum for a list of topics in French.
31. See Appendix 11.2 on Fulcrum for the list of journal questions.
32. For a list of detailed prompts for group work, see Appendix 11.3 on Fulcrum.
33. Byram, *Teaching and Assessing*, 34.
34. Milton J. Bennett, "A Developmental Approach to Training for Intercultural Sensitivity," *International Journal of Intercultural Relations* 10, no. 2 (1986): 179-196.
35. Byram, *Teaching and Assessing*, 35.
36. See question 2 in Appendix 11.2 on Fulcrum.
37. Byram, *Teaching and Assessing*, 52.
38. Byram, *Teaching and Assessing*, 52.

REFERENCES

Avgousti, Maria Iosifina. "Intercultural Communicative Competence and Online Exchanges: A Systematic Review." *Computer Assisted Language Learning* 31, no. 8 (2018): 819-853.

Bennett, Janet M. "Cultivating Intercultural Competence: A Process Perspective." In *The Sage Handbook of Intercultural Competence*, 121-140. Edited by Darla K. Deardorff. Thousand Oaks, CA: SAGE Publications, 2009.

———. A Developmental Approach to Training for Intercultural Sensitivity. *International Journal of Intercultural Relations* 10, no. 2 (1986): 179-195.

———. "Transformative Training: Designing Programs for Culture Learning." In *Contemporary Leadership and Intercultural Competence: Exploring the Cross-Cultural Dynamics within Organizations*, edited by Michael A. Moodian, 95-110. Thousand Oaks, CA: SAGE Publications, 2008.

Bennett, Milton J. "A Developmental Approach to Training for Intercultural Sensitivity." *International Journal of Intercultural Relations* 10, no. 2 (1986): 179-196.

Bessy, Marianne. "Rethinking the Teaching of Culture at the Beginning Level: The Online Francophone Cultures Portfolio Project." *French Review* 93, no. 3 (2020): 66-87.

Blake, Robert J. *Brave New Digital Classroom: Technology and Foreign Language Learning*. Washington, DC: Georgetown University Press, 2008.

Byram, Michael. *Teaching and Assessing Intercultural Communicative Competence*. Clevedon, UK: Multilingual Matters, 1997.

Byram, Michael, Adam Nichols, and David Stevens. Introduction to *Developing Intercultural Competence in Practice*, edited by Michael Byram, Adam Nichols, and David Stevens, 1–8. Clevedon, UK: Multilingual Matters, 2001.

Chun, Dorothy M. "Language and Culture Learning in Higher Education via Telecollaboration." *Pedagogies: An International Journal* 10, no. 1 (2015): 5–21.

Cutshall, Sandy. "More Than a Decade of Standards: Integrating 'Cultures' in Your Language Instruction." *Language Educator* 7, no. 3 (2012): 32–36.

Martel, Jason, and Nicole Pettitt. "Mindsets and Tools for Developing Foreign Language Curriculum Featuring Thoughtful Culture-as-Content." *French Review* 90, no. 2 (2016): 171–183.

Modern Language Association Ad Hoc Committee on Foreign Languages. "Foreign Languages and Higher Education: New Structures for a Changed World." *Profession* (2007): 234–245.

Moeller, Aleidine J., and Kristen Nugent. "Building Intercultural Competence in the Language Classroom." In *Unlock the Gateway to Communication*, edited by Stephanie Dhoneau, 1–18. Eau Claire, WI: Crown Prints, 2014.

O'Dowd, Robert. "Online Intercultural Exchange and Language Education." In *Language, Education and Technology*, 3rd ed., edited by Steven L. Thorne and Stephen May, 207–218. Cham, Switzerland: Springer International Publishing, 2017.

———. "Telecollaboration and CALL." In *Contemporary Computer-Assisted Language Learning*, edited by Michael Thomas, Hayo Reinders, and Mark Warschauer, 123–139. London: Bloomsbury Academic, 2014.

Payne, J. Scott. "Making the Most of Synchronous and Asynchronous Discussion in Foreign

Language Instruction." In *The Heinle Professional Series in Language Instruction*, vol. 1, *Teaching with Technology*, edited by Lara Lomicka and Jessamine Cooke-Plagwitz, 79–93. Boston: Heinle, 2004.

Pratt, Mary Louise, et al. "Transforming College and University Foreign Language Departments." *Modern Language Journal* 92, no. 2 (2008): 287–292.

Schenker, Theresa. "The Effects of a Virtual Exchange on Language Skills and Intercultural Competence." PhD diss., Michigan State University, 2012.

Sinicrope, Castle, John Norris, and Yukiko Watanabe. "Understanding and Assessing Intercultural Competence: A Summary of Theory, Research, and Practice (Technical Report for the Foreign Language Program Evaluation Project)." *Studies in Second Language Acquisition* 26, no. 1 (2007): 1–58.

Spitzberg, Brian H., and Gabrielle Changnon. "Conceptualizing Intercultural Competence." In

The Sage Handbook of Intercultural Competence, edited by Darla K. Deardorff, 2–52. Thousand Oaks, CA: SAGE Publications, 2009.

Thorne, Steven L. "The 'Intercultural Turn' and Language Learning in the Crucible of New Media.'" In *Telecollaboration 2.0: Language, Literacies and Intercultural Learning in the 21st Century*, edited by Sarah Guth and Francesca Helm, 139–164. Bern: Peter Lang, 2010.

Violin-Wigent, Anne, Jessica Miller, and Frédérique Grim. *Sons et sens : la prononciation du français en contexte*. Washington, DC: Georgetown University Press, 2013.

Wagner, Manuela, Dorie Conlon Perugini, and Michael Byram. Introduction to *Teaching Intercultural Competence across the Age Range: From Theory to Practice*, 1–21. Edited by Manuela Wagner, Dorie Conlon Perugini, and Michael Byram. Bristol, UK: Multilingual Matters, 2017.

APPENDICES

The appendices referenced throughout this volume share examples of course syllabi, specific course activities, and extracurricular projects that explore culinary practices, performing arts, pop culture, geolocation, digital literacy, journalism, and civic literacy.

All appendices' materials are available for free in the open access version of this volume at https://doi.org/10.3998/mpub.12217076 and www.fulcrum.org/leverpress.

CONTRIBUTORS

Aurélie Chevant-Aksoy (volume editor)
Santa Monica College
Aurélie Chevant-Aksoy's literary research interests include contemporary francophone Vietnamese writers, francophone women writers, and the graphic representations of historical trauma and exile. Additionally, her pedagogical research explores the use of technology in language instruction and the use of graphic novels and comics to teach culture in context at all levels of the French curriculum.

Kathryne Adair Corbin (volume editor)
Haverford College
Kathryne Adair Corbin's teaching and research explores the intersections of journalism, visual culture, and literature in nineteenth- and twentieth-century France. Her forthcoming book considers the spectacle and style in the works of France's first woman reporter, Séverine. Additional research has been published in *George Sand Studies*, *Romance Notes*, and *Teaching and Learning Together in Higher Education*.

Virginie Cassidy
University of Denver
Virginie Cassidy teaches all levels of French and specializes in French for professional purposes courses. Her research interest includes approaches to teaching and learning language and instructional design. She has a forthcoming publication in the *ADFL Bulletin*: "Students First: Applying Instructional Design and Technology to Foreign Language Collegiate Curriculum Building."

Christophe Corbin
Haverford College
Christophe Corbin's research and teaching interests are grounded in twentieth- and twenty-first-century French and francophone cultural studies, postcolonial studies, and women's studies. He is the author of *Revisiting the French Resistance in Cinema, Literature,* Bande Dessinée, *and Television (1942–2012)* (Lexington Books, 2019), which examines the relationship between collective memory and popular culture through the fictional representations of the French Resistance. He is currently working on cultural responses in French to terrorism from the 1940s to the present day. He is the director of the Institut d'Avignon (a six-week summer undergraduate and graduate program in French and francophone studies) under the auspices of Bryn Mawr College.

Aria Dal Molin
University of South Carolina
Aria Dal Molin's scholarly interests include sex and gender in sixteenth-century literary academies, early modern disability studies, and transnational mobility in the early modern theater of Italy and France. Her most recent book, *Early Modern Bromance: Love, Friendship, and Marriage in Sixteenth-Century Italian Academies* (Cambria Press, 2020), looks at the clash of ideals of

perfect (male) friendship and compulsory marriage in the early years of the Renaissance literary academies. She teaches upper-division and graduate-level courses in French, Italian, and comparative literature at the University of South Carolina.

Heidi Holst-Knudsen
Columbia University
Heidi Holst-Knudsen teaches all levels of language as well as a course on French language and culture through film. She presents frequently on her pedagogical practice, focusing particularly on the use of visual supports and film to integrate cultural material into language lessons. Her research is currently focused on political cinema, and she has given talks and published articles on the films of Kassovitz, Kechiche, Ameur-Zaïmeche, Bresson, Tati, Varda, and Kaurismäki, among others.

Rebecca Josephy
Oakland University
Rebecca Josephy's research is in twentieth-century French and francophone literature with a focus on mystery and detective fiction and the Québécois author Andrée Maillet. She has published numerous articles on Maillet, including "Une Traversée en théorie intertextuelle : La 'Seconde main' dans 'Les Doigts extravagants' d'Andrée Maillet" in *@nalyses* and "Mains (in)visibles : intertextualité, intratextualité et autoréflexivité dans 'Les Doigts extravagants' d'Andrée Maillet" in *Voix plurielles*. She teaches a wide variety of courses and enjoys bringing her love of literature and creative writing into French language instruction.

Jeremie Korta
Commonwealth School
Jeremie Korta taught at Miami University for five years after completing his PhD at Harvard University in early modern stud-

ies. He currently teaches French language and culture at Commonwealth School in Boston. His co-edited volume *Early Modern Visions of Space: France and Beyond* is forthcoming from University of North Carolina Press.

Audra Merfeld-Langston
Missouri University of Science & Technology
Audra Merfeld-Langston's teaching and research interests are varied and include twentieth- and twenty-first-century Francophone history, literature, and culture; digital humanities; teaching with technology; languages for specific purposes; and intercultural communication. Additionally, she is passionate about collaborating across disciplines and building relationships between K–12 and higher education language professionals.

Carrie O'Connor
Boston University
Carrie O'Connor started her second academic year in fall 2020 as a full-time lecturer at Boston University, where she had taught part-time for the two prior years. She taught a wide range of courses throughout her career, including French language, French for Business, Conversational French, French Literature in Translation, and French Culture through Gastronomy. She was a natural leader and generous colleague and was an initiator of First Mondays, a French language section gathering that invited instructors to enjoy a moment of lighthearted, remote camaraderie during the COVID-19 pandemic. She will be remembered by her students and colleagues for her firm belief in inclusion, diversity, encouragement, and community building as practices and actions at the core of teaching French and romance studies.

Eliza Jane Smith
University of San Diego
Eliza Jane Smith's research focuses on questions of language and

identity in nineteenth-century French literature. Her book, *Literary Slumming: Slang and Class in Nineteenth-Century France* (Lexington Books, 2021), is a comprehensive study on the representations of slang and its speakers in modern French literary culture. Additional research has been published in journals such as *Nineteenth-Century French Studies* and *Médias 19*.

Dr. Hongying Xu
University of Wisconsin–La Crosse
Hongying Xu teaches Chinese language courses at all levels and Chinese culture courses in English. Her research interests include the acquisition of Chinese structures by L2 Chinese learners, the use of technology in language instruction, and foreign language pedagogy. She is currently working on a monograph on the learning and teaching of the unique BA construction in Chinese.

www.ingramcontent.com/pod-product-compliance
Lightning Source LLC
Chambersburg PA
CBHW070716160426
43192CB00009B/1212